ECUADOR:
Conflicting Political Culture and the Quest for Progress

The Allyn and Bacon Series
in Latin American Politics

FEDERICO G. GIL, EDITOR
The University of North Carolina

ARPAD VON LAZAR, ASSOCIATE EDITOR
The Fletcher School of Law and Diplomacy
Tufts University

ALLYN AND BACON, INC.   BOSTON

JL
3081
.M35

Ecuador:
Conflicting Political Culture and the Quest for Progress

JOHN D. MARTZ
The University of North Carolina

WITHDRAWN
THE LIBRARY
INDIANA STATE UNIVERSITY
EVANSVILLE

0066546

© Copyright 1972 by Allyn and Bacon, Inc.
470 Atlantic Avenue, Boston. All rights reserved.
Printed in the United States of America.
No part of the material protected by this copyright notice
may be reproduced or utilized in any form or by any means,
electronic or mechanical, including photocopying, recording,
or by any informational storage and retrieval system,
without written permission from the copyright owner.

LIBRARY OF CONGRESS CATALOG CARD NUMBER: 70-189205

Contents

PACIFIC OCEAN
COLOMBIA
PERU
ECUADOR
Esmeraldas
Esmeraldas
Carchi
Tulcán
Imbabura
Ibarra
Pichincha
Quito
Manabí
Napo
Cotopaxi
Latacunga
Tena
Portoviejo
Ambato
Los Rios
Tungurahua
Puyo
Bolivar
Guaranda
Riobamba
Pastaza
Babahoyo
Guayas
Chimborazo
Guayaquil
Macas
Cañar
Azogues
Morona-Santiago
Cuenca
Azuay
Machala
El Oro
Zamora-Chinchipe
Zamora
Loja
Loja
GALÁPAGOS ISLANDS
(ARCHIPIÉLAGO DE COLÓN)
Baquerizo Moreno

Preface

As suggested in the pages which follow, the territorially small republic of Ecuador in many ways serves as a microcosm for a wide variety of problems, questions, and issues relevant to various of the other Latin American countries. Social and economic structures, ethnic and linguistic diversity, historical patterns, geographic influences, and traditions of politics are complex, presenting a rich treasure lode for social scientists concerned with contemporary Latin America. There are many lessons to be learned from the Ecuadorean experience, and it is regrettable that there have been few scholarly efforts to profit from the study of its life, society, and politics. Hopefully there will be greater future interest on the part of scholars which, without bringing about an importation of cultural imperialism, will contribute to an understanding of both Ecuadorean and Latin American reality.

It was in 1956 that I first visited Ecuador. In the course of a relatively brief stay I was captivated by its remarkable people and land, thus initiating what is frankly conceded to be a permanent fondness and admiration. After an unhappily long hiatus, I returned for more extended periods of time in 1966, 1967, and 1969. When these pages first appear in print, I expect to be in Ecuador again. The personal pleasure thereby experienced is only equaled by anticipation of many future trips to the country. In the course of past travels I have been to sixteen of its twenty provinces, including the *oriente, sierra,* and *costa* regions; thus far I have not reached the Galápagos Islands, but in due course will do so.

My indebtedness to both institutions and individuals is substantial. It is through the John Simon Guggenheim Memorial Foundation, the National Science Foundation, and the Department of Political Science at the University of North Carolina that my recent visits have been possible. On a personal level I am, as always, greatly appreciative for the encouragement, counsel, and advice of my senior colleague and the editor of this series, Federico G. Gil. In many ways I also owe much to other colleagues at the University of North

Carolina, including Henry A. Landsberger of the Department of Sociology, Harold A. Bierck of the Department of History, David G. Basile (like myself something of a transplanted *ecuatoriano*) of the Department of Geography, and my predecessor as Chairman of the Department of Political Science, Frederic N. Cleaveland. I must also add my gratitude to George I. Blanksten of Northwestern University, whose kindnesses have been unfailingly generous. Moreover, it was he who pioneered in the study of Ecuadorean politics. Even today I find the published version of his doctoral dissertation – now over two decades old – a remarkably useful treatment. I cannot realistically expect that twenty years hence, my own work will have the continuing relevance and insight which his 1951 volume retains.

My obligation to numerous Ecuadorean friends is inestimable, as well as to many political figures who consented to interviews – only a few of whom are cited in footnotes. Because of the domestic instability at this moment of writing, I have reluctantly chosen not to specify a number of essentially apolitical friends who have helped in so many ways to my study and research. I trust that they are not unaware of my deep gratitude. Most of all, let me inadequately acknowledge my sincere appreciation to Rafael Quintero, at this writing a doctoral candidate in the Department of Political Science at the University of North Carolina. Among the large contingent of Latin American graduate students who have come to Chapel Hill through the years, he is the first from Ecuador and properly anticipates a future as his country's first true political scientist.

In earlier works I have regularly appended the customary – and appropriate – acknowledgements to those who have assisted me. It must be said that the assistance of Sr. Quintero in the preparation of this volume is far greater than that of any who have worked with me in the past. His perception and knowledge of his country's politics far exceeds my own. The pages which follow are inordinately better as a result of his advice; had I not occasionally been unreasonably stubborn in the face of his suggestions, it would doubtless be better than it is. Above all else, then, my personal and intellectual debt is greatest to Rafael Quintero and, of course, to the people of Ecuador.

J.D.M.

1
Demographic and Regional Fragmentation

Ecuador is a very difficult country to govern.

The conflict between dreams and reality has been the tragedy of Spanish America. Unified by the Spanish soul, Americans have desired union, and have encountered infinite distances, huge mountains, varied climates, unhealthful valleys, and perpetually extended rivers and plains.

Evil is not essentially in dictatorship, and good is not necessarily in democracy. Evil lies in applying oppression with perverse or vain intent. Good lies in making effective the rights of man and of the citizen and in the creation of institutions which guarantee them.

Give me a balcony and the people are mine.[1]

These statements have all flowed from the lips or pen of José María Velasco Ibarra, five-time president of the Republic of Ecuador and a larger-than-life personification of its political characteristics. Physical and political fragmentation, *caudillismo* and charisma, personalism and autocracy; all of these are threads which weave colorfully turbulent patterns across the fabric of national history. Regional rivalries, linguistic and ethnic diversity, and social rigidity further contribute to the

[1] The first and fourth statements have been reiterated by Velasco Ibarra on innumerable occasions throughout his forty-year political career. The second comes from his *Experiencias jurídicas hispanoamericanas* (Buenos Aires: Editorial Americalee, 1943), pp. 137-38. The third is from ibid., pp. 64-65.

Unless otherwise noted, all translations from Spanish to English in this book are the author's own.

complex cultural and political entity known to the world as Ecuador.

There are few clear and unambiguous answers to such questions as "Who are the Ecuadoreans?," "How do Ecuadorean politics operate?," or even "What is Ecuador?"[2] To both serious scholar and casual observer, it is the very diversity of the land and its inhabitants which provides an irresistible fascination. Even more broadly, however, Ecuador is in many ways a microcosm of the customs and traits which exist in one or another part of Latin America. Beyond the intrinsic value of seeking an understanding of Ecuador, then, lies a richness of experience and insight which bears meaning elsewhere in the hemisphere.

Ecuadorean geography ranges from verdant Amazonian jungle to snow-capped Andean mountain peaks, and from coastal flood plains to desert aridity. Its inhabitants include proud descendants of white European colonizers, Indian heirs to the great Incan civilization, blacks carrying the legacy of African origins, primitive nomadic hunters and fishermen, and the racial mixture produced by generations of miscegenation and intermarriage. Political ideology runs the gamut from the unbounded radicalism of the extreme Marxist left to the reactionary falangist *Hispanidad* which worships at the grail of sixteenth-century Spain. Between these extremes one can find conservatives, liberals, populists, Christian democrats, communists, and socialists. Social elites include internationally oriented coastal bankers and merchants as well as insular owners of vast highland estates. Political functions are set within the context of advanced, progressive constitutional structures, but often devolve into exercises of arbitrary personal will by charismatic leadership.

The quest for some elemental understanding of Ecuador and its people must therefore be based on the premise that

[2] An oft-quoted anecdote, perhaps apocryphal, nonetheless bears repetition. In his *Ecuador: Portrait of a People* (New York: Doubleday, Doran and Company, Inc., 1944), Albert B. Franklin recounts his conversation with an Ecuadorean Indian:

"I told him I was a foreigner. He said he had heard of France. Not France, the United States, I said. He said, was that in Peru?

"José Manuel's idea of the world was a valley in which he lived, an outer world consisting of Cuenca, Ona, Quito, Loja, and Saraguro, and, beyond them, France on the one side and Peru on the other." (p. 200)

While this would clearly be overdrawn today, doubtless many highland Indians would be likely to respond along roughly similar lines.

diversity and complexity, even within a small geographic territory, is most pronounced. Moreover, obstacles to the search for progress and modernization in the second half of the twentieth century must be examined within the framework of competing and frequently uncompromising political and socioeconomic forces. The themes of regionalism and personalism are writ large on the pages of Ecuadorean politics. The task of integrating and assimilating physical and human resources is severe. The magnitude of the quest for a true national community of interests and attitudes is imposing, leading many to an acceptance of Velasco's dictum about the near impossibility of governing.

To spell out the nature of Ecuadorean diversity and its implications is to empathize with the obstacles to be confronted. The myriad of conflicting forces and pressures at all levels of national life pervades Ecuadorean political culture. It is this concept, as a pioneering study of "political culture" argued, which "provides structure and meaning to the political sphere in the same manner as culture in general gives coherence and integration to social life."[3] Moreover, the political culture of a society consists "of the system of empirical beliefs, expressive symbols, and values which defines the situation in which political action takes place. It provides the subjective orientation to politics."[4]

The concept of political culture is designed to help in the identification of those underlying attitudes, beliefs, and practices which guide political behavior. It accepts the complexities and contradictions of underdeveloped societies which contribute to political fragmentation and the absence of a common orientation toward political action. To quote Pye again, "political culture is to the political system what culture is to the social system."[5] While a relative dearth of reliable statistical data and attitudinal studies makes our discussion more intuitive than empirical, the concept of political culture may serve as a useful framework for the study of Ecuadorean social and political life.

[3] Lucian W. Pye, "Introduction: Political Culture and Political Development," in Lucian W. Pye and Sidney Verba (eds.), *Political Culture and Political Development* (Princeton: Princeton University Press, 1965), p. 8.

[4] Sidney Verba, "Comparative Political Culture," in ibid., p. 513.

[5] Lucian W. Pye, *Aspects of Political Development* (Boston: Little, Brown and Company, 1966), p. 105.

Variations and permutations upon the themes of fragmentation and discontinuity will recur throughout the narrative. At the outset, we will turn to those demographic and socioeconomic factors in which political orientations are rooted.

DEMOGRAPHIC BASES OF ECUADOREAN POLITICS

In November of 1950 Ecuador compiled its first national census, finding it an innovative and at times disturbing experience. There was disappointment on learning that, despite previous estimates of a population of 4 million, the final count was only 3,202,757. For some, the lower figure suggested the inadequacy and inexperience of data collection. Certainly technical problems abounded; an extreme case was recounted by Galo Plaza, the president under whose initiative the census was carried out:

> . . . a community of culturally remote Indians refused to cooperate with the census, and several dangerous uprisings took place. Local authorities and enumerators were attacked and in some cases barely managed to escape with their lives. I flew to the scene of the difficulty and spoke to the Indians, explaining in a friendly manner what the census meant in order to dissipate their fears. They finally agreed to submit to the census on the condition that I remain among them during the enumeration, and we had no further troubles.[6]

This was atypical, but suggested the difficulty of the task as well as the importance of presidential personalism.

Despite inevitable inaccuracies, the 1950 census gave a far better measure of the national population than had ever before existed. Previous figures had been little more than rough guesses, based upon the degree of general familiarity with Ecuador enjoyed by the compiler. It is believed that the population was roughly half a million when independence from Spain was established. Two widely cited sources later estimated the population at 1,108,000 in 1857[7] and in 1887 at 1,272,000.[8] By

[6] Galo Plaza, *Problems of Democracy in Latin America* (Chapel Hill: University of North Carolina Press, 1955), pp. 36-37.

[7] Manuel Villavicencio, *Geografía de la República del Ecuador* (New York: Imprenta de Roberto Craighead, 1858), p. 164.

[8] Teodoro Wolf, *Geografía y geología del Ecuador* (Leipzig: F. A. Brochkaus, 1892), p. 523.

1940, according to a North American scholar, the figure stood at 2,600,000.[9] Certainly the 1950 data, whatever its shortcomings, gave a more meaningful picture. By 1962, when a second national census was taken, the national total had risen to 4,476,007, an increase of almost 40 percent. And the most recent available official figures, estimated for November of 1968, showed a further increase to 5,776,100.[10] This represented a total growth of some 80 percent during the years since 1950 and an annual growth rate of some 3 percent.

Distribution and Density. Both the *oriente* jungle regions and the Galápagos Islands have always been sparsely inhabited, with more than 90 percent of the population located either along the coast (*costa*) or in the Andean highlands (*sierra*). Yet the distribution has been shifting perceptibly away from the *sierra* for generations. Teodoro Wolf's estimate for 1887 placed 949,800 Ecuadoreans in the highlands, or a shade under 75 percent. According to the 1968 estimates, however, there were a total of 2,894,806 *serranos* and 2,770,659 *costeños;* thus the division between the two regions is virtually equal, while the movement from *sierra* to *costa* continues. Table 1 provides a breakdown by region and by province. Given both the rapid demographic increase and the rate of internal migration, the population density has increased as well as having been redistributed. As suggested by Table 1, the most pronounced increases are found in the provinces of Guayas and Pichincha, the capitals of which are Guayaquil and Quito respectively, Ecuador's two most populous cities. The province of Chimborazo, with its own rapidly growing capital of Riobamba, has also increased significantly in recent years. Regional totals further underline the rapidity of coastal population growth.

In addition to the rapid national growth and its shifting locus from highlands to coast, a third major demographic characteristic is the trend toward urbanization. While Ecuador remains predominantly rural, growth of the cities is reducing the traditional rural-urban imbalance. This is apparent in Tables 3 and 4, which include both rural-urban breakdowns for 1950

[9] T. Lynn Smith, *Latin American Population Studies* (Gainesville: University of Florida Press, 1960), p. 75.

[10] Junta Nacional de Planificación y Coordinación Económica, *División territorial de la República del Ecuador* (Quito: Secretaría General de Planeación, 1969), p. 3.

Table 1
POPULATION OF ECUADOR BY PROVINCE AND REGION, 1950-1968

Province	1950	%	1962	%	1968	%
COSTA						
El Oro	89,306	2.8	160,650	3.6	218,663	3.8
Esmeraldas	75,407	2.3	124,881	2.8	163,585	2.8
Guayas	582,144	18.2	979,223	21.9	1,291,895	22.4
Los Ríos	150,260	4.7	250,062	5.6	328,004	5.7
Manabí	401,378	12.5	612,542	13.7	768,512	13.3
TOTALS	1,298,495	40.5	2,127,358	47.6	2,770,659	48.0
SIERRA						
Azuay	250,975	7.8	274,642	6.1	309,200	5.3
Bolívar	109,305	3.4	131,651	2.9	169,618	2.9
Cañar	97,681	3.0	112,733	2.5	130,944	2.5
Carchi	76,595	2.4	94,649	2.1	114,328	1.9
Chimborazo	218,130	6.8	276,668	6.2	352,283	6.1
Cotopaxi	165,602	5.2	154,971	3.5	228,028	3.9
Imbabura	146,893	4.6	174,039	3.9	205,058	3.5
Loja	216,802	6.8	285,448	6.4	355,868	6.2
Pichincha	386,520	12.1	587,835	13.1	779,564	13.5
Tungurahua	187,942	5.9	178,709	3.9	249,915	4.3
TOTALS	1,856,445	58.0	2,271,345	50.6	2,894,806	50.1
ORIENTE*	46,471	1.4	74,913	1.7	107,335	1.8
GALAPAGOS	1,346	0.1	2,391	0.1	3,300	0.1
NATIONAL TOTALS	3,202,757	100.0	4,476,007	100.0	5,776,100	100.0

Sources: República del Ecuador, *Primer censo de población del Ecuador 1950* (Quito: Ministerio de Economía, 1960); República del Ecuador, *Segundo censo de población y primer censo de vivienda* (Quito: Junta Nacional de Planificación y Coordinación Económica, 1964); and *Mimeo* of the Junta, November 1968.

*Provincial totals for the *oriente* are omitted, since the boundaries have been redrawn and provinces reformed several times since 1950. As of 1968 the totals were: Morona-Santiago 36,537; Napo 34,755; Pastaza 19,621; and Zamora-Chinchipe, 16,442. Percentages computed by the author.

and 1968, along with the populations of provincial capitals for 1962 and 1968. Whereas the 1950 census showed that Ecuadoreans were 71.5 percent rural, by 1968 it was estimated that less than two-thirds, or 62.4 percent, were rural. The direction of this pattern was more evident in the coastal provinces, where

Table 2
DENSITY AND DISTRIBUTION OF POPULATION OF ECUADOR, 1950-1968

Province	Sq. Km.	% Natl. Terr.	DENSITY 1950	1962	1968
COSTA					
El Oro	5,826	2.2	15	28	38
Esmeraldas	14,978	5.6	5	8	11
Guayas	21,077	8.0	28	46	61
Los Ríos	5,913	2.2	25	42	55
Manabí	18,255	7.0	22	34	42
TOTALS	66,049	25.0	20	32	40
SIERRA					
Azuay	7,804	3.0	32	35	39
Bolívar	4,271	1.6	26	31	39
Cañar	3,378	1.3	29	33	38
Carchi	3,701	1.4	21	26	31
Chimborazo	5,555	2.1	39	50	63
Cotopaxi	5,028	1.9	33	31	45
Imbabura	4,817	1.8	30	36	43
Loja	12,033	4.5	18	24	29
Pichincha	19,543	7.4	20	30	39
Tungurahua	3,212	1.2	59	56	77
TOTALS	69,342	26.2	27	33	42
ORIENTE	121,263	45.9	0.4	0.6	0.9
GALAPAGOS	7,812	2.9	0.2	0.3	0.4
NATIONAL TOTALS	264,466	100.0	12	17	22

Sources: Excepting the figures for 1968 density (calculated by the author from population data in Table 1), this is found in Junta Nacional de Planificación y Coordinación, *División territorial de la República del Ecuador* (Quito: Secretaría General de Planeación, 1969), p. 14.

there was a drop of 10.7 percent in the rural sector, while for the ten highland provinces the movement toward the city was merely 6.9 percent. Not surprisingly, only Pichincha and Guayas provinces were primarily urban, with figures of 65.2 and 63.1 percents respectively. Again the more dynamic coastal demographic pattern reappeared; Guayas had increased its urban sector by 13.5 percent, nearly double the 6.8 rise for

Table 3
RURAL – URBAN POPULATION DENSITY, 1950 and 1968

Province	% Rural 1950	% Urban 1950	% Rural 1968	% Urban 1968
COSTA				
El Oro	73.9	26.1	52.1	47.9
Esmeraldas	79.7	20.3	63.7	36.3
Guayas	50.4	49.6	36.9	63.1
Los Ríos	86.5	13.5	76.9	23.1
Manabí	71.3	18.7	79.7	20.3
TOTALS	67.4	32.6	56.7	43.3
SIERRA				
Azuay	80.4	19.6	72.9	27.1
Bolívar	89.8	10.2	89.0	11.0
Cañar	86.6	13.4	87.8	12.2
Carchi	73.0	17.0	71.7	28.3
Chimborazo	78.8	21.2	79.8	20.2
Cotopaxi	88.8	11.2	88.4	11.6
Imbabura	78.6	21.4	71.1	28.9
Loja	86.0	14.0	79.7	20.3
Pichincha	41.6	58.4	34.8	65.2
Tungurahua	79.2	20.8	68.1	31.9
TOTALS	73.8	26.2	66.9	33.1
ORIENTE	88.0	12.0	86.7	13.3
GALAPAGOS	100.0	0	100.0	0
NATIONAL TOTALS	71.5	28.5	62.4	37.6

Source: República del Ecuador, *Población urbana, suburbana y rural* (Quito: Dirección General de Estadística y Censos, 1954), and 1968 *Mimeo* cited in Table 1.

Pichincha. Moreover, it was on the coast that the more dramatic shifts had taken place. El Oro had increased its urban sector by 21.8 percent, Esmeraldas by 16.0, and Los Ríos by 9.6. In the *sierra,* only Tungurahua in addition to Pichincha showed a significant change, with an 11.1 percent rise in its urban population.

Similar characteristics are suggested by the data in Table 4 on the growth of provincial capitals, although individual variation is greater. Nationally, the percentage of the population in

Table 4
POPULATION OF PROVINCIAL CAPITALS, 1962 and 1968

Province	Capital	1962	1968
COSTA			
El Oro	Machala	30,136	50,025
Esmeraldas	Esmeraldas	33,439	51,573
Guayas	Guayaquil	510,785	716,600
Los Ríos	Babahoyo	16,369	21,035
Manabí	Portoviejo	32,435	43,305
TOTALS		623,164	882,538
SIERRA			
Azuay	Cuenca	60,817	73,407
Bolívar	Guaranda	9,597	11,243
Cañar	Azogues	8,217	8,830
Carchi	Tulcán	16,535	21,025
Chimborazo	Riobamba	41,689	50,710
Cotopaxi	Latacunga	14,936	16,666
Imbabura	Ibarra	25,806	34,289
Loja	Loja	26,657	35,332
Pichincha	Quito	355,183	483,847
Tungurahua	Ambato	53,745	69,766
TOTALS		613,182	805,115
ORIENTE	–	5,786	7,896
GALAPAGOS	–	–	–
NATIONAL TOTALS		1,242,132	1,695,449

Sources: From earlier tables, including 1962 census and 1968 mimeo.

the capitals grew by a dramatic 36.5 percent in only six years. The increase for the capitals of the five coastal provinces was 41.6 percent, while for the ten highland capitals it was 31.3. For Ecuador's two leading cities, the six-year rate of population growth stood at 40.3 percent for Guayaquil and 35.9 for Quito. While all of the coastal capitals increased markedly, the less populous highland capitals grew only slightly (especially Guaranda, Azogues, and Latacunga). Residents of these smaller capitals were presumably attracted away, if not to Quito, at least to one of the larger and more progressive provincial centers. The extent to which the overall increase in the urban sector is a result of rising birth rates rather than internal migration cannot be accurately assessed. However, the sketchy census figures on birth rates suggest that while they are higher in the cities, and especially on the coast, the major explanation for urban increase derives from the migration toward larger population centers.[11]

Occupational Characteristics. Ecuador's economically active population has shown a slight relative decline in recent years; in 1950 the labor force constituted 38.5 percent of the total population, while by 1962 it had dropped to 32.2 percent (see Tables 5 and 6). When defined in terms of persons twelve years of age and above, 59.9 percent of the population in 1950 was employed, and only 51.7 in 1962. In short, both the percentage and the gross number of unemployed Ecuadoreans increased during these years, with the dependent category growing. Regionally, employment was consistently higher in the *sierra* than on the *costa.* In 1950 40.8 percent of the total highland population was economically active, as contrasted with 35.4 on the coast. Twelve years later the respective figures were 34.1 percent for the *sierra* and 30.2 for the coast. Moreover, there was no significant difference between more and less populous regions. Indeed, figures for Pichincha were slightly below the *sierra* regional total in both 1950 and 1962, although Guayas was somewhat above the mean for the *costa* in both years.

Shifts in occupational activity also took place during the years between national censuses, although the general pattern did not vary greatly. Defined by occupational position, 53.9 percent of the active population in 1950 was listed as salaried, a figure which had dropped to 47.6 by 1962. The self-employed followed with 32.8 and 41.0 percent respectively. In both census years the percentage of salaried workers was higher on the coast, and especially in 1962. Given the nature of economic endeavors in the two regions, it was not surprising that nonremunerated farm workers constituted a larger proportion for the *sierra* than for the *costa* in both 1950 and 1962.

[11]For a careful if rapidly outdated analysis, see John V. D. Saunders, *La población del Ecuador: un análisis del censo de 1950* (Quito: Casa de la Cultura Ecuatoriana, 1959).

Table 5
ECONOMIC ACTIVITY AND OCCUPATIONAL POSITION, 1950

	ECONOMIC ACTIVITY						*OCCUPATIONAL POSITION* (percentages)				
Province	Econ. Active	%	Econ. Inactive	%	Popltn. Active (12 and over)		a	b	c	d	e
COSTA											
El Oro	31,395	35.5	57,371	64.5	57,103	55.9	1.2	52.7	35.7	7.9	4.5
Esmeraldas	26,768	35.5	48,639	64.5	46,544	57.5	0.1	43.3	42.7	5.4	8.5
Guayas	208,947	35.9	373,207	64.1	375,801	55.6	0.6	60.8	27.5	2.3	8.8
Los Ríos	51,285	34.1	98,975	65.9	90,255	56.8	0.3	63.7	21.1	4.7	10.2
Manabí	140,907	35.1	260,471	64.9	238,643	59.0	0.3	45.3	37.9	8.5	8.0
TOTALS	459,302	35.4	838,663	64.6	808,346	56.8	0.4	54.8	31.3	5.0	8.5
SIERRA											
Azuay	120,800	48.9	130,375	51.1	165,596	72.8	0.6	55.8	36.0	7.6	0
Bolívar	40,175	36.9	69,140	63.1	70,097	57.3	7.9	37.8	38.2	16.0	0.1
Cañar	50,762	52.0	46,919	48.0	63,722	79.7	0.2	51.2	37.5	11.0	0.1
Carchi	28,975	37.8	47,820	62.2	49,197	58.5	0.1	57.5	34.5	7.9	0
Chimborazo	90,336	41.4	127,804	58.6	146,635	61.6	0.6	51.0	36.5	11.5	0.4
Cotopaxi	64,078	38.7	101,524	61.3	108,432	59.1	3.3	48.6	34.3	13.8	0
Imbabura	62,627	42.6	84,266	57.4	100,462	62.3	2.3	53.3	34.0	10.4	0
Loja	81,205	37.5	135,597	62.5	134,882	60.2	1.0	44.9	40.3	14.8	0
Pichincha	146,083	37.8	240,447	62.2	260,170	56.1	1.6	69.5	21.0	3.3	4.6
Tungurahua	72,358	38.5	115,684	61.5	127,187	56.8	3.4	45.6	38.0	12.6	0.4
TOTALS	757,399	40.8	1,099,576	59.2	1,226,380	61.8	1.8	53.8	33.6	9.8	1.0
ORIENTE	19,441	41.8	27,030	58.2	29,577	63.6	0.6	43.5	40.6	8.4	6.9
GALAPAGOS	448	33.3	898	66.7	871	51.4	0.5	46.9	49.5	2.5	0.6
NATIONAL TOTALS	1,236,590	38.5	1,966,167	61.5	2,065,174	59.9	1.3	53.9	32.8	8.0	4.0

Source: Compiled by the author from a 1950 census.
Columns for Occupational Position: a, employers; b, salaried; c, self-employed; d, unpaid farm workers; e, undetermined.

Census figures also provide a breakdown into such branches of economic activity as agriculture, mining, construction, commerce, and so on (see Table 7). In 1950 49.1 percent of the economically active population was engaged in agriculture, hunting, and fishing; in 1962 this had risen to 55.6. In 1950 manufacturing and industry was second with 24.0 percent, but by 1962 had fallen to 14.5. The percentage engaged in services rose slightly, from 11.5 to 13.2 percent in 1962. All of the other categories fell below 10 percent of the active population in both census years. Closer examination shows the extent to which the provinces dominated by Quito and Guayaquil differed from the national pattern. For the former, only 28.5

Table 6
ECONOMIC ACTIVITY AND OCCUPATIONAL POSITION, 1962

	ECONOMIC ACTIVITY						*OCCUPATIONAL POSITION* (percentages)				
Province	Econ. Active	%	Econ. Inactive	%	Popltn. Active (12 and over)		a	b	c	d	e
COSTA											
El Oro	53,089	33.0	107,561	67.0	98,060	54.1	2.4	53.8	35.5	6.2	2.1
Esmeraldas	36,640	29.4	88,241	70.6	70,698	51.7	1.5	38.8	50.4	6.4	2.9
Guayas	303,437	31.0	675,786	69.0	607,600	49.9	2.1	62.1	28.8	3.1	3.9
Los Ríos	77,206	30.9	172,856	69.1	146,768	52.6	2.5	65.4	26.2	4.5	1.4
Manabí	171,274	27.9	441,268	72.1	347,514	49.3	3.7	46.7	38.8	9.1	1.7
TOTALS	641,646	30.2	1,485,712	69.8	1,270,640	50.5	2.6	56.3	32.9	5.1	3.1
SIERRA											
Azuay	96,393	35.1	178,249	64.9	178,488	54.0	0.9	27.9	57.5	12.0	1.7
Bolívar	43,739	33.2	87,912	66.8	85,986	50.9	1.9	27.9	56.0	13.3	0.9
Cañar	42,375	37.6	70,358	62.4	72,151	58.7	1.1	24.8	61.0	12.0	1.1
Carchi	31,873	33.7	62,776	66.3	59,338	53.7	1.3	45.1	43.3	8.2	2.1
Chimborazo	95,540	34.5	181,128	65.5	184,311	51.8	0.8	35.2	52.5	10.0	1.5
Cotopaxi	54,129	34.9	100,842	65.1	101,486	53.3	0.9	36.3	53.2	8.4	1.2
Imbabura	63,648	36.6	110,391	63.4	116,950	54.4	1.1	39.7	50.9	6.9	1.4
Loja	89,787	31.5	195,661	68.5	172,605	52.0	1.1	24.6	63.8	9.4	1.1
Pichincha	198,094	33.7	389,741	66.3	381,119	52.9	2.4	64.9	25.1	2.8	4.7
Tungurahua	59,861	33.5	118,848	66.5	117,780	50.8	1.4	41.1	47.6	7.4	2.5
TOTALS	775,439	34.1	1,495,906	65.9	1,470,214	52.7	1.4	40.9	47.3	7.9	2.5
ORIENTE	24,691	32.9	50,222	67.1	45,453	54.3	2.7	34.9	51.5	9.1	1.8
GALAPAGOS	815	34.0	1,576	66.0	1,460	55.8	2.1	53.0	38.9	4.0	2.0
NATIONAL TOTALS	1,442,591	32.2	3,033,416	67.8	2,787,767	51.7	2.2	47.6	41.0	6.7	2.5

Source: Compiled by the author from 1962 census.
Columns for Occupational Position: a, employers; b, salaried; c, self-employed; d, unpaid farm workers; e, undetermined.

and 28.1 percent of the Pichincha population was engaged in agricultural pursuits in the two census years, while 25.2 and 26.2 percent were employed in services. The figures for manufacturing and industry stood at 21.3 for 1950 and 20.7 for 1962. In the province of Guayas, 33.5 and 35.2 percent pursued agricultural activities, while the service sector was well above both regional and national means, at 17.9 percent and 17.8. Manufacturing and industry accounted for 17.2 in 1950 and 15.6 in 1962. Finally, both provinces were above the national figures for the commercial sector. Pichincha had 9.4 percent and 8.1 so occupied, and in Guayas the figures were more than double the national totals, at 11.6 in 1950 and 13.7 in 1962.

Such data, imprecise though they may be, give some suggestion of changing dimensions over time. The increased number of Ecuadoreans engaged in agriculture is accounted for largely by the expansion of banana activities, as well as the opening of previously unoccupied lands elsewhere on the coast. Manufacturing, while slowly increasing, has not maintained its proportion of the growing population. Quito and Guayaquil are, of course, the centers for such activities, although there are lesser concentrations in Cuenca, Riobamba, and Otavalo. Elsewhere the emphasis has been on small handicrafts, and these are

Table 7
BRANCHES OF ECONOMIC ACTIVITY, 1950 and 1962

	1950								
Province	a	b	c	d	e	f	g	h	i
COSTA									
El Oro	60.3	1.3	9.3	1.6	0.1	4.9	2.1	15.5	4.9
Esmeraldas	64.4	0.1	7.0	1.2	0.1	4.7	2.1	11.5	8.9
Guayas	33.5	1.1	17.2	8.0	0.2	11.6	4.9	17.9	35.6
Los Ríos	70.8	0.1	4.4	0.6	0.1	3.7	1.3	7.6	11.4
Manabí	56.8	0.1	19.3	1.1	0.1	4.0	1.7	8.2	8.7
TOTALS	48.4	0.1	15.0	1.9	0.1	7.5	3.1	13.2	10.3
SIERRA									
Azuay	44.3	0.1	45.1	1.1	0.7	2.6	0.7	5.4	-
Bolívar	80.9	0.2	8.8	0.7	0.1	2.3	0.9	6.1	0.2
Cañar	38.4	0.2	54.1	1.2	0.1	1.3	0.8	3.8	0.1
Carchi	51.5	0.4	27.0	2.3	0.1	5.0	1.4	12.1	0.2
Chimborazo	57.5	0.1	26.8	1.7	0.1	3.6	2.0	8.1	0.1
Cotopaxi	62.5	0.4	21.3	2.2	0.1	5.5	0.8	7.1	0.1
Imbabura	40.1	0.2	42.7	2.1	0.1	4.6	2.2	7.8	0.2
Loja	64.6	0.1	21.7	1.3	0.1	2.8	0.7	8.6	0.1
Pichincha	28.5	0.5	21.3	5.5	0.3	9.4	3.6	25.2	5.7
Tungurahua	58.7	0.2	22.8	2.9	0.1	4.7	1.5	9.0	0.1
TOTALS	50.1	0.2	29.9	1.3	0.1	4.6	1.7	10.6	1.5
ORIENTE	71.6	2.8	5.8	1.0	–	1.8	0.3	10.4	6.3
GALAPAGOS	74.6	–	8.0	–	–	0.9	1.8	13.6	1.1
NATIONAL TOTALS	49.1	0.1	24.0	1.5	0.1	5.7	2.3	11.5	5.7

Table 7 (Continued)
BRANCHES OF ECONOMIC ACTIVITY, 1950 and 1962

	1962								
Province	a	b	c	d	e	f	g	h	i
COSTA									
El Oro	62.8	0.8	7.6	2.9	0.1	6.4	4.4	12.3	2.7
Esmeraldas	69.1	0	7.9	2.9	0.1	4.9	3.9	10.7	0.5
Guayas	35.2	0.6	15.6	4.5	0.8	13.7	5.6	17.8	6.2
Los Ríos	78.2	0	4.7	1.2	0.1	4.8	1.9	7.6	1.5
Manabí	73.6	0	7.5	1.7	0.3	5.3	1.6	7.9	2.1
TOTALS	54.8	0.4	11.2	3.2	0.4	9.1	3.9	12.9	4.1
SIERRA									
Azuay	59.1	0	21.1	2.4	0.2	3.5	1.5	10.5	1.7
Bolívar	83.7	0.1	5.7	1.3	0	1.9	0.5	6.2	0.6
Cañar	61.2	0.2	25.6	1.8	0.1	2.2	1.4	6.6	0.9
Carchi	61.3	0.5	15.1	2.9	0	4.2	2.2	12.1	1.7
Chimborazo	72.3	0	11.4	2.3	0.3	2.7	1.9	7.5	1.6
Cotopaxi	66.6	0.2	16.6	2.1	0.3	3.6	1.8	7.4	1.4
Imbabura	50.1	0.3	28.0	2.8	0.1	4.9	2.5	9.9	1.4
Loja	73.9	0	9.8	1.7	0.1	3.6	1.1	8.9	0.9
Pichincha	28.1	0.3	20.7	7.1	0.5	8.1	4.2	26.2	4.8
Tungurahua	55.9	0.1	16.6	2.1	0.3	3.6	1.8	7.4	1.4
TOTALS	55.8	0.2	17.9	3.4	0.3	4.4	2.3	13.5	2.2
ORIENTE	74.7	0.2	4.4	3.8	0.1	1.4	0.6	14.4	0.4
GALAPAGOS	58.0	3.8	5.9	3.8	0.1	2.1	1.0	25.1	0.3
NATIONAL TOTALS	55.6	0.2	14.5	3.3		6.7	3.0	13.2	3.1

Source: Compiled by the author from 1950 and 1962 censuses.
Columns are the following: a, agriculture, hunting, and fishing; b, mining; c, manufacturing and industry; d, construction; e, electricity and water; f, commerce; g, transportation and communications; h, services; i, miscellaneous. All figures are percentages.

presently in decline. Urbanization, primarily in Quito and Guayaquil, has brought about predictable increases in services, as well as in transportation and in commerce, but these figures still represent but a small proportion of the total economically active population.

Educational and Living Conditions. Historically Ecuador

has suffered from endemic illiteracy. Table 8 gives some measure of the problem, although data from the 1950 and 1962 census are not directly comparable. In the former year, based on the population of age ten and above, 43.7 percent was listed as illiterate. The regional total of 45.9 for the highlands exceeded the 40.1 percent for the coast, while 57.8 of the sparsely inhabited *oriente* was illiterate. The more rural provinces were generally marked by lower rates of literacy, as exemplified by

Table 8
RATES OF LITERACY AND ILLITERACY, 1950 and 1962

Province	1950[a] (lit.)	1950[a] (illit.)	1962[b] (lit.)	1962[b] (illit.)
COSTA				
El Oro	72.9	27.1	79.1	20.9
Esmeraldas	48.8	51.2	55.2	44.8
Guayas	70.7	29.3	76.0	24.0
Los Ríos	42.3	57.7	55.6	44.4
Manabí	49.1	50.9	57.1	42.9
TOTAL	59.9	40.1	67.3	32.7
SIERRA				
Azuay	54.6	45.4	65.6	34.4
Bolívar	51.2	48.8	57.6	42.4
Cañar	47.4	52.6	56.2	43.8
Carchi	70.6	29.4	74.2	25.8
Chimborazo	40.5	59.5	44.9	55.1
Cotopaxi	39.0	61.0	52.2	47.8
Imbabura	46.1	53.9	54.0	46.0
Loja	58.8	41.2	68.7	31.3
Pichincha	68.4	31.6	75.3	24.7
Tungurahua	52.6	47.4	66.4	33.6
TOTALS	54.1	45.9	63.6	36.4
ORIENTE	42.2	57.8	56.4	43.6
GALAPAGOS	80.8	19.2	86.7	13.3
NATIONAL TOTALS	56.3	43.7	65.3	34.7

Sources: Censuses for 1950 and 1962.
Data for 1950 (a) represent the population of age ten and over; for 1962 (b) represent the population of age six and over.

Los Rios, Chimborazo, and Cotopaxi. Twelve years later census figures were based on age six and above, with the national illiteracy figure 34.7 percent. The *sierra* rate of illiteracy remained higher than the *costa,* by 36.4 to 32.7 percent. Provincial rankings were similar to those for 1950. Thus El Oro remained the most literate in the country, with Guayas second. The lowest literacy rates were again in Chimborazo, Cotopaxi, Los Rios, and Imbabura, although the range between extremes had shrunk somewhat.

A review of data on housing conditions illustrates the level of inadequacy; Table 9 summarizes by province the percentage of homes with and without water, hygienic, and electrical services. Little elaboration is necessary. For 1962, 62.3 percent of all homes were without indoor water, 67.1 lacked sanitation facilities, and 67.7 were without electric light. Regional totals are variable. There are slightly more coastal than highland homes without water. However, conditions of sanitation and electricity in the *sierra* are worse. In highland homes, 76.2 percent lack hygienic facilities, with 70.4 without light, while on the coast these figures are 54.7 and 63.7 percent. In the *oriente,* of course, relatively few homes have any of these services. Predictably, Pichincha and Guayas stand out in the availability of such facilities, far exceeding those elsewhere in Ecuador. Judged by these criteria the province of Esmeraldas is generally the least developed on the coast, while for the *sierra* Bolívar, Cañar, and Loja – all provinces in the more remote south – are the least developed.

REGIONAL BASES OF ECUADOREAN SUBCULTURES: THE ANDES

The regional and subregional fragmentation of Ecuador underlies the cultural, socioeconomic, and political divisions which have persisted throughout recorded history. The geographic contrasts between the Andean highlands (*sierra*) and the coastal plains (*costa*) have spawned perhaps the most intense regionalism in the hemisphere, and to these are added subregional characteristics which are nearly as deeply rooted. Inade-

Table 9
HOUSING CONDITIONS, 1962

Province	Water Service		Hygienic		Elec. Light	
	with	w/o	with	w/o	with	w/o
COSTA						
El Oro	49.2	50.8	34.1	65.9	30.3	69.7
Esmeraldas	12.2	87.7	16.4	83.6	13.0	87.0
Guayas	61.4	38.6	65.2	34.8	58.8	41.2
Los Ríos	17.9	82.1	22.7	77.3	16.7	83.3
Manabí	4.6	95.4	31.2	68.8	13.4	86.6
TOTALS	36.5	63.5	45.3	54.7	36.3	63.7
SIERRA						
Azuay	23.6	76.4	17.4	82.6	21.2	78.8
Bolívar	16.1	83.9	7.6	92.4	9.8	90.2
Cañar	15.5	84.5	6.3	93.7	12.7	87.3
Carchi	38.5	61.5	15.8	84.2	32.5	67.5
Chimborazo	29.2	70.8	14.9	85.1	15.2	84.8
Cotopaxi	27.1	72.9	9.2	90.8	17.7	82.3
Imbabura	37.7	62.3	12.6	87.4	28.0	72.0
Loja	23.2	76.8	7.2	92.8	12.8	87.2
Pichincha	75.9	24.1	57.6	42.4	61.8	38.2
Tungurahua	40.0	60.0	26.7	73.3	31.9	68.1
TOTALS	39.1	60.9	23.8	76.2	29.6	70.4
ORIENTE	9.6	90.4	9.6	90.4	11.9	88.1
GALAPAGOS	45.6	54.4	27.3	72.7	47.9	52.1
NATIONAL TOTALS	37.7	62.3	32.9	67.1	32.3	67.7

Source: 1962 census.

quate transportation and communications, racial diversity, religious and political cleavages, and conflicting social practices blend in a mosaic of dazzling if disruptive discontinuity. The bulk of the population has been placed in a situation of marginality which has endured to modern times and, despite recent advances, constitutes a major impediment to meaningful national development. The political manifestations of disunity are discussed in later chapters, but can only be understood within the context of geographic and socioeconomic subcultures.

On the broadest dimensions, Ecuador is divided into highlands, coast, eastern jungle (*oriente*), and the Galápagos Islands (known officially as the Archipelago de Colón).[12] Of these, the latter two have little present importance, although the potential for development of the *oriente* has been enhanced by the recent uncovering of petroleum deposits there. The archipelago of the Galápagos consists of twelve islands and numerous islets of volcanic origin centered some six hundred miles west in the Pacific. Noted for the nineteenth-century studies by Charles Darwin and leased to the United States for an air base during World War II, the Galápagos remain sparsely populated today. Despite the richness of the surrounding waters for fish, there are only some three thousand permanent residents. Regular air service from the mainland has been recently inaugurated as an intended stimulus to tourism, but the islands remain peripheral to national life, and their status is unlikely to change in the near future.

The *oriente* comprises roughly half of the national territory, extending from the descending slopes of the eastern Andes into dense jungle foliage reaching the headwaters of Amazon tributaries. Although the population more than doubled in the years between 1950 and 1968, it still totals but a little above 100,000 inhabitants, with a density of 0.6 per square kilometer. While rainfall is plentiful and much of the land is fertile, most of the *oriente* remains inaccessible and, other than a few outposts along jungle streams, is inhabited by nomadic Indians. It has received increasing public attention through the discovery of petroleum on the eastern mountain slopes and beyond (for details see chapter 5). But as with similar regions in the other Pacific coast countries of South America, the obstacles in tapping its potential are formidable.

Ecuadorean life in all its manifest shapes and forms, in short, lies primarily in the *sierra* and westward to the Pacific. The manifest contrasts will be reiterated throughout this volume. To understand the bases of existing subcultures, then, requires a close examination of these two regions. Their respec-

[12]Among several standard Ecuadorean geographies, the reader is directed to Ulpiano Navarro Andrade, *Geografía económica del Ecuador,* 2 vols. (Quito: Editorial "Santo Domingo," 1966), and Girardo Nicola L., *Síntesis de la geografía del Ecuador* (Ambato: Publicaciones de la Sección Nocturna del Colegio Nacional "Bolívar," 1965).

tive geographic conditions, resultant economic activities, and emergent social attitudes and values testify to the enormity of developmental problems.

The Reality of Geography. The rugged Andean chain runs north and south across the entire length of Ecuador in two parallel ranges, the Eastern and Western Cordilleras. Among the many majestic snow-capped volcanoes are Cotopaxi (19,500 feet), Cayambe (19,200 feet), and Tungurahua (16,700 feet) in the former, while the more spectacular of the Western Cordillera include Chimborazo (20,500 feet), Iliniza (17,400 feet), and Cotocachi (16,300 feet). Between the *cordilleras* lies a mountainous plain of some 7,000-9,500 feet in elevation, divided in turn by mountain spurs running east and west. The resulting *hoyas,* as Ecuadoreans term these basins, provide the setting for the larger population centers of the *sierra.* It is along this "valley of the volcanoes" that the cities of Tulcán, Ibarra, Quito, Latacunga, Ambato, Riobamba, Cuenca, and Loja are located (running in order from north to south). In varying degrees each has its own features and characteristics, although constrained by the Andean topographic and climatic setting common to all. Given the elevation, temperatures are chilly; in the mid-fifties by day, they drop sharply after nightfall, but there is little seasonal change during the year. Rainfall is variable in different parts of the Andes, although in many of the basins it is relatively light.

The two northernmost provincial capitals are Tulcán and Ibarra. The former, situated a few miles from the Columbian border where the historic natural bridge of Rumichaca crosses the Carchi River, is at some 9,800 feet the highest city in Ecuador. Inhabited by just over 20,000 persons, Tulcán serves as the marketing center for nearby dairy farms, and surrounding lands also support barley, wheat, and other grains. As ties with southern Colombia are fairly close, smuggling has often flourished as a consequence. Tulcán has sometimes served as the city of reentry for returning political leaders. One of José María Velasco Ibarra's many arrivals from exile proceeded triumphally from Tulcán along the Pan American Highway to Quito.

Approximately eighty miles south of Tulcán is Ibarra, a city of roughly 35,000 residents. Located 7,300 feet above sea level, it serves as the center of an area in which cereals, cotton, and sugar cane are grown. Perhaps its greatest significance is the rail connection to the northern coastal port of San Lorenzo. Completion of the line in 1957 linked the northern highlands with that coastal area for the first time. While the potential for development has been only partially realized, it has served to introduce change and growth to both cities, while commerce has begun to move north and to the coast from Quito for the first time. Only fifteen miles further south is Otavalo, one of the more unique towns in the republic.

With a population of no more than 10,000, Otavalo is famed for its Indians, among the most industrious and progressive of all Latin America. Energetic and hard-working, the Otavaleños are productive and skilled at their looms, and are known to travel throughout Ecuador and beyond to sell their wares.[13] Weekly fairs on Saturday, beginning at daybreak, are among the most colorful in a country replete with such market days. Singularly active and animated, the Otavalans place a high value on their own land, putting the profits from the sale of their fabrics into its purchase. Otavalo itself and its immediate environs are dotted with cleanly painted homes, and the fields are worked more intensively than is the usual custom in the *sierra.*

Still in the northern Andes some seventy-five miles from Otavalo is the capital city of Quito. Nearly two miles high at about 9,350 feet elevation, it is the world's second highest capital, lying in one of the most beautiful of settings. Surrounded by yet higher mountains dotted by grain fields and overshadowed by the volcano of Pichincha, Quito is within sight of several spectacular snow-crested peaks. Historically the center of Ecuadorean national life since the arrival of the Spanish *conquistadores* in 1534, its population of nearly a half-million is second only to that of Guayaquil. Its *serrano* climate is typified by a mean temperature of 56 degrees Fahrenheit; the months of February through April and October through November are marked by moderate rainfall, while the rest of the year is generally dry.

[13]A friend of the author insists on his having seen an Otavalan, dressed in typical garb, enter the First National City Bank offices in New York City to deposit several thousand dollars! This is by no means unimaginable. The author has seen Otavalans on the streets of Santiago, Chile, and Rio de Janeiro, as well as at market places throughout Ecuador.

Despite the construction of new and modern buildings in recent years, Quito still possesses the colonial charm which is increasingly rare in Latin America.[14] The Plaza Independencia in the heart of the city retains the traditional arrangement whereby it is faced by the Government Palace, Municipal Palace, the Cathedral, and the Archbishop's Palace. Within a short distance are narrow, cobblestoned streets dating back to colonial times, and many buildings of that vintage survive. Quito is also dotted by more than fifty churches, including some of the most ornate and elaborately sculptured in Latin America. Many are rich in art treasures as well, including exquisite carvings and sculpture dating back to the colonial era.

Lying but a few miles south of the Equator, Quito has expanded and spread toward the northern end of the Quito basin, acquiring modern residential sections as well as outlying commercial sections. Among the more notable buildings are the Hotel Quito and the Legislative Palace, both of them erected for the scheduled Eleventh Inter-American Conference which was never held. The former, placed on the mountain rim to the east of the city, provides a remarkable panoramic view of the city. Despite such modern structures, Quito remains in many ways a colonial city. The pace of daily life – especially in contrast with that of rival Guayaquil – is customarily measured, and after nightfall it soon becomes still, only to reawaken with the coming of dawn. Entertainment and social life are largely restricted to the home except for national holidays and the celebration of the city's founding in early December.

While the beauty and charm of Quito reflects the characteristics of traditional highland life and social customs, its historic governmental and political role has led to the introduction of modern life in a fashion and extent alien to other highland cities. Fifty miles to the south, Latacunga is an unremarkable and slumbering provincial capital of fewer than 20,000 residents dominated by the majesty of nearby Cotopaxi. Further to the south, however, both Ambato and Riobamba are important centers. The former, known as the Garden City of Ecuador, is

[14] A useful review is Filoteo Samaniego Salazar, "Colonial Art of Ecuador," reproduced in Richard E. Greenleaf (ed.), *The Roman Catholic Church in Colonial Latin America* (New York: Alfred A. Knopf, Inc., 1971), pp. 251-56.

eighty miles from Quito at a height of 8,400 feet overlooking the Ambato River. The country's fourth most populous city at some 70,000, Ambato receives sufficient rainfall to nourish orchards and floral gardens. The home of the nineteenth-century writer Juan Montalvo, Ambato contains several commemorative busts and statues as well as a mausoleum and adjoining Montalvo historical museum. While serving as the market and commercial center for the region, Ambato also includes the colorful suburb of Miraflores where prosperous Guayaquil families own summer homes.

A road runs east from Ambato toward the *oriente,* passing the town of Pelileo which was rebuilt following the devastating 1948 earthquake. It then drops torturously to Baños and continues to Puyo in the *oriente,* in 1972 the easternmost town in Ecuador accessible by all-weather road. A few miles along this road between Ambato and Pelileo is the home of the Salasacas, one of Ecuador's more distinctive Indian tribes. Numbering some 2,500, they remain protectively aloof from whites and *mestizos,* tilling their own lands while weaving primitive if strikingly unusual tapestries. Resisting the encroachments of westernized life, the independent-minded Salasacas only reluctantly adjusted to the extent necessary to move the products of their looms into the hands of buyers.

Riobamba, the provincial capital of Chimborazo, is the home of 50,000 inhabitants roughly forty miles south of Ambato. Founded shortly after the Spanish arrival in Quito, it lies amid a region characterized by subsistence agriculture and occasional cattle raising. Typically colonial in outlook, Riobamba has grown through the stimulus of the Quito to Guayaquil railway. The trip from the coast to Riobamba covers 150 miles, and it is the usual custom to spend the night there, after which the train continues to Quito the following morning. The local fair on Saturdays deliberately caters to travelers, although local tourist facilities are poor.

The Indians of Riobamba provide a classic illustration of the gradual breakdown of indigenous insularity. Although long existing without enjoying access to the benefits of national society, the Indians of Riobamba and the canton of Colta are coming into increasing contact with the outside world. In Riobamba even more than in Cuenca or Loja to the south, the vertical north-south divisions are being crosscut increasingly by horizontal east-west relations. Within the past decade the physical mobility between Riobamba and the coast has gone far to open up the region. Patterns of migration show a much greater flow between Riobamba and Guayaquil, while economic ties have grown apace. This growing horizontal interaction is a forerunner of similar movements elsewhere in Ecuador, heralding the future prospect of a more natural regionalization of Ecuador than now exists.[15]

The road south of Riobamba continues all the way to the Peruvian border, but is an increasingly lonely and difficult trip as one travels along. Thus the two cities of importance in southern Ecuador – Cuenca and Loja – stand isolated from the rest of the country. Only in recent years has the introduction of regular air service brought them closer to the mainstream of national life. Cuenca, the capital of Azuay, is Ecuador's third city with nearly 75,000 residents, and is known for its own individuality. Founded in 1557, the city today epitomizes the Ecuadorean Andes. At 8,500 feet a crisply colonial center for the windswept farmlands of the surrounding basin, Cuenca is representative of the traditions and customs of Ecuadorean conservatism. Its inhabitants, commonly known as *morlacos,* have long been among the most stubbornly independent conservatives in every sense of the term.

The Catholic Church exerts a powerful influence on local life and society, while Cuenca through the years has produced many prominent leaders of the Conservative party, including its 1960 presidential candidate, Gonzalo Cordero Crespo. *Cuencanos* have also firmly resisted Quito's inevitable highland domination. Although unable to defy the national capital with impunity, Cuenca has employed its geographic isolation to pursue an independent course when possible. While favorable to *serrano* interests when threatened by the coast, Cuenca has generally advocated a measure of regional autonomy in opposition to central governmental control. In 1961, for example, the initiation of antigovernment demonstrations and riots in Cuenca

[15]An excellent study which documents such shifting patterns in detail is Hugo Burgos Guevara, *Relaciones interétnicas en Riobamba; dominio y dependencia en una region indígena ecuatoriana* (México: Instituto Indigenista Interamericano, ediciones especiales 55, 1970).

triggered the movement forcing the resignation of President Velasco. The city's role was also of consequence two years later in the ouster of Carlos Julio Arosemena Monroy from power.

Somewhat similar traits have also been evidenced by Loja, Ecuador's southernmost population center.[16] A city of approximately 35,000, Loja in its solitude has maintained its autonomy far from distant governmental authority. Nestled in a valley at 7,300 feet, it is the central focus for agricultural activities of the surrounding province. Inevitably separated from their fellow Ecuadoreans, *lojanos* have long been threatened historically by the menace of Peruvian incursions, and last experienced military invasion in 1941. Such experiences have etched even more deeply the traits of rugged self-confidence, notwithstanding the impoverished soil and unsympathetic climate. Local leaders bridle if slighted by the central government, while the law school of the University of Loja has produced eminent figures. Although provincialism is gradually eroding, the city remains far removed from major transportation arteries. Even today it is served by an airfield nearly an hour's drive away by twisting mountain road, and flights connecting with Guayaquil are restricted to early morning hours in twin-engined planes.

Economic and Social Patterns. If there are pronounced differences between a Loja and Ambato, for example, this is not to deny the similarities of life and society in the Ecuadorean Andes.[17] Since the time of the Incas agriculture has been the lifeblood of Andean life, and the patterns of land use and ownership are fundamental to an understanding of regional and localist subcultures. Land is unevenly distributed, with large holdings concentrated in the hands of a few. Figures compiled in 1963 for a national developmental plan revealed that 0.4 percent of all agricultural holdings in Ecuador covered 45.1 percent of the total land area. Moreover, nearly three-fourths of the total holdings were under twelve acres, constituting a mere 7.2 percent of the total area. For the *sierra,* roughly 250,000 peasants (largely Indian) worked plots of land smaller than

[16]For an excellent study by one of Loja's most distinguished sons, see Pío Jaramillo Alvarado, *Historia de Loja y su provincia* (Quito: Casa de la Cultura Ecuatoriana, 1955).

[17]An outstanding anthropological study of a Quechua-speaking village in Pichincha province is Ralph L. Beals, *Community in Transition: Nayón-Ecuador* (Los Angeles: University of California Press, 1966).

twenty-five acres. At the other extreme, some four hundred large estates of over 2,500 acres covered 40 percent of total agricultural lands.

Much of the land on these large *haciendas* lies uncultivated. The social prestige of land ownership, the availability of cheap labor, and impoverished living conditions of most *campesinos* (peasants) have all been influential factors. Productive and accessible land is therefore controlled for the most part by a small handful of *hacendados,* many of whom are absentee landowners. Such *haciendas* are commonly operated by a *mestizo* overseer, with field labor provided by Indian peasants. The system of *concertaje* and *huasipungaje,* traditional to the highlands, requires tenant farmers (*huasipungueros*) to work most of the week for the landowner.[18] Compensation for the *huasipunguero* consists of partial pay or, more commonly, the right to work his own subsistence plot of land (*huasipungo*) during what few hours he has to himself. The *huasipungo* itself is too small to support the peasant adequately, and is customarily the least productive land on the *hacienda.* The fortunate *huasipunguero* may occasionally have a small surplus to sell to the local fair, but customarily he lives outside the money economy.

Methods of farming are primitive, and only infrequently mechanized. In the absence of modern methods, crop yields are low. While figures for recent years show some increase in agricultural output, this derives less from greater productivity than from the extension of land under cultivation. The excess supply of agricultural labor contributes to the maintenance of cheap labor, and peasants working small plots of land are deeply attached to them. Generations of isolation from the outside world and allegiance to traditional methods of farming further support long prevailing practices. Despite efforts in the last decade to introduce a national program of agrarian reform (see chapter 5), there is little to suggest a major alteration in the deep-rooted patterns of Andean ownership and usage.[19]

[18]In October of 1964 the government decreed the abolition of the *huasipungo.* However, this legal action has by no means alleviated the conditions and customs attendant upon *huasipungaje.* For an overly optimistic report on initial progress, see *El Comercio* (Quito), March 18, 1968.

[19]A discussion of *indigenista* writings appears in chapter 2. For the moment, the reader is directed to a recent work stressing generally qualitative socioeconomic

The most important crops on the *sierra* have been grains, with two-thirds of the acreage devoted to maize, barley, and wheat. These staples of the Indian diet have proven adaptable to the highland climate. Maize was being cultivated when the Spaniards arrived, is more extensively planted than any other crop, and is found most abundantly in the provinces of Pichincha, Tungurahua, and Azuay. Barley was introduced by the Spaniards and is found extensively throughout the highlands, especially in Chimborazo. Wheat has become increasingly important and, unlike maize and barley, is grown on medium-sized farms with somewhat less primitive methods and higher productivity. It is nonetheless inadequate to meet domestic needs.

Other highland crops include sugar cane, potatoes, and a variety of fruits and vegetables. The cane is used primarily for the production of distilled liquor and for *panela,* a hard brown-sugar substance. Of the vegetables, potatoes are easily the most important. Sufficiently hardy to survive in the cool and arid mountains, potatoes have been increasing in productivity since the 1950s. Less important vegetables include assorted types of beans, peas, yucca, and sweet potatoes. Of nontropical fruits, the more common include avocados, pears, and peaches. Inadequate irrigation has been a major drawback to the cultivation of such crops.

The population of the *sierra,* as already seen, is growing less rapidly than that of the *costa,* and its composition is distinctive. Ethnicity can be only roughly estimated, but a large segment of the highland population is pure-blooded Indian. One highly imperfect measure came from the 1950 census which, although avoiding explicit questions on race, inquired into linguistic characteristics. As Table 10 shows, 16.3 percent of the highland population spoke Indian languages (in most cases Quichua). This figure included bilingual speakers who used an Indian language in their homes. Indian languages were thus found most extensively in Chimborazo, Imbabura, and Cotopaxi. Such figures give but a pale reflection of ethnic background, however.[20]

---

analysis of indigenous Ecuador, especially on the *sierra:* Gonzalo Rubio Orbe, *La población rural ecuatoriana* (Quito: Talleres Gráficas Nacionales, 1966).

[20]For a discussion of the problems involved in using such linguistic characteristics as an indicator of ethnic composition, see John V. D. Saunders, *The People of*

Table 10
PERCENTAGES OF LANGUAGES SPOKEN, 1950

Province	Spanish[a]	Indian[b]
COSTA		
El Oro	100	0
Esmeraldas	97.3	2.7
Guayas	100	0
Los Ríos	100	0
Manabí	100	0
TOTALS	99.9	0.1
SIERRA		
Azuay	92.7	7.3
Bolívar	83.8	16.2
Cañar	77.9	22.1
Carchi	99.8	0.2
Chimborazo	64.6	35.6
Cotopaxi	71.8	28.2
Imbabura	65.1	34.9
Loja	96.7	3.3
Pichincha	93.0	7.0
Tungurahua	83.2	16.8
TOTALS	83.7	16.3
ORIENTE	50.7	49.3
GALAPAGOS	100	0
NATIONAL TOTALS	89.7	10.3

Source: 1950 national census.
In the columns, a includes bilingual speakers who use Spanish in their homes; b, in contrast, includes bilingual speakers who use an Indian language in their homes.

Estimates of the national racial composition vary widely, ranging from 40 to 60 percent Indian, 10 to 15 percent European, 3 to 10 percent Negro or mulatto, and 20 to 50 percent mixed Indian and white, or *mestizo*. It is generally agreed that, with only minor exceptions, Ecuador's Indians are centered on the highlands. The original inhabitants of the land, rapidly sub-

Ecuador; a Democratic Analysis (Gainesville: University of Florida Press, Latin American Monograph #14, 1961). For a more narrow and detailed discussion drawn from the same data, see Saunders, "Man-Land Relations in Ecuador," *Rural Sociology*, Vol. 26, No. 1 (March, 1961), 57-69.

jugated by the European conquerors, have historically been treated as a subhuman source of cheap labor. Despite the existence of such distinctive groups as the Otavalans, the Salasacas, and the Saraguros in Loja province, most of the Indians have seemed culturally homogeneous, especially in the eyes of whites and *mestizos*. Most of the Indians are rural, living in communities of less than 2,500. Largely tied to agricultural subsistence, they have been restrained both legally and socially from extending their horizons.

For the Indian, social interaction is related to his own family and narrowly circumscribed community. His value patterns stress communal responsibilities, and the collective role is more important than the individual. The highland Indian is constrained from upward mobility which might elevate him from economic and social subjugation. Rural-based as he often is, the Indian is effectively removed from many aspects of political authority. The overseer on the large *hacienda* exercises power little short of life and death itself. Moreover, the role of the local political and security officers, especially the *teniente político*, is supportive of the economic elite.

Cooperative arrangements which exist informally between local political authorities and socioeconomic leadership are common. Moreover, ecclesiastical officials are also prone to assist in the maintenance of serflike conditions. The Indians, in short, exist in a dependency relationship on the *sierra*, constituting the bulk of the impoverished *serrano* masses. Living apart from the mainstream of national life, working outside the money economy, and existing in subservience to local Hispanic elites, they have responded by defensive withdrawal into the life of their immediate family. Suspicious of outsiders – even other Indians – they are similarly unresponsive to political appeals. With little basis for interpersonal trust or cooperation, the Indians are exceedingly resistant to change. Cultural conservatism prevails, and the heritage of generations works against forces of potential progress. Effectively powerless to alter their own position, tied to customs and beliefs dating back several centuries, the Indians are enured to life's physical and psychological deprivations. Historically they have been subjects rather than participants in the national culture.

Standing in stark contradistinction to the Indian masses is

the *serrano* social elite. Characteristically centered in the urban areas, its membership has long been fundamentally conservative. Having evolved from an agricultural economy, the elite soon settled in Quito, Ambato, Riobamba, and Cuenca. Building its society on Hispanic colonial foundations, its leadership became inculcated with values and attitudes which have largely survived to the present day. Wealth and power are based upon land ownership and domination of the Indian, and this group has insisted upon its role as cultural purveyor and preserver of Hispanic customs and beliefs in all their presumed purity. Numerically small, the upper class of the *sierra* has been willing to absorb the small number of foreigners and upwardly mobile businessmen and entrepreneurs who have become economically successful.[21] Yet it remains a closed group in many of its inclinations; the rigidity of class distinctions have been maintained, and full acceptance into this elite comes only infrequently, and with difficulty.

While political influence is sometimes exercised indirectly, many members of the highland elite have been politically prominent. Family relationships and personal friendships have contributed to a pride of exclusivity which characterizes the *gente decente,* or "decent people." While Quito is its natural locus, the elite includes similar people in the larger provincial capitals, many of whom spend considerable time in the capital city away from their property and personal holdings. Others maintain their provincial residence most of the time, exercising political and socioeconomic power on a subregional basis. In any case, the customary social values hark back to the patterns of white, Spanish-speaking society which were implanted under Spanish colonial rule. The durability of this Hispanic social tradition has been remarkable in withstanding culturally alien influences.

In contrast with the Indian proclivity toward narrowly defined communal allegiances is the Hispanic preoccupation with the inner worth and importance of the individual. The concept of *dignidad* emphasizes personal qualities above broader loyalties. Every person is seen as uniquely endowed with individual qualities, which carry with them the perqui-

[21]See the report of a recent study in Emily M. Nett, "The Functional Elites of Quito," *Journal of Inter-American Studies and World Affairs,* Vol. 13, No. 1 (January, 1971), 112-21.

sites of privilege and power. Personal honor becomes an innate endowment, and human relationships must not be permitted to violate this honor. There are clear implications for the workings of the political system, with personal loyalties stronger than party organizational ties. Thus, personalism is reinforced by the necessity of observing commitments of trust to given personalities. These again take precedence over more formal institutional loyalties.

Social life for this elite also incorporates concepts of authority and hierarchy which spill over into the political arena. Ideals of forceful personality, individual charisma, and strong leadership are encouraged, often clashing with the egalitarianism of democratic principles. The relationship of *patrón* to employee is also tied in with these attitudes. Whether landowner, businessman, or political leader, the upper-class *patrón* assumes a position of power and authority; although related to bonds of personal respect and trust, there is an unqualified status inequality. The deference shown to the *patrón* by the lower-class worker or employee further confirms his elitist status and its many antiegalitarian and hierarchical assumptions. The clearest explicitly political manifestation of such values is the *caudillo,* whose decisive personal leadership has been so common. A contemporary personification is five-time President José María Velasco Ibarra (see chapter 5).

Between the paternalistically inclined highland elite and the populous masses lies a small and heterogeneous middle group.[22] Concentrated in the urban centers, it is comprised of professional people, intellectuals, small businessmen, white-collar office personnel, and bureaucrats. An ethnically mixed group, it includes not only upwardly mobile *mestizos* (or *cholos,* the more common term in much of Ecuador) but also occasional whites whose families have lost their wealth and prominence. Education is an important prerequisite, although

[22]One of the more detailed examinations of social stratification in Ecuador is Georg Maier and Gunther Remming, "Social Classes in Ecuador: An Analysis of Social Stratification and Social Mobility under Conditions of Incipient Change," as quoted in Georg Maier, *The Ecuadorean Elections of June 2, 1968* (Washington: Institute for the Comparative Study of Political Systems, 1970), p. 14. Maier and Remming divide the Ecuadorean population into six class levels, ranging from 0.2 percent in upper-upper to 55.0 in the lower-lower. As reproduced in his monograph, Maier does not incorporate regional or subregional distinctions into the analysis.

sometimes limited to the secondary level. While entrance into this middle sector can be achieved by an individual of lower-class origins, upward mobility beyond the middle level is difficult. Frequently this will be accomplished, if at all, through the marriage of children rather than as a result of an individual's occupational activity or his success in pursuing it.

As in many other Latin American republics, the middle group in Ecuadorean society cannot properly be termed a class.[23] Its occupational characteristics are widely varied, and values do not comprise a distinctive class consciousness. There is little identification with the masses from which individual members may have come, and those of the middle sector share with the upper class a general disdain for manual labor. Indeed, the drive for greater security and status leads many to adopt upper-class values, even if impossible of realization. As one long-time resident of Ecuador has written:

> The larger section of the middle class enjoys neither economic independence nor security. Yet many people struggle hard to join it because of the prestige attached to it . . . The middle class does not allow many to climb through it up the highest rungs of the ladder.
>
> It is a dissatisfied, restless class, which constantly suffers from insecurity.[24]

Given such conditions, the urban middle groups on the highlands, although gradually increasing in number and in influence, remain more of a latent than an active force for modernization and development.

REGIONAL BASES OF ECUADOREAN SUBCULTURES: THE COAST

The Reality of Geography. The Ecuadorean coastal region, covering one-quarter of the country's surface, extends over 400

[23]Two somewhat dated but generally perceptive essays appear in Theo R. Crevenna (ed.), *Materiales para el estudio de la clase media en la América Latina,* Vol. 6 (Washington, D.C.: Unión Panamericana, Departamento de Asuntos Culturales, 1951). See Humberto García Ortiz, "La clase media en el Ecuador," pp. 15-35, and Angel Modesto Paredes, "Estudio de la clase media en el Ecuador," pp. 36-57.

[24]Lilo Linke, *Ecuador, Country of Contrasts,* 2nd ed. (London: Royal Institute of International Affairs, 1955), p. 72.

miles in length and 50 to 150 in width. With an altitude seldom surpassing 2,000 feet, the *costa* is largely tropical although there is some subregional variation. Numerous small streams drain toward the Pacific from the Andes, but the two major systems are the Guayas and the Esmeraldas. Rainfall tends to be heaviest along the latter, which is near the northern border with Columbia. It becomes less pronounced as one moves south, however, and the lands adjoining the Peruvian frontier are decidedly arid. It is along the Guayas river basin, however, that the heart of the *costa* is located. The Guayas lowlands are among the most fertile such regions on the continent, standing out as Ecuador's most important section economically and commercially. The location of Guayaquil on the west bank of the Guayas river provides a natural hub for such activity.

At the same time there is considerable potential for development elsewhere along the coast. Expansion of the national economy depends importantly upon those resources most accessible along the coast. As one scholar has written – although *serranos* would take umbrage – "For Ecuador to develop as a nation, the coastal potential must be tapped. . . . Responsible Ecuadorians are well aware of this, and they are striving to develop their coastal lands and to bridge the socio-cultural gap between Serranos and Costeños."[25] One of the subregions which might well experience significant growth is the province of Esmeraldas, in the northernmost region. With neighboring Manabí to the south the site for the most advanced Indian coastal societies in pre-Columbian times, Esmeraldas has experienced an unusual history, one which has contributed to its present situation.[26]

In addition to its original coastal Indians, the province received an influx of Africans during the 1600s. Historians disagree, some maintaining that the wreck of a slave ship along the coast brought the Africans; some even put forth twenty-three as the precise number of survivors to reach the shores.[27] In any

[25]Norman E. Whitten, Jr., *Class, Kinship, and Power in an Ecuadorian Town; The Negroes of San Lorenzo* (Stanford: Stanford University Press, 1965), p. 11.

[26]For an informal overview see Misuel Acosta-Solis, *Nuevas contribuciones al conocimiento de la provincia de Esmeraldas* (Quito: Publicaciones Científicas, n.d.).

[27]According to one writer, the Negroes intermarried with local Indian women and were able to gain political control of the entire province in a short time. This

event, the African ethnic strain is in evidence throughout the province. Esmeraldas, the capital city, has been growing rapidly in the last two decades, today numbering slightly over 50,000 inhabitants. A busily untidy town which has only acquired fully adequate centralized municipal and electrical services since the 1950s, Esmeraldas stands at the mouth of the river of the same name. The opening of a road connecting with Quito has helped to reduce the town's isolation, and today it is in more direct contact with Carchi and the northern *sierra* than with much of the coast.

Largely underdeveloped lands in the province support cattle, timber, and a variety of crops, all of which could be expanded substantially. Banana plantations near the provincial capital have contributed to the relative boom of the 1960s, and despite the need for frequent dredging, port facilities are being gradually improved. *Esmeraldeños* speak of the day when Guayaquil will be rivaled as a port city. While realizing the disparity between the two cities as immense, however, they are correctly optimistic in projecting the possibilities for future growth. Moreover, the rivalry between Quito and Guayaquil has encouraged some in the national capital to support the development of Esmeraldas and the entire northern coast as a partial counterweight to Guayaquil. If the northern sector could be developed as an economically important center in its own right, the resultant rivalry with Guayaquil could presumably be healthy for highland interests.[28]

Esmeraldeños adamantly claim that Guayaquil interests have deliberately discouraged the development of the northern coast, and there is evidence to substantiate the charge. Certainly Guayaquil has no desire to further the progress of another port city at its own expense. There may be further friction in the coming decade as a result of oil-related activities, moreover. In the summer of 1969 an agreement between the government and a Texaco-Gulf consortium stipulated the construction of a pipeline from the eastern oil fields to the Pacific, reaching the sea at

---

version appears in Victor Wolfgang Von Hagen, *Ecuador and the Galápagos Islands* (Norman, Oklahoma: The University of Oklahoma Press, 1949).

[28]An exceptional account of daily life in a small river village a few miles from the town of Esmeraldas is in Moritz Thomsen, *Living Poor; A Peace Corps Chronicle* (Seattle: University of Washington Press, 1969).

the provincial capital. By 1971 construction had begun on the artery. With the expansion of petroleum exploitation in the immediate future, there are bound to be major effects for the entire northern coast.

Intermittent *quiteño* encouragement of potential coastal rivals to Guayaquil is characteristic of regional interests impinging upon developmental issues. The northern coast experienced a similar episode with the construction of a railroad from Ibarra to the tiny port of San Lorenzo. Although originally authorized by legislative decree in 1861, the bulk of the work was only carried out from 1952 to 1957.[29] Its completion linked the coastal north to the rest of the country by rail for the first time, and was intended to nourish the growth of San Lorenzo as a port. However, the town has not progressed as anticipated. Inhabited by no more than 5,000, virtually all black, San Lorenzo has not lived up to the optimistic forecasts. Its potential nonetheless endures, especially should the rail facilities attract increased foreign trade from the northern *sierra* to the Pacific.

The politics of Esmeraldas province also display a distinctive flair. While the traditional coastal party, the Liberals, has enjoyed substantial strength for some years, it has been forced to share power with the Socialists. In many cases rivalries have been tied more to kinship and family bonds than to party loyalty, however, and the personalistic element is predominant. Years of disagreement among a handful of families have made possible the recent emergence of newer leadership, notably in the provincial capital itself. Populist appeals have increased in demagogic content and have incorporated ethnic overtones. Given the lower status of blacks – especially in the riverside slums of Esmeraldas – along with rapid growth in the city, politicization based on ethnic divisions might well exacerbate *esmeraldeño* public affairs.

To the immediate south of Esmeraldas lies Manabí, second most populous coastal province. A varied area in both climate and economic activity, its main port is Manta. An active town

[29]The first serious renewal of long-shelved plans for the railroad came in 1940, and is described in Mariano Suárez Veintimilla, *El ferrocarril Quito-San Lorenzo,* a report appended to Jorge A. Garces G., *Plan del camino de Quito al Río Esmeraldas* (Quito: Publicaciones del Archivo Municipal XIX, 1942). For further details see Whitten, *Class, Kinship, and Power,* chapter 1.

serving as a commercial center for western Ecuador, Manta has been seeking to attract tourist trade by its beaches.[30] Some thirty miles east is the provincial capital of Portoviejo, a city of some 40,000 which houses processing plants as well as providing customary commercial services. There is considerable banana-growing in the area, and the volume of fruit being shipped abroad from Manta and from Bahia de Caraquez has been on the upswing despite Guayaquil's continuing dominance. The province also includes the small towns of Jipijapa and Montecristi, sources of the famous if misnamed Panama hats. The toquilla straw from which the hats are made originates here before shipment to Cuenca, where much of the weaving and blocking is done by *serrano* Indian women.

Los Ríos, although regarded as a coastal province, does not actually front on the Pacific. A small territory wedged between Cotopaxi and Bolívar to the east and Guayas to the west, it is largely tropical in climate and vegetation. Plantations of bananas, sugar, cacao, and a variety of fruits are found, but the province is not richly endowed. Moreover, it has several towns of roughly comparable size and resources, thus avoiding domination by any. Los Ríos' capital, Babahoyo, situated on a northern branch of the Guayas river, has less than half the population of any other coastal provincial capital. Political traditions have been marked by local *caciques* whose influence is largely external to party control. Intricate arrangements and personal understandings link together town leaders to one another in a fashion which confounds the outsider and seeks to maintain autonomy from national government.

In addition to its other products, Los Ríos has flood plains used for the cultivation of rice. National developmental plans in the early 1960s called for extensive rice milling, and this has increased as a provincial activity. Yet despite the dietary importance of rice and favorable conditions, it has progressed slowly. It is perhaps inevitable that the province is overshadowed by Guayas, Ecuador's largest, most populous, and wealthiest province. Guayas plays a role of inordinate importance in the coun-

[30]An interesting picture emerges in Rhoda and Earle Brooks, *The Barrios of Manta; A Personal Account of the Peace Corps in Ecuador* (New York: The New American Library, Inc., 1965).

try's past, present, and future. At its core is the teeming, throbbing vitality of the city of Guayaquil. Chief seaport and commercial city, it has grown to a population of over 700,000 while casting a long shadow across the national body politic.

The city lies on the west bank of the Guayas river thirty-five miles above the Gulf of Guayaquil, which itself is nearly one hundred miles long. Consistently tropical in climate and oppressively hot during the rainy season from December to April, historically Guayaquil was notoriously unhealthy. From its founding in 1538[31] the city lacked sanitation facilities, and was periodically wracked by disease and epidemic. Its typical wooden and bamboo structures were susceptible to fires, and on several occasions much of the city was consumed by flames, only to be rebuilt once again. Yet Guayaquil's development as a port was inevitable, and by the coming of independence it had emerged as a center of political agitation and resistance to the imposition of outside authority, a tradition which survives to this day. It also entered the pages of hemispheric history in 1822 as site for the famed if mysterious interview between the two great continental liberators, Simón Bolívar and José de San Martín.

Only in the twentieth century, however, has Guayaquil come fully into its own. Eradication of malaria and yellow fever, along with improved sanitation facilities, removed its perils to health, while the highly flammable buildings were replaced by more modern structures. The former "pesthole of the Pacific" was thus transformed into a new city physically. As the most rapidly prospering city in the republic, Guayaquil exudes an air of bustling activity which starkly contrasts with highland cities. It is also experiencing the manifestations of urban growth – burgeoning slums, housing shortages, high birth rates, unemployment, crime, and political discontent. The prevalence of newly erected modern architecture but short distances from the squalor and poverty of cardboard and tin hovels is a measure of both the city's unquenchable vigor and of the magnitude of its problems.

Port facilities along the waterfront, known as the Malecón,

[31]Although officially founded in 1535, it was not until 1538 that a permanent settlement was established.

have been improved through the addition of new piers and frequent channel dredging. Of greater importance, however, is Puerto Marítimo, which was opened a few miles away in 1963. The subsequent acceleration of trade has been rapid. Development of the river basin was also furthered greatly in October 1970 with the inauguration of a bridge across the river, providing direct motor transportation to the town of Eloy Alfaro, situated across from Guayaquil proper. It is from Eloy Alfaro that the 288-mile railroad to Quito begins; an engineering triumph at the time of its opening in 1908, it provides regular service which is used extensively. In the opposite direction, to the west of the city, lie the beaches of the province, most notably the popular resorts of Playas and Salinas. There are salt and oil refineries as well, but the peninsula is better known as a pleasant weekend escape from the city.

To the south of Guayas is El Oro, the least populous of the coastal provinces and of only secondary importance economically. Extending toward Peru from the southern banks of the Gulf of Guayaquil, it is reached only by boat or by a lengthy drive out of the Andes from Cuenca. The capital city, Machala, numbers some 50,000 and serves as commercial center for agricultural environs. The province's future presumably depends upon its mineral resources, however. Gold and silver, copper and lead have been found, and there are also magnesium deposits. Gold has been mined commercially for years in the nearby Portovelo area, but productivity is limited. Although realistic expectations are not high, the sheer presence of mining in El Oro helps to underline the relative diversity of economic activity on the coast as contrasted with the *sierra*.

Economic and Social Patterns. Major economic products of the *costa* remain the tropical crops, particularly bananas and cacao. The latter provided the country with its first important export commodity. Developing as a major economic resource late in the nineteenth century, cacao rapidly emerged as the source of coastal fortunes. Its peak year of production came in 1914, but soon after, the onslaught of pests, especially witchbroom, ravaged the plants. By the early 1930s cacao exports were no higher than they had been in the mid-1800s, and not until World War II were concerted efforts undertaken to revive productivity. It was during the administration of Galo Plaza

(1948-52) that the cultivation of bananas was undertaken on a massive basis, and Ecuador soon became the world's leading exporter.

While long a staple of the coastal economy, bananas achieved rapid and dramatic growth through the confluence of several forces: plant disease and Caribbean hurricanes which nearly decimated production in Central America; the resultant desire of international banana interests to develop holdings away from the Caribbean; rising demand on the international market; and a determined commitment by the Plaza government and by coastal economic interests.[32] Climatic conditions were favorable to rapid expansion, while virgin lands along coastal rivers and streams permitted rapid colonization and development. In contrast to the Central American pattern, banana plantations in Ecuador are generally small, with parcels of land owned by a large number of small farmers. While data are imprecise, it is estimated that perhaps 75 percent of banana cultivation comes from farms under 250 acres in size. The total acreage planted in bananas grew tenfold in the years from 1948 to 1954, leveling off in more recent years.

Coffee has also been important for the export trade, and is grown most extensively in Guayas, Manabi, and El Oro. Like bananas it is cultivated on landholdings of moderate size, and has received considerable government support and encouragement during the last quarter-century. The yield per acre is lower than in such coffee producers as Columbia and Costa Rica, but improved methods of cultivation have increased productivity while acreage has remained fairly constant. Rice, cotton, and sugar cane are products of lesser importance to the export economy. The first is raised largely for domestic consumption through simple methods of cultivation, especially in the flood plains of the Guayas basin. Cotton production also employs rudimentary methods, and is used largely for the country's young and struggling textile industry. Sugar cane, in contrast, is a product grown primarily on large plantations, and improved technology has led to a gradual increase of production.

[32]For a detailed if highly favorable account, see Stacy May and Galo Plaza, *The United Fruit Company in Latin America* (Washington: National Planning Association, 1958).

As already implied, the *costeño* pattern of land tenure differs from that in the highlands. The greater availability and fertility of land has encouraged small and medium-sized farms. Yet there is destructive exploitation of the land, for slash-and-burn practices are common, and land misuse is more the exception than the rule. Government programs to improve agricultural technology have made some inroads, but to a considerable degree methods are still simple, unscientific, and wasteful.

Official development plans in recent years have placed growing emphasis on the role of industry in the national economy. Just as with Quito in the highlands, so is Guayaquil the major coastal center. More than four-fifths of Ecuador's total industrial output comes from the provinces of Pichincha, Guayas, and Manabí. Light industry and textiles have received attention, although producing almost entirely for the small domestic market. Manufacturing, the most important productive sector after agriculture, has grown much more rapidly on the coast than in the highlands. In addition to textiles, activities include canning, refrigeration, beverages, sugar and rice milling, and tobacco products. Mining activities remain secondary, owing in some measure to the relative inaccessibility of many deposits.

The racial composition and social structure of coastal Ecuador stands in contrast to that of the *sierra*. The Negro admixture on the coast, while most striking in the north, is found all along the Pacific, while once numerous Indian tribes have nearly vanished. The only remaining groups are the Cayapas, Colorados, and Caranquis, believed to have come originally from the Caribbean. The mixed-blood coastal peasant, who largely comprises the lower social stratum, is known as the *montuvio*. Descended from coastal Indians but reflecting generations of intermarriage with both Europeans and Negroes, he has long since abandoned his native culture. Living in more of a Hispanic than Indian fashion, he is in contrast to the *sierra* Indian an active, zestful, and fiercely independent being.

The *montuvio*, whether as agricultural farm hand or urban laborer, is highly mobile. Flexible and adaptable, he does not establish close ties with a particular locality or a small plot of land. Familiar with both city and rural life, he gravitates between the short harvest seasons on the plantations and manual labor in the cities. Although sometimes acquiring his own plot of land, the *montuvio* has little reluctance in moving from it, and will frequently sell his belongings to travel to the city for employment. With the exception of those who live in fishing communities and establish firm roots there, the coastal lower class is therefore both mobile and unstable. His ties to vested authority, whether economic, political, or clerical, are loose; opportunities for upward social mobility are thereby broadened. As one observer has written:

> Economically, the *montuvio* farm-hand on the coastal plantation may not be much better off, living also a hand-to-mouth existence, but he would never consider himself to be on the same rung of the ladder as the Sierra Indian. . .
>
> On the whole, the *montuvios* are as lightly burdened with possessions as the Sierra Indians, but they feel no sorrow when carrying a bundle which contains all their property and their bushknife from one bamboo hut to another. . . .[33]

This spirit of independence and a life style of physical and occupational movement for the lower-class *costeño* nourishes the volatility and instability so endemic to coastal society and politics. Especially in Guayaquil (also see chapter 6) he introduces an element of uncertainty and unpredictability, which is uncommon to the highlands, as well as more responsiveness to populistic demagoguery. He is also confronted with an elite which differs significantly from that of the highlands. With its membership generally wealthier than its Quito counterparts, the Guayaquil upper class has largely achieved its prosperity in the twentieth century. Certainly the colonial ancestry and aristocratic aura of Quito's leading families is absent.

Espousing the precepts of the Liberal party as firmly as do the traditional *quiteño* elites for the Conservatives, the wealthy of Guayaquil are nonetheless careful to guard and to preserve their own commercial interests and social standing. Yet the fragmentation and divisiveness which have so typified Ecuadorean life, society, and politics go beyond the familiar *costa-sierra* contrasts. Subcultural variation within each of these regions is pronounced, a factor of quintessential relevance for an under-

[33]Linke, *Ecuador, Country of Contrasts,* pp. 61-62.

standing of Ecuador. As already outlined, such intraregional rivalries as those of Guayas and Esmeraldas on the coast or Quito and Cuenca in the *sierra* are the warp and woof of Ecuadorean life. Today the trend is in the direction of integrating east-west relationships, such as those of Esmeraldas to Carchi and Chimborazo and Azuay to Guayas. Thus the historic subcultural fragmentation is assuming new shapes and forms, strongly molded by local and provincial interests. This theme will be developed further in the concluding chapter. For the present it suffices to underline these old and new distinctions, for it is only through a recasting of traditional fragmentation that the several subcultures can be brought into an integrative balance. Until this takes place, historical rivalries and competition will continue to impede the Ecuadorean quest for progress and modernization.

2
The Legacy of Political Disunity

The fragmentation of Ecuadorean political culture is traceable far back into the colonial period, and the legacy of disunity has been intensified by both historical events and by broad intellectual trends. For generations the dominant elite has exerted a powerful influence in the shaping of national attitudes and orientations. In openly political terms, the storied division between Conservatives and Liberals has long been manifest, while more contemporary trends have included variations on Marxist themes. Intellectual bases have helped significantly to form attitudes which persist to this day. Before examining historical experience, therefore, we must first turn to these bases.

INTELLECTUAL SOURCES OF CONFLICT

Foundations of Contemporary Thought. While a panoramic view of intellectual and cultural life might reach back into the past of the original indigenous inhabitants, major foundations in Ecuador were laid by Spain during its three centuries of colonial rule. The role of the Spanish-born *peninsulares* had become pronounced by the coming of the eighteenth century, although that impact can be traced back to the arrival of the *conquistadores* in 1532. Early writings emanated largely from religious centers of learning, with primary attention directed at highly abstract formulations within the existing tradition of scholasticism. As an intellectual concern scholasticism survived in Ecuador long after its European decline in the late 1500s. Similarly, the intellectual impact of the European Enlightenment lagged far behind, not becoming prevalent in Ecuador until the eighteenth century.

As the orientation of intellectual thought gradually turned more fully toward the thought of the Enlightenment, the most noted spokesman in Quito was Francisco Eugenio Javier de Santa Cruz y Espejo (1747-95). Educated in medicine, Espejo in time assumed prominence as a critic of the colonial system, becoming a prominent advocate of proindependence views. During his four-year exile in Bogotá beginning in 1787 he became acquainted with Antonio Nariño and other Colombian precursors of independence. In 1791 he joined in the establishment of the *Sociedad Patriótica de Amigos del País,* a body dedicated to the encouragement of both intellectual and economic activities. Composed of members of the wealthy *criollo* leadership in Quito, the Sociedad under his leadership became the champion of individual freedom, the rule of law, and the right of local self-government. Espejo was again arrested in 1795 on charges of conspiracy and died a political prisoner shortly thereafter. The independence movement was already well established and gaining support, however, with the intellectual elite assuming unto itself the leadership.

Ideas from the French and North American revolutions were gaining in currency by the beginning of the nineteenth century, and eloquent poetic voice to the aspirations of freedom and of popular sovereignty was articulated by José Joaquín Olmedo (1789-1847). Although most of his writings were apolitical, Olmedo wrote a few lyric poems, such as *La Victoria de Junín, Canto a Bolívar,* which idealized the exploits of revolutionary liberators. Within a few years of the expulsion of the Spanish, a series of newspapers and periodicals provided an outlet for intellectual expression, perhaps the best known being *El Quiteño Libre.* First published on May 12, 1833, it soon became an outspoken critic of President Juan José Flores. While expressing sentiments of nationalism in its attacks on the Venezuelan-born Flores, *El Quiteño Libre* helped to establish a tradition of strongly oriented political journals, many of which flourished later in the century.

Liberal spokesmen attacked the material wealth and political influence of the Church, while advocating essentially decentralized government and *laissez faire* economic policies. The Conservatives hotly disputed their opponents, defending the primacy of the Church and of centralized government, while also supporting a modicum of administrative intervention. By mid-century Gabriel García Moreno had become a leading Conservative spokesman through the columns of several publications. Upon his assumption of political power in 1860, García Moreno himself became the leading target of intellectual and political criticisms. His establishment of a virtual theocracy, as described below, helped to produce perhaps the preeminent intellectual of independent Ecuadorean history, Juan Montalvo (1832-89).

While becoming an embattled critic of Conservative hegemony, Montalvo in the process established himself as one of Latin America's leading intellectual figures.[1] Writing largely from exile in Europe or Columbia, he conducted a ceaseless campaign against García Moreno, his political authoritarianism, and religious fanaticism. Montalvo's own journal, *El Cosmopólita,* was suppressed by García Moreno in 1866, but his pen was not to be silenced. Montalvo continued the attack in essays and pamphlets, including *El Antropófago* (1872), *Judas* (1873), and *La Dictadura Perpetua* (1874). Upon the assassination of García Moreno in 1875 he exulted, "My pen has killed the tyrant." Returning to Ecuador as editor of the newspaper *El Regenerador,* Montalvo soon alienated the continuing Conservative leadership and was driven into exile for the remainder of his days.

Montalvo's best-known statement was published in 1882 under the title *Siete Tratados,* or *Seven Treaties.*[2] Eternally the social and political rebel, he demanded that liberation of man from clerical influence which lay at the heart of the Liberal

[1] For a discussion of Montalvo which places him within the context of philosophical currents, see Miguel Jorrín and John D. Martz, *Latin-American Political Thought and Ideology* (Chapel Hill: The University of North Carolina Press, 1970), pp. 156-59.

[2] For a collection of Montalvo's writings, see his *Obras escogidas* (Quito: Casa de la Cultura Ecuatoriana, 1948). Among the more recent editions of *Siete tratados* is that prepared by Antonio Acevedo Escobedo and published in Mexico by the Secretaría de Educación Pública in 1942.

platform. Defending his view of democracy as a means of assuring social justice for the masses, he advocated a variety of reforms, many of which were introduced by the Liberals following the 1895 revolution which ousted the Conservatives from power. However, Montalvo was more deeply concerned with the moral than the economic bases of liberalism. Among the first Ecuadoreans to be concerned about the condition of the Indian, he was at the same time unwilling to accept the romanticized concept of the noble savage living blissfully in an untouched state of nature. Rather, in anticipation of the later emergence of *indigenista* thought in Ecuador, he argued that the oppression of the Indian was among the major sources of national backwardness.[3]

Philosophically Montalvo was essentially an iconoclast. He demonstrated wide familiarity with both ancient and contemporary writers while expressing an intellectual idealism which was at once utopian and skeptical. Certain of his essays carried the flavor of Tom Paine and other critics of the Enlightenment. His own faith in progress was boundless, and a spirit of optimism pervaded much of his writing. At the same time, there was an intellectual questioning which prevented him from unqualified acceptance of all the liberal beliefs of the day. Neither a logically rational nor systematic thinker, Montalvo's was a wide-ranging intellect from which ideas flowed in abundance. Infusing all his writings with an indomitable belief in the intrinsic worth of the individual, he was less an original thinker than, in the words of an Uruguayan intellectual, a fencer with ideas (*esgrimidor de ideas*).[4]

Following a few years' hiatus preceding the turn of the century, political agitation found itself accompanied anew by intellectual activity. There was a concomitant revival in avowedly academic inquiry, both characterized and to a considerable degree propelled by Federico González Suárez, a clergyman who in 1906 became archbishop of Quito. His interest in anti-

[3] A brief but characteristic Ecuadorean assessment of Montalvo's literary and moral qualities by an eminent intellectual is found in Alfredo Pérez Guerrero, *Semillas al viento* (Quito: Editorial Publitécnica, 1966), pp. 37-45.

[4] For a thoughtful analysis by an equally noted Latin American writer, see José Enrique Rodó, *Hombres de América* (Barcelona: n.p., 1920). Another excellent study is Gonzalo Zaldumbide, *Montalvo y Rodó* (New York: Instituto de las Españas en los Estados Unidos, 1938).

quity led him to project a massive study of the history of America, although his official duties limited him to the writing of four volumes on the pre-Columbian and colonial period in Ecuador.[5] Relying on local as well as Spanish archival sources, he created considerable furor with his critical analysis of the colonial clergy; indeed, his writings were received more sympathetically by Liberal intellectuals than by Conservatives. González Suárez' own quest for knowledge, coming as it did from an eminent Church figure, did much to encourage scientific investigation and historical study. Through the first quarter of the twentieth century, less stress was placed upon polemical writings; at the same time, the modernist movement in poetry and prose began to develop. The gifted Gonzalo Zaldumbide was instrumental in the introduction of modernism into Ecuadorean literature, and this in turn provided inspiration for the school of realism which arose.

The Rise of Indigenismo. In the decade following World War I there was a perceptible movement toward fictional realism; this encouraged critiques of Ecuadorean society. A growing consciousness and the contemporary impact of European ideas also contributed to the sociopolitical dimension; by the 1950s the cultural and intellectual community was rife with new ideas, perspectives, and interpretations of national life. There was an absorption with the common man; Marxist ideology became a familiar intellectual staple; student protests and labor work stoppages grew more frequent; and this general recrudescence of agitation and discontent provided a new context within which a rising generation of young intellectuals took shape. While both Marxism and xenophobic nationalism became common, there were divergences centered upon the role of the Indian in national society. It was from this that expressions of both *indigenismo* and *Hispanidad* leapt to the fore.

The literature of *indigenismo* – a broad-based concern for the plight of the indigenous peoples – received great impetus from the 1934 publication of Jorge Icaza's celebrated *Huasipungo*. In detailing the life of a landless Ecuadorean Indian,

[5] González Suárez' multivolume work was *Historia general de la República del Ecuador* (Quito: Imprenta del Clero, 1890 ff.). To see another characteristic expression of his intellectual interests, see González Suárez, *Notas arqueológicas* (Quito: Imprenta del Clero, 1915).

Icaza (1906-) wrote of "the brutal exploitation of man by man, with both exploiter and exploited enmeshed. . ."[6] This tale of violence, sex, and naked force gained international renown and has been widely translated.[7] In addition to the recognition won, Icaza at the same time helped to direct intellectuals' attention toward the Indian. A more scientific *genre* of *indigenismo* began to appear, with its most eminent practitioner the sociologically inclined Pío Jaramillo Alvarado (1889-1968). A pioneering figure whose classic *El Indio Ecuatoriano* first appeared in 1922,[8] the prolific Jaramillo blended the talents of historian, sociologist, essayist, and man of letters.[9]

In the original edition of *El Indio Ecuatoriano* there was a broad consideration of Indians elsewhere in Latin America, although the author included descriptions of his own country. His recitation of Indian customs, traditions, and individual characteristics was enhanced from firsthand observation of economic and agricultural realities. With the publication of the third edition in 1936 he also included his *Del Agro Ecuatoriano.*[10] The intuition of his early analysis was supplemented by precise data, notably that of Italo Paviolo, an Italian agronomist who had undertaken extensive studies under contract to the Ecuadorean government.[11] After documenting Ecuadorean *latifundismo* and the conditions of exploited *huasipungueros,* Jaramillo concluded – as he was to insist throughout his career – that the dispersed rural population of more than a million Indians (in the 1920s) constituted Ecuador's single most serious problem. Moreover, the exploitative system had rendered the

[6] Jean Franco, *The Modern Culture of Latin America; Society and the Artist* (New York: Frederick A. Praeger, 1967), p. 166.

[7] For the English version, see Jorge Icaza, *Huasipungo; The Villagers, a Novel,* authorized translation and introduction by Bernard M. Dulsey, foreword by J. Cary Davis (Carbondale, Ill.: Southern Illinois University Press, 1964).

[8] Because of major additions to the 1922 original, one should consult Pío Jaramillo Alvarado, *El indio ecuatoriano,* 4th ed. (Quito: Casa de la Cultura Ecuatoriana, 1954).

[9] Among his many works, those with relevance for this discussion would also include *Estudios históricos* (Quito: Casa de la Cultura Ecuatoriana, 1960); and *La nación quiteña: biografía de una cultura* (Quito: Imp. Fernandez, 1947).

[10] Jaramillo Alvarado, *Del agro ecuatoriano* (Quito: Imprenta de la Universidad Central, 1936).

[11] The most extensive source for Paviolo's findings, aside from later editions of Jaramillo's *El indio ecuatoriano,* is found in a series of studies published in 1927 by the *Revista de la Sociedad Nacional de Agricultores* in Quito.

Indian impotent as a creative producer of economic wealth for Ecuador.

Pío Jaramillo Alvarado advocated a radical transformation of Indian cultural life. While quoting the famed Mexican José Vasconcelos to the effect that the future of the Indian lay with his introduction to modern culture, Jaramillo argued that the major responsibility lay with the whites. Demanding a major and enduring commitment on the part of national government, in later years he became a more acerbic critic. By the 1950s he was expressing the opinion that national concern for the Indian had been largely intellectual rather than practical. He observed that the *Instituto Indigenista del Ecuador,* of which he had long been director, had achieved but modest results as a consequence of inadequate budgetary support. He also remarked that the Constitution of 1945 – long since superceded – had been the only such document to recognize in any detail the rights and needs of the Indian. And although having represented "a marvelous constitutional conquest for Indian protection," it was subsequently ignored rather than implemented.[12]

Unlike later *indigenistas,* Jaramillo did not argue that the redemption of the Indian assured national salvation, but rather that it was necessary if there were to be any possibility of true social justice and economic development.

> For Ecuador, the decisive epoch has arrived for the planning and execution of new forms of economic life, which means a profound transformation of the ancient systems of working the land and the labor of the Indian population. May the servitude of Indian *concertaje* disappear, for it has enslaved them and has kept them in the misery of routine to their *patróns*; may the land be a just extension of all that he works; and may Ecuador – even today an essentially agricultural country – reach prosperity by peaceful Agrarian Reform or by the right of insurrection.[13]

Jaramillo encouraged younger *indigenista* writers, and studies of the Indian became more scholarly and systematic in nature. There was also a growing effort to proffer specific policy recommendations. Luis Monsalve Pozo (1904-), for one, undertook an historical review of Indian society and culture, presenting a profile of economic and agricultural patterns identified by geo-

[12]Jaramillo, *El indio ecuatoriano,* 4th ed., p. 509.
[13]Ibid., p. 526.

graphic zone. Noting that the Indian in Ecuador followed one of two separate patterns of life style – either that of the communal village or of the individual *minifundio* – he provided a careful assessment which implied clear policy recommendations.[14]

Angel Modesto Paredes (1899-), placing somewhat greater emphasis on cultural and psychological factors, was distressed over the silent withdrawal of the Indian in the face of dominant white interests.[15] Víctor Gabriel Garcés (1905-68) reflected a more explicit concern with political issues, discussing at length the role of governmental authority vis-à-vis the Indian, as well as the relationship between the Indian and administrative representatives of the state. Deeply moved by existing conditions on the *sierra*, he wrote tellingly:

> There are enormous human zones within our country which have no meaning, neither substance nor form... These human zones are, as is logical, those of the *campesinos* and the Indians for whom not even distant and remote echoes of changes or alterations in the country are known, not even major political events. For the *campesino* and Indian masses there is generally no difference between one regime and another, between one man and his successor. Thus, for a substantial quantity of Ecuadorean men there is neither a creative nor a positive feeling when one governmental system is ended and a new one replaces it. While in the cities and urban centers the expectant citizenry and especially the bureaucratic ranks are affected and shaken with nervous uncertainty, in the *campos*, in the rural areas, man realizes his continuing and immutable life, without change of any sort... Nothing is altered in the unvarying rhythm of rural Ecuadorean life...[16]

Among the more anthropologically oriented indigenistas has been Gonzalo Rubio Orbe (1909-).[17] In *Punyaro* he

[14]Luis Monsalve Pozo, *El indio; cuestiones de su vida y de su pasión* (Cuenca: Editorial Austral, 1943).

[15]Angel Modesto Paredes, *Problemas etnológicos indoamericanos* (Quito: Casa de Cultura Ecuatoriana, 1947). See especially his discussion of "*pertenencia,*" those Indian values relating to the feeling of being owned by those who enjoy a "superior" life style, pp. 160 ff.

[16]Víctor Gabriel Garcés, *Indigenismo* (Quito: Casa de la Cultura Ecuatoriana, 1957), pp. 120-21.

[17]Gonzalo Rubio Orbe, *Aspectos indígenas* (Quito: Casa de la Cultura Ecuatoriana, 1965); *Promociones indígenas en América* (Quito: Casa de la Cultura Ecuatoriana, 1957); and *Punyaro; estudio de antropología social y cultural de una comunidad indígena y mestiza* (Quito: Casa de la Cultura Ecuatoriana, 1956).

undertook a microcosmic examination of a small *serrano* community to the south of Imbabura, employing interviews, observation, and compiling a mass of statistical data. The result was a case study which included major sections on material, religio-cultural, and sociopolitical aspects of Indian life. In the final section he summed up the implications of his findings:

> The sharpest and most critical problem in Punyaro is that of land. The Indian is a farmer *par excellence*; the great part of his economy revolves about this activity and, if we consider that in Punyaro there are plots so small and that people live in an unqualified condition as rural proletariat, . . . one can only deduce that the land problem is the most grave of all. The economic conditions of the community are so precarious precisely because of the lack of lands. Therefore we judge that it is of urgent necessity to study the possibility of the parceling of lands near the community, on the basis of a cooperative organization and with bank loans incorporating a social consciousness.[18]

In later writings Rubio Orbe has attempted to generalize more broadly. In *Aspectos Indígenas* he reported the findings of an extensive questionnaire circulated and administered from the *Instituto Indigenista Interamericano*. Included was a wealth of statistical data, as well as a close analysis of various Ecuadorean and inter-American agencies working with the Indians.[19]

One of the more singular spokesmen of Ecuadorean *indigenismo* was José de la Cuadra (1903-41), who was among the few to examine Ecuadorean racial questions beyond the Andean context. Concentrating upon life and society as he found it along the banks of the littoral rivers, he wrote of the coastal *montuvio* as one whose ancestors included ethnic and cultural attributes predating the Incan civilization. Estimating that one-tenth of the Ecuadorean population consisted of *montuvios,* De la Cuadra wrote that although not tied to the land and the *patrón,* the *montuvio* was little better off materially than was his Andean counterpart. In *El Montuvio Ecuatoriano,* De la Cuadra characterized him as more independent and less passive than the highland Indian, and as more eager to depart from past traditions in an effort at self-improvement. Yet external aid was

[18]Rubio Orbe, *Punyaro,* pp. 393-94.

[19]Among those cited, attention was directed to the *Instituto Indigenista Ecuatoriano,* the *Instituto Ecuatoriano de Antropología y Geografía,* the *Sociedad Ecuatoriana de Antropología,* and the *Junta de Defensa del Indio.* Cf. pp. 186 ff.

necessary. Local communist and socialist parties had failed in their efforts as the result of internal rivalries and therefore, De la Cuadra believed, conditions would be slow to change. In the meantime, "social revolution will never attract the *montuvio* if it does not guarantee him exclusive domain over a plot of land that he works and cultivates, and over the fruits that he makes it produce."[20]

An even more striking figure has been Segundo B. Maiguashca, himself a full-blooded Indian. Educated in law and dedicated to the improvement of the country's native population, his major work appeared in 1949.[21] To incorporate the Indian into national culture, a broad-based approach to the whole panoply of psychological, economic, juridical, and educational problems was urged. A major difficulty at the outset would stem from inherent Indian distrust of the white; yet mutual trust would be necessary, and the instinctive white repudiation of the Indian had to be dissipated. Economically, the Indian should receive those lands which had once been his, while receiving credits and agricultural assistance from the government. In the juridical sphere, protective agencies would be created and special legislation would be enacted. Educationally, the Indian required opportunities in special schools, including vocational training as well as outlets for artistic self-expression.

Maiguashca rejected several of the approaches advocated by others. Thus he was unimpressed with the argument that compulsory military service would train and prepare the Indian for an assimilated adulthood. Furthermore, he opposed the sending of Indian children to schools with whites, arguing that in practice the Indian would be left out. He believed that the Indian would not be transformed or "modernized" through mere contact with whites, and rejected as well the argument favoring extensive employment of Indians in domestic service. Ultimately, Maiguashca urged the Indian not to be ashamed of his heritage or race, but to strive for social improvement. He was asked to initiate a campaign for the vindication of his personality and race. In Maiguashca's words:

[20]José de la Cuadra, *El montuvio ecuatoriano* (Buenos Aires: Ediciones Imán, 1937), p. 92.

[21]Segundo B. Maiguashca, *El indio, cerebro y corazón de América; incorporación del indio a la cultura nacional* (Quito: Edit. "Fray Jodoco Ricke," 1949).

> My purpose is to put within the reach of the Indian all the elements that are necessary to bring about a species of social osmosis, letting the vernacular form of attitudes toward us disappear in the minds of the other social classes, a thing which would mean our true injection . . . into the Ecuadorian nation. My fundamental thesis is: ALL OR NOTHING.[22]

In the writings of the *indigenistas* there has been a wide variation in interpretation and in policy recommendation. Yet an additional strain may be that of dependency and domestic colonialism (see below). Underlying all of these writings, however, has been a belief in the necessity of incorporating the marginal Indian into national life. This is based upon a normative commitment to the equality of man, but is also expressed as a practical necessity for the development and ultimate transformation of Ecuadorean society. Twentieth-century Ecuadorean intellectual life has thus extended its quest for reconciliation of the Indian heritage of Tahuantinsuyo[23] with the legacy of Spain. In purely political terms, only the Marxists have given continuous attention to the indigenous peoples, even going so far as to provide for specifically "Indian" representatives to national Socialist congresses. Yet this commitment has been largely verbal. As Jaramillo prophetically remarked earlier in the century, concern for the Indian remains more intellectual than pragmatic. *Indigenistas* themselves have sometimes been guilty of a patronizing attitude which assumes that definitive solution of the Indian question requires intermarriage, westernizing education, and in effect the eventual replacement of the Indian by the *mestizo*. Even so, *indigenismo* remains an important current in contemporary Ecuadorean thought. An element of nationalism has become increasingly evident as well; this is, however, a very different form than that which has appeared in the contrasting body of literature known as *Hispanidad*.

Hispanidad *and the Clash of Ideologies.*[24] Consistent with the long domination of a white, Spanish-speaking social elite are the views of *Hispanidad*, also referred to as *Hispanismo*. Al-

[22] Ibid., p. 83.

[23] This quechua name for the Incan empire is variously spelled through transliteration into Spanish.

[24] I am particularly indebted to the careful analysis of ARNE and the ideology of *Hispanidad* by Rafael Quintero, whose dissertation when completed in 1972 will be the definitive study of the subject.

though less extensively articulated than *indigenista* views in recent years, there is still in evidence a perceptible residue. The durability of the Hispanic social tradition in Ecuador is such that the unity of the westernized elite still finds expression in social attitudes and values. Despite clearly contradictory evidence, it is still argued, for example, that the pre-Conquest Indian in what was to become Ecuador existed at a lower level of civilization and social development than were others in the Andes. As essentially inferior beings, they required the socializing influence and guidance of a higher and external civilization, presumably the Hispanic. Prominent in the twentieth-century intellectual affirmation of *Hispanidad* was César Arroyo,[25] while major political expositions have come from Jorge Luna Yepes, leader of the movement known as ARNE (see chapter 4).

In various of his writings,[26] Luna has sought to align the *arnista* movement to the Spanish cultural heritage. The affirmation and vindication of *Hispanidad* has long preoccupied his thinking, reflecting in part the fear that traditional Hispanic values are being threatened by the inroads of new social forces and particularly through communist or socialist intervention. The ultimate objective of *Hispanidad* is seen as the resurrection of a commonwealth of states sharing the cultural values derived from colonial Spain. The unity of the colonial system, although in some ways more latent than actual, is to be reestablished in modern times, with Spain destined to occupy a privileged place of honor. The social preoccupation with individuality, with the worth of each man, and with his own innate inner dignity or *dignidad* are all seen as transcendental values stemming from Iberian values.

A particularistic concept of *raza,* or race, is also central to Hispanic values. In Ecuador it is therefore argued that the Indian must be totally integrated into essentially western cultural patterns. More precisely, in fact, the Indian should be assimilated into the community of *Hispanismo,* losing his orig-

[25]Cited by Jorge Luna Yepes in his *Mensaje a las juventudes de España* (San Sebastián: Ediciones Maravillas, Coleccion Americana, 1949), p. 43.

[26]In addition to ibid., Luna's writings include *Explicación del ideario de ARNE* (Quito: Gráficas Sánchez, 1949); *Prologo: Proyecto de constitución para la Republica del Ecuador* (Quito: Talleres Gráficos Nacionales, 1964); and *Tres pueblos mesianicos: Rusia, España, Israel* (Quito: Publicaciones de Cultural Popular del Movimiento ARNE, 1958).

inal indigenous identity in the process. The argument is not presented in racial and ethnic terms, but rather within the conception of cultural and spiritual values. Presumably the process of acculturation must be realized if Ecuador is ever to become sufficiently unified socially to permit the achievement of truly national growth and development. For the advocates of *Hispanidad,* the sympathy for oppressed indigenous living conditions is essentially temporal. What is necessary is not the providing of support and assistance whereby the Indian may reach the fullest realization of his own cultural values and belief. Rather, acculturation ideally should bring about a kind of reintegrated utopia in which Hispanic values will be uniformly shared, accepted, and practiced by all members of society.

If the exponents of *Hispanidad* have been less vocal than the *indigenistas,* this is not to deny their presence, especially in a number of literary and artistic clubs and associations. Moreover, reflecting as they do some of the values long practiced by members of the traditional white elite, they enjoy continuing support even in the absence of frequent intellectual expression. Thus the competing forces of *Hispanidad* and *indigenismo* lie at the root of intellectual divisions which themselves are intimately connected with existing social discontinuities. The magnitude of such disagreement runs deep, and has been further exacerbated by a more recent recrudescence of nationalistic sentiment in Ecuador. Much of this has emanated from Marxist statements, although these expressions have been articulated in various ways.

Marxist Nationalism and Internal Colonialism. Rival schools of Marxist thought and affiliated political movements not only vie with one another for legitimacy as spokesmen of the political left, but also draw upon the divisions inherent in the competing statements of *indigenismo* and *Hispanidad.* Marxist interpretations of national history stress the exploitation of the native masses, a condition which in turn is blamed upon North American policy and upon the impact of international capitalism. It is continuing external support for the local oligarchy, especially as represented by coastal interests, which has been alleged to maintain and indeed to increase the state of subservience in which the Indian still lives. As early as the 1920s, Ecuadorean Marxists were issuing appeals for the redemption of the Indian. The Socialist party in particular has long claimed unto itself the mantle as defender and protector of the Indian.

There have been characteristic charges of external imperialism against the United States, as well as treatments linking international capitalism in a causal chain to the internal colonialsim of national elites (also see chapter 6). To cite but one example, Jaime Galarza Zavala (1942-) has described Ecuadorean peasant life as a re-creation of Dante's inferno, largely created and constantly aggravated by North American imperialism. The Alliance for Progress is described as "protecting United States interests and privileges, accentuating imperialist *concertaje* and Ecuador's colonial dependency. . ."[27] Even more significant than such fairly predictable critiques, however, has been the contemporary emergence of less ideological discussions of internal colonialism and dependency relationships.

Hugo Burgos Guevara's study of the Riobamba Indians exemplifies this growing intellectual orientation. In his introduction Burgos describes the history of the world's indigenous masses as that of colonized peoples.

> This history is nothing less than the struggle between dominion and dependency unleashed among culturally heterogeneous peoples. I use the term dependency as a synonym for exploitation of natural resources, of products and of the labor of men of a culture technologically and economically less evolved, by men of a society whose technology, economy and cultural organization are more complex.[28]

In the specific case of Riobamba, economic dependence rests with the coast, while in turn international interests are found behind coastal ones. Given the growing mobility of Riobamba society, internal colonialism is in the process of a historical redefinition. This presumes an emerging transformation from paternalism to competition, thereby altering the present structure of unbalanced relations. Finally, creation of conditions for a more balanced development requires "a breaking of internal

[27]Jaime Galarza Zavala, *El yugo feudal; visión del campo ecuatoriano* (Quito: Imprenta Argentina, Ediciones Solitierra, 1966), p. 140.

[28]Hugo Burgos Guevara, *Relaciones interétnicas en Riobamba; dominio y dependencia en una región indígena ecuatoriana* (Mexico: Instituto Indigenista Interamericano, ediciones especiales 55, 1970), p. 1.

colonialism, and this is related to the external dependence of Ecuadorean society."[29]

With some variations, this theme is increasingly preoccupying Ecuadorean intellectuals as they seek explanations in the diagnostic quest for progress and modernization. Developmental studies emphasize the marginality of the masses – especially the highland Indians – as well as the persisting qualities of socioeconomic dualism. A study by the *Instituto Ecuatoriano de Planificación para el Desarrollo Social* (INEDES) in 1969 argues that foreign encouragement of industrial development, in stressing import substitution, has led to a transferral of *hacendado* mentality to the commercial and entrepreneurial elite. It also expresses the increasingly common view that dependency relations and national integration are gravely impeded by the incapacity of the political system. In the meantime, "structural vices and maladjustment impede the participation of vast social sectors which remain . . . on the margin of national life."[30]

Contemporary intellectual currents, then, share in common an underlying hostility to alien influence. While *indigenistas,* Marxists, and developmental theorists speak of international capitalism, dependency, and domestic colonialism, the champions of *Hispanidad* are also troubled by existing external influences. While supporting strengthened ties with Spain, *Hispanistas* have also held Anglo-Saxon civilization as bearing a responsibility for the retardation of national cultural integration. The slowness of socioeconomic development is often blamed upon the untoward receptivity of national leadership to foreign interests. For the *Hispanistas,* it has been the historical failure to revive the practices and policies of colonial Spain which explains the inadequacy of national institutions and the failure to free the republic from decelerating influence of the indigenous masses.

Contemporary nationalism therefore includes positive as well as critical components. Many have argued – contrary to the *Hispanistas* – that even in colonial times there has never existed a true national community. Thus the task is not that of reviving in modern form what in fact has never existed. Rather,

[29]Ibid., p. 381.

[30]Oswaldo Hurtado (ed.), *Dos mundos superpuestos; ensayo de diagnóstico de la realidad ecuatoriana* (INEDES, 1969), p. 249.

the necessity becomes that of helping Ecuador to realize its potential as an integrated and unified society. This requires development of untapped resources, including all sectors of the population, in order to bring into being a meaningful sense of community incorporating both European and indigenous values. Much as Vasconcelos argued in his writings on Mexican national history and culture, Ecuadorean nationalists call for the development of a new Ecuadorean man, blending the most constructive and positive elements of both heritages. Given the existence of these varying schools of thought, the resultant disunity and discontinuity contributes to an intellectual dissensus. An examination of Ecuador's historical evolution provides manifest testimony to such discord.

HISTORICAL EVOLUTION OF POLITICAL FRAGMENTATION

In pre-Conquest times a mosaic of small and diverse groups of Indians lived in the lands which were to become Ecuador. Only shortly before the coming of the *conquistadores* did the Incan Empire extend its reach this far north of its original base in the mountains of southern Peru. In 1493 Huayna Capac had become Incan monarch; by the time of his death in 1526, amid wild rumors of bearded white men along the coast, he had established his rule nearly as far as the region of today's border between Ecuador and Colombia. A contest for authority between his two sons, Atahualpa in Quito and Huascar in Cuzco, led to hostilities between the half-brothers which raged in the late 1520s. Eventually Atahualpa reunited the Empire under his own dominion, and the Quito-born chieftain was in the process of renewing Incan expansion to the north when the Spaniards arrived.

The famed *conquistador* Francisco Pizarro being occupied otherwise, one of his lieutenants, Sebastián de Benalcázar, in November 1533 led some two hundred men into the Ecuadorean highlands.[31] Easily winning control of the valley of Quito and environs, the Spaniards continued their explorations. In

[31]See Alfredo Pareja Diezcanseco, *Historia del Ecuador,* Vol. 1 (Quito: Casa de la Cultura Ecuatoriana, 1958), pp. 134-35 for more details.

1542 Francisco de Orellana led a trip of over 2,000 miles to the mouth of the Amazon and back, providing the historical basis for later Ecuadorean claims to status as an Amazon republic with territorial possessions along the upper waters of the river. Consolidation of the conquest followed, with Quito itself becoming the seat of a colonial *audiencia* in 1563. Essentially a high administrative court with widespread powers, the *audiencia* became a major mechanism of Spanish rule.

A tracing of colonial history lies beyond the scope of this work. Suffice it to say that, in common with the rest of the colonies, the eighteenth century showed a progressive deterioration with the concomitant decline of the Spanish monarchy. Administrative fragmentation, relaxation of colonial economic controls, and the introduction of non-Spanish foreign influences became evident. Resentment toward Spanish authorities among the native-born *criollo* elite became noticeable, and by the opening of the nineteenth century rebellion was in the air. A local junta was secretly established in Quito in December of 1808; by August of 1809 it had ousted the Spanish president of the *audiencia,* although before the close of the year the junta itself had been toppled. After further turmoil, a congress in December of 1811 declared independence from Spain and proclaimed the founding of the nation of Quito.

These early efforts proved abortive, for in December of 1812 the royalists regained control. However, a second phase in the independence struggle was precipitated in 1820 by a *cabildo* of local leaders in Guayaquil. The forces of Simón Bolívar, under the leadership of Antonio José de Sucre and Juan José Flores, soon launched an assault against royalist troops. Winning the climactic battle of Pichincha on the mountains overlooking Quito on May 24, 1822, independence forces assured liberation from colonial rule. Five days later loyalty was sworn to Gran Colombia, and for eight turbulent years that federation survived amid the internal rivalries of the future Ecuador, Venezuela, and Colombia. When in 1830 Venezuela withdrew from Gran Colombia, Ecuador promptly followed suit. A *cabildo* in Quito proclaimed independence and convened a constitutional convention in Riobamba. On September 11, 1830, the twenty-one-man assembly named General Juan José Flores its ruler. Shortly thereafter he proclaimed the first constitution of the republic of Ecuador.[32]

Genesis of Postcolonial Disunity. With the initiation of the republican period came the accompanying fruits of discord, although admittedly many seeds had been sown during the colonial past. Thirty-year-old General Juan José Flores (1800-64), a Venezuelan-born *mestizo* of humble origins who had proven himself an able and ambitious soldier, found himself widely mistrusted as a foreigner. Furthermore, he was suspect to *guayaquileños* through his residence in Quito, and socially unacceptable to the *quiteño* aristocracy despite marriage into a prominent family. Quito was already conservative and clerical, Guayaquil liberal and rebellious; the military was divided, the treasury thin, and the economy stagnant. The newly independent republic also lacked a common political will; some advocated the renewal of ties with Colombia, others proposed union with Peru, and there were even a few who lamented the passing of Spanish authority. It is small wonder that Flores' response was autocratic, harsh, and tough-minded.

Determined to establish sound and orderly government, he suppressed opposition and tightened his control over the military. National pride was fed by Ecuador's seizing control of the Galapagos islands in 1832, although a brief campaign by Flores against Colombia in the Cauca valley was unsuccessful. Flores was also protective of Church interests, honoring the constitutional pledge of 1830 that it was "the duty of the government, in the exercise of the right of *patronato,* to protect this religion, excluding any other." Flores' single-minded pursuit of his own ambitions inevitably rankled liberal opposition in both Guayaquil and elsewhere. Nationalistic criticisms appeared in *El Quiteño Libre,* while elements in Guayaquil followed the leadership of Vicente Rocafuerte (1783-1847) in demanding individual freedoms, a reduction of Church authority, and a curtailment of centralized power from Quito.

Sensitive to this intensification of opposition, Flores nego-

[32]Unless otherwise indicated, citations for specific historical events or dates are drawn from Ecuadorean historiographical sources. For the interested reader, the more useful include Pedro Fermín Cevallos, *Resumen de la historia del Ecuador desde su orijen hasta 1845,* 5 vols. (Lima: Imprenta del Estado, 1870); for a massive if selective compendium of data, see Federico E. Trabucco, *Síntesis histórica de la república del Ecuador: legislación y principales hechos* (Quito: Editorial "Santo Domingo," 1968); the rather informally written account of Pareja Diezcanseco, (see fn. 31); and the more systematic interpretation of G. Cevallos García, *Visión teórica del Ecuador* (Puebla, Mexico: Editorial J. M. Cajica Jr. S.A., 1959).

tiated an agreement whereby Rocafuerte came to the presidency in 1835 but Flores himself remained as military commander. Rocafuerte, a well-to-do liberal journalist and political leader from Guayaquil, agreed to this arrangement in anticipation of subsequent alternation in the presidency. A new constitution was adopted, embodying such cherished liberal principles as anticlericalism, popular sovereignty, and the enshrinement of individual freedoms. Political liberty was generally observed, immigration was encouraged, and a number of schools were built. Throughout this period General Flores preserved much of his own power, and toward the end of Rocafuerte's four-year-term influenced him in renewed restriction of political rights. In 1839 Rocafuerte completed his term and returned the presidency to Flores. The liberal then assumed the governorship of Guayas province.

During his second period in power Flores exercised even more despotic authority. Drawing fully upon the conservative sentiments of the *quiteño* elite, he became more hostile toward the coast while reviving the old Indian tribute system. Scheduled to return the presidency to Rocafuerte in 1843, Flores instead instituted a new constitution. While doubling the presidential term to eight years and removing the prohibition against immediate reelection, the document called for congress to meet only at four-year intervals. Adoption of this constitution and the bribery of Rocafuerte presumably assured Flores' preeminence for years to come, but the result was an exacerbation of domestic unrest. Anti-Flores elements in Quito were centered among Conservative university students belonging to the *Sociedad Filotécnica* (Philotechnical Society); for them, the constitution was Flores' "Charter of Slavery." Guayaquil liberal opposition could not be bought off as neatly as had been Rocafuerte, and coastal rebellion in 1845 led to Flores' resignation. His defeat was assuaged by retention of his military rank, salary, and 20,000 pesos to establish residence in Europe.

This early republican period helped to establish patterns of disunity which have their parallels in twentieth-century Ecuador. The highland-coastal rivalry was apparent from the outset, as was the temporary marriage of convenience between rival political leaders; if Flores and Rocafuerte were Machiavellian in their pact, others have been no less calculating in more recent years. In addition to Liberal-Conservative divisions, Guayaquil's readiness to rebel against central authority as personified by its Quito rival was also firmly established. Constitutionalism was formally recognized as paramount but either ignored in practice or altered for personal convenience, while popular participation was held to a minimum. And while divisions were deepening, political maneuvering was increasing, with personalistic leadership pursuing its own ambitions in the absence of concerted or systematic attention to socioeconomic needs. The use of force was being employed both to preserve and to overthrow governmental power, in neither case responding directly to popular opinion.

The departures of Rocafuerte in 1843 and Flores two years later, both under circumstances providing them considerable financial consolation, ushered in fifteen years of economic stagnation and political disorder. Some eleven governments of varying brevity seized and lost power, while three further constitutions (1845, 1851, and 1952) were drafted, adopted, and discarded. Civil strife rose, and border skirmishes with both Peru and Colombia added to the turbulence. Military rule was frequent, and the Liberals held the upper hand. Normally their community of interests went little further than general opposition to a return by Juan José Flores, who periodically threatened to launch a drive for yet a third period in power. Perhaps the most recurrent name on the political scene was that of José María Urbina, a *guayaquileño* and onetime military protegé of Flores who occupied the presidency from 1851 to 1856.

Liberal sentiment led to a restriction of the Church and expulsion of the Jesuits. This blow to the backward educational system was nominally offset by official support to expanded public facilities, but little real improvement was achieved. Economic conditions remained unsatisfactory, and foreign trade was largely ignored. Among the few positive actions was Urbina's abolition of slavery, which congress approved on September 18, 1852. Through Urbina's influence greater attention was given to the military, both for support of the regime and for an extension of hostilities with Ecuador's neighbors. Tension with Peru ultimately led to the latter's proclamation of a blockade of the Ecuadorean coast in 1858, and intermittent fighting continued for two years. By that time there was little semblance of national government whatever, and the Liberal cause had fallen into deep disrepute as a result of fifteen years' disorder, repression, and anarchy. When Guillermo Franco of Guayaquil actually signed a treaty ceding that city and Ecuador's southern territory to Peru, governmental authority had reached its nadir.

At that juncture the erstwhile ex-*caudillo* Flores hastened back from exile to join with Conservative forces led by Gabriel García Moreno (1821-75). Swiftly defeating Franco on the coast and winning control of the country, the rebels established their own provisional government. Flores was soon pushed aside by García Moreno and, on April 8, 1861, a new constitutional assembly named the latter president of the republic. This marked the introduction of nearly four decades of Conservative hegemony, with its foundations laid and institutions formalized by Gabriel García Moreno. One of the most remarkable and in some ways bizarre figures to pass across the political stage in Ecuador, he is well characterized by the following words of a twentieth-century Ecuadorean historian:

> The new President, endowed with extraordinary talent, great probity and admirable administrative and organizing talents; a man of science and letters, but of profoundly conservative and absolutistic ideas, mystic, impulsive, arbitrary, cruel and despotic . . . in his hands politics and religion would be weapons and instruments destined for the execution and realization of his beliefs. . .[33]

Theocracy, Absolutism, and Conservative Rule. Born in Guayaquil to a nonaristocratic family, Gabriel García Moreno was largely educated in Quito, where he studied theology and law. Exposed from an early age to strict religious teachings and austere living conditions, he developed a staunch conservatism which was deepened by firsthand observation of Europe's revolutionary upheavals of 1848 while studying abroad. Returning home in 1850 he became rector at the University of Quito. Later in the decade he served as mayor, and for a time was a member of the Senate. Throughout this period he astutely built his own personal power, isolated his conservative rivals, and maintained an energetic attack upon the Liberals. An avowed

[33]Francisco Huerta Rendón, *Historia del Ecuador* (Guayaquil: Editada por Publicaciones Educativas "Ariel," 1966), pp. 236-37.

proponent of civilian as well as Conservative rule, he ended the 1850s as a dominant figure and, with the successful removal of Flores from the scene, became the unchallenged ruler of the country. Serving in the presidency 1861-65, he stepped into the background until 1869, when he reassumed the presidency. Throughout the years from 1861 until his death in 1875, García Moreno was the unquestioned leader of the country, whether or not formally occupying the presidential chair.

It was under García Moreno that the Conservative party enjoyed its greatest hegemony, although retaining political control for two decades after his death. It was an era of religious fanaticism, absolutism in its most autocratic garb, and notable advances in major policy areas. García Moreno is perhaps most widely known for his dedication to Catholicism, for his regime was the most theocratic in all the independent history of Latin America. While drawing important political support from the Church, he effectively clericalized it as never before. Large numbers of foreign priests were brought to Ecuador, most notably the Jesuits. Educational facilities were more than doubled and became almost totally dominated by the Church.

His 1861 Constitution proclaimed Catholicism to be the *only* religion, and powers of censorship were turned over to Church authorities. A concordat was signed with the Vatican in 1863 whereby ecclesiastical courts were introduced and control over education was granted without qualification. A new constitution was adopted in 1869 which restricted citizenship to practicing Catholics and denied civil rights to all others. The Ecuadorean congress authorized a financial payment to the Vatican, and in 1873 García Moreno climaxed his earlier measures by officially dedicating the republic to "The Sacred Heart of Jesus." This action, in the words of one historian, successfully perpetuated "the ties between the Ecuadorean community and the outward symbol of divine mercy . . . the highest manifestation of devotion to the Catholic faith."[34]

As Herring has written, García Moreno deeply believed that Catholicism provided the morality and faith on which Ecuador should be rebuilt; the country was to become, in short,

[34]A lengthy treatment of the García Moreno era is that of Richard Pattee, *Gabriel García Moreno y el Ecuador de su tiempo* (Mexico: Editorial Jus, 1944).

"a theocratic state in which the Church would exercise moral and spiritual authority in the name of the Almighty."[35] Moreover, this required a ruler of dedication and strength, one who would impose that discipline necessary for the furthering of the faith. Political opponents were dealt with harshly. Congress was merely an appendage of the dictator's personal will, and criticism was forbidden. An Ecuadorean historian has quoted a letter in which García Moreno instructed one of his followers to bear in mind that "prompt, energetic, and terrible repression is the only way to curb wrongdoers."[36] Freedom of speech and press were nonexistent, while intellectual activity was restricted to properly Catholic thought and writing. While constitutional order was violated by the dictator with impunity, he nonetheless introduced an extreme degree of governmental centralization, especially in the 1869 charter. Predictable Liberal protests brought severe retaliation, and the most vocal critics – such as Montalvo – were expelled from Ecuador.

Granted the single-minded authoritarian Catholicism of the period, García Moreno must nonetheless be credited with a variety of domestic improvements. Internal communications and transportation were extended. Both railways and ordinary roads were constructed, including the initiation of the link from Quito to Guayaquil. This latter engineering feat, when later completed, was a major step in combatting regional isolation. Guayaquil's port facilities were also expanded and enlarged; agriculture was encouraged through the introduction of new crops, while early attempts at light industry were undertaken. The educational system was enhanced from primary through the university levels, notwithstanding the rigid curricular emphases. A sound financial base was achieved for the first time, encouraged through the adoption of a national currency, the payment of long-outstanding foreign debts, and the introduction of both efficiency and fiscal integrity to the treasury.

Gabriel García Moreno therefore succeeded far beyond his predecessors in the fostering of national unification, a sense of community, and a spirit of national identity. This, of course, reached only a small sector of the population, but nonetheless

[35]Hubert Herring, *A History of Latin America from the Beginnings to the Present,* 2nd ed. (New York: Alfred A. Knopf, 1961), p. 530.

[36]Alfredo Pareja Diezcanseco, *Historia del Ecuador,* Vol. II, p. 127.

represented an achievement which none of his predecessors had been willing or able to achieve. On August 6, 1875, he was assassinated on the steps of the presidential palace, thus marking the end of an extraordinary personal career. Such was the impact of his character and his policies that another twenty years passed before the Conservatives were swept from political power. During those two decades the country gradually slipped back into the turbulent and unsettled pattern which had become common prior to 1860. Ten governments and two more constitutions marched across the scene, while embattled Liberals slowly drained away Conservative strength. General Ignacio de Veintimilla, calling himself a "radical," provided a fairly popular government for seven years, but in 1883 was overthrown after a six-month-long civil war. Central authority was never effectively reestablished by the Conservatives, and finally, in 1895, the Liberals gained power after long years in the political wilderness. Their leader was a man who, like García Moreno, cast a long shadow across Ecuadorean history – Eloy Alfaro.

The 1895 Revolution and a Half-Century of Liberal Rule. Eloy Alfaro (1842-1912) is revered by Ecuadorean Liberals much as the Conservatives idolize García Moreno. An opponent of the Conservatives from the days of his youth in Guayaquil, he had been embroiled in rebellion during the years following the killing of García Moreno. Returning from Nicaraguan exile in 1895, the "Old Campaigner" assumed the leadership of Liberal forces in Guayaquil and, following an uprising there on June 5, 1895, rapidly proceeded to gain control of the country. Like García Moreno earlier, he was to remain the dominant force in Ecuador until his own death by assassination. Serving as president 1895-1901 and 1906-11, he was largely responsible for shaping the Liberal policies which were to be continued until 1944. The excesses of Conservative years logically led to a harsh and exaggerated response once the Liberals came to power. An anticlerical reaction was legitimized in the constitutions of 1896 and 1906, and a sweeping secularization undertook to restrict Church influence. A 1906 document in particular, largely dictated by Alfaro himself, provided for separation of church and state while recognizing freedom of worship and a wide range of civil liberties.

Alfaro's vision of Ecuador included the strengthening and

maintenance of constitutionality, observance of individual liberties, and the reestablishment of fiscal integrity.[37] Committed to the extension of education, attention to the Indian, and an improvement of health and sanitation, he also maintained his unwavering conviction that traditional Church preeminence had been fraught with perils for the republic. A notable achievement was completion of the railway from Quito to Guayaquil,[38] an engineering feat that linked the coast to the highlands. Alfaro's broad commitment to modernization also brought striking improvements to Quito, where electricity and a potable water supply were introduced. Additional anticlerical measures included abrogation of the government tithe which had been paid the Church, confiscation of many Church estates, and an end to public support for Catholic schools.

Although outspoken in his support of constitutionality, Alfaro himself was inclined to personalistic rule. Intolerant of criticism, he sometimes disregarded legal niceties in the pursuit of his goals. At one juncture he reportedly exclaimed that he would not lose by ballots what had been won by strength of arms. By the turn of the century there was growing rivalry between Alfaro and another Liberal leader, General Leónidas Plaza Gutiérrez (1865-1932). Alfaro was mistrustful of Plasa's relative cordiality with certain Conservative elements but in 1901 did accept the transfer of power to Plaza. With Alfaro withdrawn to Guayaquil in temporary retirement, Leónidas Plaza adopted a more conciliatory approach. An efficient administrator, he extended Liberal reforms on several fronts, including laws on marriage and divorce.

By the time of Alfaro's return to the presidency in 1906 the rift between the two Liberal leaders was more evident, and political dissension spread. While Alfaro continued to exert a magnetic appeal for the masses, he also presided over an increasingly acrimonious regime. Although leaving office in 1911, he soon returned to the fray at the head of another irregular force.

[37]For insight into *alfarista* reforms, the 1906 constitution is especially revealing. See *Constitución política de la república del Ecuador decretada por la asamblea nacional de 1906-1907,* 2nd ed. (Quito: Imprenta y Encuadernación Nacionales, 1910).

[38]As noted in chapter 1, the railway ends at Duran, a town across the Guayas river from Guayaquil.

Defeated and imprisoned, he was dragged from the Quito penitentiary by angry mobs and killed on January 28, 1912. Later in the year Plaza returned to office again, serving four years until the conclusion of his term in 1916. The two decades of rule by Alfaro and Plaza had established the predominant Liberal orientation, and it was to survive nearly three decades more.

Allegiance to the Liberals, who had been formally organized as a political party in 1878, became fairly widespread. Liberal anticlericalism, the dogged tenacity and drama of Alfaro's career, and the more placid but generally progressive rule under Plaza, all served to strengthen the existing patterns. The fluctuations of the economy also began to register a greater impact on political affairs. Several years of relative prosperity as a result of the booming cacao market soon gave way to growing recession as a major blight attacked the plant pods. Public works projects had drained government resources, and private banks lent increasingly large sums of money to Liberal governments. During the World War I years, Guayaquil's Commercial and Agricultural Bank became a major creditor, and as such exerted great influence on political affairs. This underwrote the national role of the wealthy Guayaquil elite, permitting a serious challenge to more traditional *quiteños*.

From 1914 through 1925 the financial situation became increasingly unsound. Domestic unrest increased, as society's dispossessed demonstrated less passivity in the fact of governmental insensitivity to their everyday problems. A major coastal strike in November of 1922 cost the lives of more than one thousand, and in 1925 a brief but symbolically meaningful *golpe de estado* by young reformist military officers ousted the existing Liberal government. Another change soon brought to the presidency Isidro Ayora (1879-1963), who exercised virtual dictatorship until 1931. A somewhat neglected administration in national history, it was nonetheless productive. Ayora energetically initiated a number of fiscal and economic reforms, including establishment of the *Banco Central,* reorganization of the monetary system, currency devaluation, debt collection, and the founding of several administrative agencies. Much of this stemmed from the recommendations of the so-called Kemmerer Mission, which was invited by Ayora to study and to reorganize the financial situation. Solid progress was also achieved in education, health, and highway construction before Ayora's forced resignation in 1931.

While the Liberal-Conservative polarity remained, its bitterness was lessened somewhat by the growing intensity of intraparty fissures. A variety of factions, movements, and mini-parties appeared on the scene, running the ideological gamut from radical Marxism on the left to Falangist reaction on the right. Over a dozen individuals held the presidency during these years, including a fiery young congressman named José María Velasco Ibarra, of whom more will be said later. There were extended discussions of social justice, of popular education, and of public works projects; but administrative disorganization, limited resources, and political instability vitiated such goals. Not until 1940 did the situation become more promising, with the inauguration of Carlos Arroyo del Río (1893-1969). A skilled Liberal politician and lawyer with long experience at the national level, Arroyo del Río initially promised reinvigorated leadership and more rational economic policy. Instead, he was to be overtaken by events which led to great national humiliation and brought to a shuddering halt the long era of Liberal domination.

Ecuador had already endured several additional losses of territory during the preceding half-century. Brazil had seized disputed land in the *oriente* in 1904, while Colombia had also insisted upon its own claims in 1916. Historic differences with Peru were revived in 1935 when Colombia ceded to Peru a sliver of territory still claimed by Ecuador. Provocations inflamed popular imaginations in both Peru and Ecuador, while the border situation became increasingly unsettled. Peruvian troops were mobilized along the frontier, and in early July of 1941 their forces marched into Ecuadorean territory. Fearful of an internal coup, President Arroyo sent little aid to the disputed area, retaining his better military units in Quito. There had been scant preparation despite warnings of impending danger, and Arroyo also rejected the offer of retired military men to return to active duty. The outnumbered Ecuadorean forces were unable to repel the better-equipped invaders, and most of the province of El Oro was rapidly occupied.[39]

The fruits of Peruvian aggression were accepted with belated intervention by the United States and several Latin American countries. The Protocol of Rio de Janeiro was signed in January of 1942, whereby the transfer of more than 200,000 square kilometers to Peru was recognized and guaranteed by Argentina, Brazil, Chile, and the United States. The Peruvians withdrew their troops from occupied portions of El Oro and Loja after having sacked and ravaged the countryside. The Arroyo government yielded to strong international pressures by signing the Protocol. Its initial unpreparedness and subsequent lack of a will to resist provoked great popular resentment; Arroyo was bitterly attacked for the debacle, the military vented its embarrassment in opposition to the president, and national morale collapsed. Emotions were still inflamed as the 1944 elections approached, and the impassioned torment produced by the territorial loss was channeled and capitalized upon by Arroyo's longtime critic, José María Velasco Ibarra (1893-).

Perhaps the most remarkable figure of twentieth-century Ecuadorean politics,[40] Velasco Ibarra had been in self-imposed exile following a disputed defeat by Arroyo del Río in the 1940 elections. By 1943 the opposition to Arroyo was being organized under the initiative of Camilo Ponce, a rightist who had been secretary-general of the *velasquista* electoral committee in 1939-40. Communists, Socialists, dissident Liberals, and Conservatives banded together as the *Alianza Democrática Ecuatoriana* (ADE) and, after months of disagreement, settled on Velasco as their candidate. The "Great Absentee" slipped across the border from Colombia during a major outbreak of rioting and demonstrations in Guayaquil on May 28, 1944, and Arroyo del Río resigned. Velasco, greeted by cheering roadside throngs during a three-day trip from the frontier to Quito, arrived in the capital on May 31. Standing in a drenching rain, he pledged himself to social justice and a national resurrection, while promising to

[39]For a detailed treatment which stresses the military operations, see David H. Zook, Jr., *Zarumilla-Marañon: The Ecuador-Peru Dispute* (New York: Bookman Associates, 1964).

[40]For further discussion of Velasco as personifying many fundamental traits of Ecuadorean political leadership, see chapter 4.

punish those responsible for staining the national honor. Although having served briefly as president in 1933-34, it was the May 1944 revolution which catapulted Velasco to national prominence.[41] The course of national politics from that point forward has deeply reflected the qualities of his personality and leadership. Either from the presidency or from foreign exile, he has been a dominant factor in national affairs.

Velasquismo, Populism, and Social Protest. More than a quarter-century has passed since Velasco's triumphant arrival in Quito. His unquestioned talent for building widespread national support has been equaled by an inability to provide constructive leadership once having assumed power. Each time Velasco has aroused popular passions, has broadened the base of support for the political system, and has then brought progressive disillusionment with both his own leadership and with the efficacy of national government. Traditional parties have increasingly fragmented, the military role in politics has increased, and personalism has become ever more prevalent. At the same time, economic and social problems have been largely unresolved, and growing discontent has led to dissension and discontinuity within the system.

Velasco's second presidential tenure survived until August of 1947, when he was deposed by the armed forces. At the outset he had persecuted prominent members of the previous administration; in later terms he was also to take punitive action against opponents, whom he customarily viewed as evil and antinational. A constituent assembly dominated by leftists and independent Liberals met to draft a new constitution, but the document was suspended by Velasco barely a year after its adoption. Velasco's autocratic inclinations became swiftly evident, and the disparate elements within his administration began to turn on one another. Typical was a dispute between leftist Minister of Government Carlos Guevara Moreno and rightist Foreign Minister Camilo Ponce, which nearly resulted in a duel between the two.

As the incongruous elements of the ADE gradually fell

[41]A detailed discussion of the events surrounding Velasco's 1944 assumption of power appears in George I. Blanksten, *Ecuador: Constitutions and Caudillos* (Berkeley: University of California Press, 1951), pp. 42-51.

upon one another, the president turned away from his earlier leftist support. Elections for a new constituent assembly in June of 1946 were won by the Conservatives, and they were influential in the drafting of the 1946 constitution. By 1947 Velasco had also alienated many Conservatives, his popular support had deteriorated, and there were few protests when Colonel Carlos Mancheno engineered his overthrow. After an interim period preceding 1948 elections, the country returned to the constitutional path with the inauguration of Galo Plaza Lasso, son of the former Liberal president.

Ecuadorean politics since 1948 can be divided into two periods: the first, from 1948 to 1960, saw the remarkable feat of three successive elected presidents serving out their full terms of office; the second, from 1960 to the present, experienced a revival of extreme governmental instability. Thus the superficial appearance of growing continuity in government from 1948 to 1960 proved to have been a mere interlude, during which existing divisions remained largely unchanged. The election of the moderate Galo Plaza brought to office a man of democratic commitment, and his energy was devoted to the strengthening of representative institutions.[42] Plaza regarded political democracy as the necessary prerequisite to socioeconomic reforms; much of his time was occupied with his own political survival.

Plaza also recognized the prevailing ignorance about national resources and problems. He therefore eschewed grandiose planning to concentrate on modest programs of reform, in the meantime gathering together a cataloguing of Ecuadorean needs. The 1950 national census was but one such manifestation of his efforts. It was also during his administration that bananas were rapidly developed as the country's major export. Plaza's commitment to democratic processes was further illustrated by his neutrality in 1952 elections, despite his antagonism toward Velasco Ibarra, who won the contest and returned for a third time to the presidency. It was from 1952 to 1956 that Velasco for the first time served his full constitutional term. Having drawn primarily upon the political right on this occasion, Velasco for a time included members of the rightist

[42]A personal account of his experiences appears in Galo Plaza, *Problems of Democracy in Latin America* (Chapel Hill: University of North Carolina Press, 1957).

ARNE in his government, and also leaned heavily on the astuteness of Camilo Ponce in a key ministry.

Launching a massive public works program, Velasco relied on the rising income from bananas to finance his government. However, gross mismanagement and dishonesty in government – despite Velasco's own personal austerity and rectitude – dissipated the economic gains produced by banana exports. At the close of his term Ecuador had a deficit of more than $30 million, and his characteristic failure at political organization had prevented the implementation of projected reforms. It was his last-minute support which helped bring Camilo Ponce to the presidency in 1956 after a close race rife with charges of electoral fraud. With Ponce, the Ecuadorean right returned to political power after sixty-one years.

Ponce was confronted by limited popular support, deep-seated mistrust of the Liberals, an empty treasury, and *velasquista* denunciations which began immediately following inaugural ceremonies. His survival through four years was a measure of his considerable political acumen. At the same time, however, both Ponce's own inclinations and the reality of the political situation held social and economic reforms to a minimum. His attention was largely held by the struggle to avoid total bankruptcy in the wake of *velasquista* errors. Budgetary austerity, restricted public investment, and increased foreign investment helped in the recovery of fiscal well-being. Having served out his term, Ponce was unable to provide the necessary support for the 1960 Conservative candidate. Instead, the irrepressible Velasco Ibarra won yet another term of office, this time with the greatest popular mandate of the century.[43]

With Velasco's inauguration to a fourth term, political instability returned with a vengeance and has been omnipresent ever since. A startling array of personalistic leaders, military officers, and obscure governmental caretakers have sped in and out of power. In 1960 Velasco came to office committed to major socioeconomic change, and at the outset seemed prepared

[43]Brief biographical sketches of Ecuador's presidents through 1958 appear in Julio C. Troncoso, *Odio y sangre; la descalificación del sr. Neptalí Bonifaz y la batalla de los cuatro dias en Quito; esbozo histórico-biográfico de los presidentes del Ecuador de 1830 a 1958* (Quito: Editorial "Fray Jodoco Ricke," 1959). Vignettes of Velasco, Plaza, and Ponce are found on pp. 92-97 and 108-113.

to follow a leftward course. He soon proved characteristically unable to convert electoral support into meaningful policy, however. The *velasquista* movement itself fragmented, with Vice-President Carlos Julio Arosemena Monroy turning against his president and building his own personal following. The military was insulted when Velasco removed forty-eight senior officers on his first day in office. Protests and demonstrations became common by the close of 1960, and Velasco's ambitious call for industrialization, agrarian reform, and public works failed to get beyond the planning stage. Pro-Castro manifestations and North American pressures, along with the growing hostility of Arosemena Monroy, impelled Velasco to move toward the political center.

With the economy sagging dangerously, in October of 1961 Velasco decreed extensive taxes on some thirty consumer items. Protests broke out, rapidly mounting in both Cuenca and Guayaquil. Several weeks of strikes, work stoppages, military retaliation by the government, and personal interventions by Velasco finally led to the collapse of the government on November 8, 1961. Velasco was replaced by his vice-president, scion of a wealthy Guayaquil family, erstwhile ex-*velasquista,* and a powerful personality in his own right. His ascent was widely hailed, drawing support from such leftist-controlled organizations as the student federation and the labor confederation. Paradoxically, both the political left and the economic elites felt comfortable with Velasco's successor. Arosemena's cabinet appointments were impressive, including all sectors but the radical left and far right.

The new president's sympathy for the Cuban revolution gradually created growing suspicion, however. Ecuador voted against the expulsion of Cuba from the inter-American system in January 1962, and only strong pressure from the military in April forced Arosemena to break relations with Poland and Czechoslovakia, which he had only recently established. The President's leftist inclinations proved less pronounced than his practical sense of political survival, and in early 1962 he shifted toward the political center without difficulty. While rumors of his fondness for alcoholic beverages became commonplace, there was a wave of sympathetic support when, following Arosemena's rejection of the left, Fidel Castro publicly called him a "drunken coward." The president reiterated earlier pledges of major structural reforms, and the economic elite became alarmed. By the close of 1962 the president had lost Liberal support, and the right intensified its charges of communist infiltration of his administration. Allegations of public drunkenness were aired in congress and the press, and by early 1963 military conspiracy was afoot.

On July 11, 1963, following Arosemena's after-dinner insults of the North American ambassador and the president of the Grace Line Steamship Company, the military deposed the president and seized power. While widespread knowledge of Arosemena's personal vices contributed to the military *golpe,* more fundamental issues were also involved. In the wake of their action the military claimed to have saved the country from communist influences; some of its members, however, had also been disappointed by Arosemena's failure to implement meaningful reforms.[44] Contrary to tradition the military, instead of acting as temporary custodians of government, opted for the initiation of basic reforms before relinquishing power.[45] The *Junta Militar* announced that elections and the reestablishment of constitutionality would await their introduction of major reforms.

The junta encountered growing resistance, while finding the tasks of governance more political and less technical than it had anticipated.[46] Degenerating into a regime of force, the junta was further handicapped by rivalries within its own leadership. Eventually pressured to promise elections in 1967, the regime was unable to withstand student protests, labor strikes, and unqualified opposition from the political parties. On March 28, 1966, disheartened by massive opposition and frustrated in the extreme, the *Junta Militar* announced its resignation. After some twenty-four hours without any effective government, a small group of prominent national figures chose as interim president Clemente Yerovi Indaburu. A prominent economist of

[44]A searching evaluation of the factors involved in the ouster of Arosemena appears in Martin C. Needler, *Anatomy of a Coup d'Etat: Ecuador 1963* (Washington: Institute for the Comparative Study of Political Systems, 1964).

[45]An initial statement of policy appeared in República del Ecuador, *Plan político de la junta militar de gobierno* (Quito: Talleres Gráficos Nacionales, 1963).

[46]Also see the discussion of the military in chapter 3.

liberal leanings who had served the country effectively in a variety of posts, Yerovi harbored no political ambitions and promised nonpartisan leadership until the convening of a new constituent assembly.

Yerovi provided a scrupulously neutral setting during the next eight months. Following the first national elections since 1962, the Constituent Assembly – Ecuador's sixteenth[47] – met in October of the year. In addition to drafting a new constitution, it was charged with selecting a new interim president until national elections were held. With the assembly evenly divided between Liberals and Conservatives, the latter formed a pact with the *Coalición Institucionalista Democrática* (CID) of former Liberal Otto Arosemena Gómez (a cousin of Carlos Julio). Rightist forces thereby succeeded in electing Arosemena Gómez to the provisional presidency, and he immediately replaced Yerovi.[48] Arosemena remained in office for the following twenty months while the 1967 constitution was adopted, new election laws were passed, and national elections were held in June of 1968.[49]

During those months Arosemena continued Yerovi's efforts to regularize national government, stimulate the economy, and restore a modicum of stability to the political scene. The youthful Arosemena, forty-one years old and desirous of establishing himself more clearly as a politician of national stature, provided forceful leadership. Asserting Ecuador's independence in hemispheric affairs, he also attempted to energize the government through school construction and industrial growth. Although preferring a Conservative victory in 1968 which would presumably maximize his own chances for 1972, he remained at least publicly neutral during the 1968 campaign. On September 1, 1968, he turned over the presidential sash to

[47]The first had been the body which elected Juan José Flores in 1830. For a listing of constituent assemblies, see *El año ecuatoriano, 1966* (Quito: Talleres Gráficos de Editorial Santo Domingo, 1967), p. 53.

[48]Details are found in chapter 4. For another description of the details of Arosemena's election, see ibid., pp. 48-52 and 54-60.

[49]A listing of presidents from 1830 to 1967 appears in Trabucco, *Síntesis histórica,* pp. 10-13. A table which includes provisional regimes and method of election is found in Georg Maier, *The Ecuadorian Presidential Election of June 2, 1968* (Washington, D.C.: Institute for the Comparative Study of Political Systems, 1969), pp. 32-33.

his elected successor. On that date, some six months after returning from his most recent period of foreign residence, the ubiquitous José María Velasco Ibarra was inaugurated, moving for the fifth time into the presidency of Ecuador.[50]

This last *velasquista* government, as discussed later, was characteristically volatile. Constitutional rule was abrogated in June of 1970, after which Velasco survived largely on the sufferance of the armed forces. On February 15, 1972, the military ousted Velasco, suspended the elections scheduled for June, and proclaimed a "revolutionary nationalist" junta under General Guillermo Rodríguez Lara. Thus, for the second time in less than a decade, Ecuador was governed by the military.

[50]See the concluding chapter for a discussion of the fifth *velasquista* administration. A discussion of the transition from the *Junta Militar* through two interim presidents to the 1968 elections is narrated by a sympathizer of Velasco in Joaquín Mena Soto, *Enfoques universitarios; de la dictadura militar al quinto velasquismo; hombres, hechos y proyecciones* (Quito: Editorial "Fray Jodoco Ricke," 1968).

3
The Political Framework: Theory and Practice

> The monarch in republican dress who carries on Ecuador's monarchical tradition is called the *caudillo*. Both monarchical systems upon which the Ecuadorean political process partly rests – the system of the non-American Spaniards and that of the pre-Hispanic Americans – contained the hereditary principle of legitimacy as the vehicle for replacing defunct monarchs. . . *Caudillismo*, unplanned and unpremeditated, sprang from the Ecuadoran cultural milieu spontaneously and chaotically as a method of selecting "natural" rulers, a substitute vehicle of succession.[1]

Although written two decades ago, these words are by no means inappropriate to contemporary Ecuador. Certainly political personalism and the role of the *caudillo* continue to loom large in the country. The prototype of such *caudillos*, José María Velasco Ibarra, returned in 1968 for the most recent such exercise of personalism. Yet the concept of monarchical authority can be exaggerated, exemplifying, as it does, virtually unchallenged authority of the chief executive.

Ecuadorean *caudillos* have enjoyed unlimited authority only when prepared to violate constitutional norms. The most recent constitution,[2] for example, placed substantial restric-

[1] George I. Blanksten, *Ecuador: Constitutions and Caudillos* (Berkeley: University of California Press, 1951), p. 34.

[2] As described later, the 1967 constitution was suspended by President Velasco in June of 1970. Thus its treatment in this chapter is framed as a means of illustrating the republic's constitutional traditions and practices rather than the specific details of this particular document.

tions on executive power, and today the domination of a García Moreno is impossible. Indeed, the 1967 constitution was intended to guard against undue executive personalism. And beyond constitutional constraints, the dynamics of contemporary Ecuadorean politics are such that a host of largely self-interested pressure groups and social sectors operate as mutually countervailing powers. A mass of strong and generally conflicting pressures and demands surround the chief executive. Given relative equality of strength, these tend to impose an equilibrium which is difficult to alter. *Serrano* landowners, Guayaquil businessmen and financiers, the Church, armed forces, organized labor, students, and an expanding middle sector all compete within the political arena, with the president the final arbiter. Such forces often may exercise an effective veto power, but none can gain domination for more than a brief interlude. Political dynamics tend to offset one another; the president, while able to play them off against one another, can rarely weave a consensus sufficiently broad to introduce new or innovative policies.

Both systemic political dynamics and constitutional restrictions, then, mitigate against effective executive direction and policy formation. Excepting periods of extraconstitutionality, personal authority in contemporary Ecuador has not been limitless. This reinforces the innate conservatism of the system; it may be possible to tinker with details of programs or policies, but bold new departures are not easily susceptible to implementation. Furthermore, the elitist domination of important pressure groups further assures the continuation of policies which contemplate no more than modest reforms, thereby providing still firmer undergirding for the existing status quo. Both constitutional forms and political elitism contribute to the maintenance and preservation of the system.

STRUCTURES OF CONSTITUTIONAL AUTHORITY

The 1967 constitution, Ecuador's sixteenth,[3] was officially published following adoption by the constituent assembly

[3] Some sources refer to the 1967 constitution as Ecuador's seventeenth. The difference of opinion is based upon the 1938 document, which was written but never

on May 25, 1967. Its immediate predecessor, the 1946 document, had survived longer than most, while that of 1967 was set aside by Velasco three years after its inception. Most of the nineteenth-century charters had reflected either explicit Liberal or Conservative views, depending upon the relative power of the two groups at the time of writing. Basic issues therefore centered largely about the relationship between civil and church authority. Conservative proclericalism was evident in most of the documents through that of 1884, while the next four emphasized the Liberal credo of state–church separation.

The 1967 constitution, drafted in the wake of a half-decade of unstable provisional government, violation of constitutional precepts, and the avoidance of legality, was a product of its times in view of the drafters' strong anti-*velasquismo*. Executive authority was restricted more than had previously been the case; as will be seen, legislative powers previously granted the congress were increased, and the balance was tilted away from the president. He was also denied control over many of the semiautonomous state agencies which had been proliferating. The government was described as "presidential and republican, and is elective, representative, responsible and alternating" (Title I, Article 1).[4] The constitution defined the primary function of the state as "establishing social conditions in which those who compose the community can enjoy by necessary means the realization of their goals" (Article 10).

The Executive. Elected directly for a four-year term and forbidden from reelection until an additional term has passed, the president must be at least forty years old and in full exercise of his normal political rights.[5] In a major departure from past practice, the 1967 constitution effectively stripped the presi-

promulgated. For a listing which excludes the 1938 document, see Federico E. Trabucco, *Síntesis histórica de la república del Ecuador* (Quito: Editorial "Santo Domingo," 1968), pp. 87-89.

[4] *Constitución política del estado ecuatoriano dictada por la asamblea nacional constituyente de 1966-67 y ley de elecciones dictada por el congreso nacional de 1967* (Quito: Talleres Gráficos Nacionales, 1967).

[5] Anti-*velasquistas* in the 1966-67 assembly had hoped to block his return by banning multiple terms, but *poncistas* and others understandably objected. Some even spoke of an age restriction of seventy, thereby rendering Velasco ineligible. In a bitingly sarcastic radio attack, Velasco suggested that, since he was bald and had a mustache, these attributes might be written into the constitution as a ban on presidential eligibility!

dent of the veto power he had long enjoyed. Thus, although he was able to reject a legislative bill on grounds of "inadvisability," this veto could be overridden through straight majority vote by congress in joint session. No longer was a two-thirds vote necessary to override, as had been true with the 1946 constitution. Presidential objection on the grounds of "unconstitutionality" was subject to decision by the Supreme Court.[6]

Another innovation was provision for national plebiscites under specified circumstances. The president was empowered to call for a plebiscite when: (a) congress rejected a constitutional amendment he had initiated; (b) when he himself opposed a legislatively initiated constitutional amendment; (c) when presidential legislation had been rejected or blocked by congress for two consecutive sessions; and (d) where the president sought a mandate from the electorate concerning "matters of transcendental importance to the interest of the nation." The president, although lacking a meaningful veto, could have recourse to the plebiscite should a truly vital measure be blocked by congress.

As a practical matter, the substitution of plebiscitory for veto powers realistically weakened the executive. President Velasco's experience in 1970 was doubtless typical of the new constitutional pattern. As further detailed in the concluding chapter, he proposed a set of controversial fiscal and tax reforms to congress. When the legislators failed to act, Velasco proclaimed the measures by executive decree. The Supreme Court subsequently overrode his action, at which point he assumed dictatorial powers, suspended the constitution, and set up a civilian dictatorship. Intractable in such a situation, Velasco in the absence of effective veto power had little constitutional authority to implement his reforms. The organizing of a plebiscite would have been time-consuming, while the economic situation required prompt action. The 1970 episode suggests that the plebiscitory changes introduced in 1967 exacerbated rather than moderated traditional conflict between congress and president.

Beyond the above, executive powers in the 1967 constitu-

[6] The author is indebted in particular to conversations on the 1967 constitution with Dr. Andrés F. Córdova (who played a major role in its framing) and to Lic. Luis E. Robles Plaza (Secretary of the Senate when interviewed in 1969).

tion followed past traditions more closely. The president retained the power to appoint ministers of state to head the eleven cabinet departments, and, in this, congress was denied the power of review. The legislature was, however, empowered to require ministerial presence for questioning at congressional sessions, and could force a cabinet resignation by a three-fifths vote. However, the fragmentation of congress into numerous parties and factions made the requisite 60 percent extremely difficult to achieve. Although ministerial instability is a characteristic of Ecuadorean politics, it derives from the collective instability and lack of cohesion of the executive rather than from direct congressional action. The president's appointive powers included governors of the twenty provinces and administrative directors of both the cantons and parishes. Like ministers of state, these officials were not subject to congressional approval. Appointments to the judiciary, in contrast, were entirely the constitutional responsibility of the legislature.

In common with most other Latin American states, the Ecuadorean president could assume extensive powers during periods of national emergency. Article 186 of the 1967 constitution conferred upon the president several extraordinary powers, including mobilization of the armed forces, the contracting of loans, transferral of the seat of government from Quito to another location within national territory, the temporary closing of ports, the arrest of those favoring invasion from abroad or supporting internal turbulence, and suspension of constitutional guarantees. Should congress be in recess, the president would immediately notify the Tribunal of Constitutional Guarantees (below), which might either limit or revoke the presidential declaration of a state of siege. Should congress be meeting at the time, the president would have to secure its assent before any such declaration, specifying the length of time and the constitutional guarantees which he proposed to suspend.

A departure from tradition introduced in 1967 related to the vice-presidency, which had been dropped in 1906 but was restored in the 1946 constitution. Drafters of the constitution remembered the role played by Vice-President Arosemena in 1960 and 1961, when Velasco's erstwhile running mate had used his power as presiding officer in congress to build his personal strength while working covertly against Velasco. Consequently the vice-presidency was stripped of all powers save the responsibility of succeeding to the presidency should it be vacated. As stated in Article 175, the vice-president "will be able to undertake whatever public or private function he desires, with the exception of that of legislator." Vice-President Jorge Zavala Baquerizo frequently complained after his 1968 election that his single official function was to remain alive in case the president did not.

Although this diminution of vice-presidential functions helped protect the president, the situation was worsened by the decision to permit voters to choose their president and vice-president separately. The victory of the Liberal Zavala over Velasco's running mate in 1968 therefore created a situation in which bitter political animosity divided the country's two ranking elected officials. Before long Zavala was being excluded from all official functions, and his contact with the president consisted of frequent exchanges of angry public communications. When Velasco assumed dictatorial power in 1970, the vice-president was among the "dangerous leftists" names, and his arrest was ordered.

The Bureaucracy. One of the most frustrating limitations on presidential power in Ecuador has been executive inability to control the extraordinary number of autonomous and semi-autonomous agencies which have come into being through the years. As Velasco correctly noted during his fifth administration, at least 50 percent of all tax revenues were being absorbed by the operation of these agencies, which operated in blithe indifference to the wishes of the president. Thus to the government ministries and their administrative staffs are added an astonishing array of organs numbering over 1300.[7] A 1967 study categorized some four dozen agencies alone under the single heading of "decentralized dependencies."[8] The range of

[7]When Velasco seized dictatorial powers in 1970, he promptly intervened in 703 of an official total of 1364 such bodies! See *El Universo* (Guayaquil), September 24, 1970.

A detailed listing of only a few of the more important agencies was prepared by the Institute of Administrative Studies of the Central University in conjunction with United States officials from the Agency for International Development. See *Manual de gobierno* (Quito: Editorial Universitaria, 1965).

[8]Instituto de Estudios Administrativos, *Directorio de dependencias del estado ecuatoriano* (Quito: Universidad Central, 1967).

these organs is staggering; a few of these include the National Association of Sheep Growers; the Port Authority of Guayaquil; Center of Industrial Development; Center of Economic Reconversion for the Provinces of Azuay, Cañar and Morona–Santiago; Ecuadorean Tourist Corporation; National Finance Corporation; Polytechnic School of the Coast; Ecuadorean Institute of Electrification; National Junta for the Defense of Artesans; Ecuadorean Institute of Hydraulic Resources; National Meteorological and Hydrological Service; and so forth, *ad infinitum.*[9]

The impossibility of meaningful centralization of authority and rational national planning amid this welter of largely independent bodies has been nearly as serious as the budgetary drain. Moreover, the opportunity for nepotism and political patronage is substantial. The same 1967 report listed 14,024 employees of the decentralized dependencies, 30.7 percent of whom were outside the civil service law. Moreover, of a total of 67,853 public servants in all the dependencies identified, 45.1 percent of the total were without the protection of "administrative career" jurisdiction.[10] Further insight into bureaucratic problems and attitudes comes from a recent analysis of upper-level government officials.[11]

From a sample of ninety-four interviews with section chiefs (generally two to three steps below the minister) drawn from eight ministries and three nonministerial organs, data indicated substantial official discontent, especially as the result of low prestige and poor morale. The government work "suffered on key factors such as salary employment security, opportunities to exercise initiative, political intervention, and recognition for work accomplishments."[12] Furthermore, the role of politics in bureaucratic appointments remained prevalent while turnover was high. There had been sixty-nine changes of ministers in the eight offices studied over a seven-year period beginning in 1960, and at lower levels job instability was nearly as extreme. The

[9] Several of these, most importantly the Port Authority of Guayaquil, were intervened by Velasco following his 1970 *autogolpe.* Most can be expected to be reestablished in due course, however.

[10] Instituto de Estudios Administrativos, *Directorio,* pp. 107, 109.

[11] Freeman J. Wright, *The Upper Level Public Administrator in Ecuador* (Quito: Editorial "Fray Jodoco Ricke," 1968).

[12] Ibid., p. 26.

presence of *palanqueo* – the gaining of bureaucratic employment through influence – was strong. Seventy-three of the respondents cited either political contacts or friendship as having been relevant in securing their appointments.

There is clear sentiment favoring a nonpolitical, merit-based administrative service for virtually all those beneath ministerial and subministerial levels. A collective consciousness has also been developing which may result in greater independence of action as well as defiance of ranking elected officials. During the sessions of the 1967 constituent assembly there were rumors that its budget committee was planning to eliminate some 4,000 positions as an economy measure. Public employees responded with a work stoppage, and the assembly swiftly reversed itself and announced its commitment to a merit bureaucracy. The employees promptly returned to their desks. Further evidence of concern appeared in Article 76 of the 1967 constitution, promising creation of an administrative career system "to ensure the stability of public employees and administrative efficiency, based on capability, merit and honesty . . . as a system for selection and promotion." Ultimately the 1967 constitution provided civil servants the opportunity to defend their interests either through the Tribunal of Constitutional Guarantees or the Tribunal of Administrative Disputes.

The Legislature. The 1967 constitution retained the bicameral tradition with a senate and chamber of deputies. Membership of the upper house was for a four-year term, with each of the provinces represented by two popularly elected senators but for the one allotted to the Galápagos Islands. In addition, another fifteen so-called "functional" senators were chosen, based on certain interest groups whose role was thereby institutionalized in the senate. There were four representatives of labor, chosen from both rural and urban workers as well as artisans. The economic interests of agriculture, commerce, and industry were also represented by two senators, one each from the *sierra* and from the coast. And, finally, five more functional senators represented additional groups; these included one apiece for the national police, the armed forces, public education, private education, and cultural bodies (defined in the constitution as "media of collective communication and scientific and cultural academies and societies").

Functional representation had first appeared in the 1929 constitution, and has survived in later documents. The functional senators – whose number has grown through the years – are selected through a kind of electoral college. As Blanksten noted years ago, the rationale for this constitutional oddity is based heavily upon a desire to maintain the balance between coast and highlands. Moreover, such functionalism provides further protection "to such instruments of power underlying the political process as the pattern of landownership, the armed forces, and the political role of formal education peculiar to countries like Ecuador."[13] The combination of provincial with functional senators in 1967 brought the national total to fifty-four. Unlike most of their provincial colleagues, the functionals are generally freer of party affiliation, but their socioeconomic commitments are unavoidably strong. The functional senators for *sierra* agriculturalists and for coastal urban workers are normally among the most influential.

In the lower chamber, election is for two-year terms, selected through a system of proportional representation derived from provincial population, with one per 80,000 inhabitants and one for a remainder of 40,000 or more. By 1967 the membership had grown to eighty, with Guayas' delegation composed of sixteen deputies, followed by Pichincha and Manabí with ten apiece. Several provinces had but two deputies, and the Galápagos Islands only one. It is in the chamber of deputies that all draft bills are initiated, whether introduced by the membership or, in certain cases, by the Supreme Court or the president. On a number of procedural matters, the two houses meet in joint session; among the more important are constitutional amendments, declarations of war, passage of the national budget, or compromising of disparate drafts on the same subject. The 1967 constitution intended to streamline congressional action on matters of urgency by providing for such joint action. Following the enactment of this constitution, however, such joint sessions were infrequent.[14]

Meeting twice annually for sixty-day sessions beginning

[13]Blanksten, *Ecuador,* p. 107.

[14]The Legislative Palace, constructed a decade ago, is among the few in the world with three chambers inside: one for each body sitting separately, and a third for joint sessions.

March 6 and August 10, congress has had limited time to enact important legislation; in recent years it has squandered much of its time and energy on minor business. The 1967 constitution established a permanent commission (*Comisión Legislativa Permanente*) to function regularly while congress was out of session. Composed of four senators and five deputies, this body may issue decrees and rulings on many matters. The practice drew heavy criticism after 1967, however, for many politicians were more concerned about a possible loss of congressional prerogatives than about legislative functioning throughout the year. In any event, the commission lacked the authority to appoint judges or to consider constitutional questions. Congress alone could name members of the judiciary, and also enjoyed sole authorization of constitutional interpretation "to resolve doubts that may arise with regard to the meaning of its precepts" (Article 257).

Despite efforts to strengthen the legislative function, congress has remained a center for bickering, haggling, and an energetic drive for narrow political advantage. If, on the one hand, congressmen have enjoyed authority sufficient to stalemate the president, this has been interpreted by some as an important defense against undue executive authority. However, the tradition of ineffective and opportunistic politicking has continued to prevail. Congress has only rarely exercised responsible leadership during constitutional periods. Moreover, the very fragmentation of political parties, the weakness of party discipline, and the large number of floating, semiindependent representatives have rendered legislative performance even less constructive. While educational backgrounds have improved and there is some nonelitist representation, this has done little to improve the calibre of performance. As a consequence, public attitudes toward congress are singular in their cynicism and disillusionment.

Tribunal of Constitutional Guarantees. A peculiarity of twentieth-century constitutions in Ecuador has been the Council of State.[15] A body which was granted extensive powers in the 1946 constitution, it was vested with both legislative and

[15]For a review and background, see Milton Alava Ormaza, "El Consejo de Estado," *El Universo* (Guayaquil), October 2, 1970. The tribunal was dismissed on June 22, 1970, by President Velasco following his *autogolpe*.

judicial functions, including primarily the resolution of jurisdictional disputes among or between administrative organs. The 1967 charter transformed the council into the Tribunal of Constitutional Guarantees (*Tribunal de Garantías Constitucionales*), charging it in Articles 219-223 with responsibility for the integrity of the constitutional process. However, tribunal power was largely restricted to the moral authority of condemnation or denunciation.

The Tribunal of Constitutional Guarantees was empowered to "formulate observations" and to report them to the responsible governmental authority, customarily the president or congress. Lacking the ability to impose sanctions, however, it could merely announce its opinions in print. In addition to its watchdog function, the tribunal performed certain minor duties when congress was out of session. Its approval was necessary before the president could call a plebiscite; he was also required to notify the tribunal before declaring a state of siege, in which case it might be restricted or disapproved. The ten-man tribunal was composed of the president of the Supreme Electoral Tribunal, the president of the Supreme Court, the Solicitor General, an appointed representative of the national president, two deputies, one senator, and three private citizens chosen by the congress meeting in joint session.

Although seriously intended as a meaningful organ for the maintenance and preservation of major constitutional guarantees, the tribunal, like the Council of State in earlier years, has lacked both the formal power and independent prestige to play an effective role. Even with its added powers concerning a possible plebiscite or presidential declaration of a state of siege, it has been ineffective. It is also unrealistic to expect a chief executive to feel constrained by the tribunal. Most likely he would ignore it completely. Unless or until such a body might establish independent prestige and political responsibility, its declarations are unlikely to be effective.

The Judiciary. Although somewhat apart from the mainstream of politics, Ecuador's judiciary enjoys a surprising degree of respectability. At the apex of the hierarchy is the Supreme Court of Justice (*Corte Supremo de Justicia* – CSJ), whose members are selected by congress for renewable six-year terms. The number of justices is not specified by the constitution, but eligibility for appointment includes either fifteen years' experience as a lawyer or twelve years as a sitting judge. Alternatively, eligibility can be met by service of at least a dozen years as a university professor of law. The composition of membership in practice is balanced between highland and coast, and the court in turn is divided into four separate *salas* or chambers.

The Supreme Court of Justice may temporarily suspend a law on the grounds of unconstitutionality, but must then direct it to congress for interpretation. Only the congress can actually render final judgment on questions of constitutionality. Thus judicial review is far from extensive. The constitution does permit the Supreme Court to collaborate with congress under specified conditions. It may introduce bills directly to congress, while justice may be present for floor discussions. When a constitutional amendment is under consideration, they may attend sessions and, under certain circumstances, may actually vote. Judicial-legislative collaboration is also encouraged by the annual message on the state of judicial administration, delivered to congress by the presiding officer of the court.

By tradition the judicial system is highly centralized. Beneath the Supreme Court of Justice are superior courts of appeal; then come provincial courts and cantonal courts, while at the local level the political lieutenants exercise judicial authority in minor cases. In moving down the judicial ladder, the degree of legal expertise and experience diminishes rapidly. Despite efforts to encourage a career judiciary, little progress has been achieved. The normal backlog of cases is often a year or more, and periods of unconstitutional government aggravate the situation. Moreover, while judicial integrity in the higher courts is substantial, at lower levels political influence or outright bribery is unexceptional.

On balance the judicial system has been freer from serious political intervention than in many other Latin American countries. This is at least partially the result of the distance between the courts and the politics of the country. The Supreme Court of Justice is not frequently drawn into major disputes. The most recent exception came with the events surrounding Velasco's establishment of a dictatorship in 1970. His rejection of the CSJ's declaration that his emergency decrees were unconstitutional dramatized the political weakness of the judiciary.

Clearly it cannot experience such episodes with impunity. In the long run, repetitions of such actions could well divest Ecuador's courts of the limited political influence which they now exercise.

Local and Provincial Government. While the republic is described in Article 1 as "sovereign, democratic and unitary," it is divided administratively into provinces (plus the Galápagos Islands), 103 cantons, and 846 parishes. The system blends locally elected officials with presidentially appointed authorities. The president names provincial governors, cantonal political chiefs (*jefes políticos*), and political lieutenants (*tenientes políticos*) in the parishes. Such appointees are generally supporters of the president, who is free to remove or replace them at will. Customarily there has been greater stability of tenure for governors than for cabinet ministers. In practice the governors are responsible for the choice of both political chiefs and lieutenants, although presidential intervention on the part of a friend or relative is not unknown.

For the everyday concerns of the ordinary citizen, especially in rural areas, the political lieutenant may well be the central figure. His authority includes such diverse matters as arrests and fines, issuing of marriage licenses, decisions over inheritance disputes, and the requisitioning of labor for community work projects. The last is especially relevant in the *sierra,* where small-scale public works and construction projects are often manned by local citizens. This leads to frequent abuses, particularly in largely Indian highland regions where the large landowner or his manager is in collusion with political authorities. In such areas the most powerful men will be the landowner, political lieutenant, and the local priest.

While appointed officials carry considerable weight in more isolated and rural regions, in the urban settings elected officials generally hold greater power. All of the provincial capitals have an elected mayor, who in turn presides over municipal councilmen (*concejales*). The councils range in number from five to eleven members (the maximum is found in Quito and Guayaquil). Terms run for four years, with neither mayors nor councilmen eligible for immediate reelection. The mayors of Guayaquil and Quito in particular wield both local and national power, numbering among the very most prominent political leaders of the country. In comparison with many Latin American republics, municipal authorities enjoy considerable freedom of action, including the right to levy local taxes for local purposes. Many local services are, of course, funded by the central government, but the larger cities do attempt to collect revenue for local projects. In addition to municipal officials, there are also provincial councilors (*consejeros*) and a prefect elected every four years. Their authority is spelled out less clearly than that of municipal officials, and practice varies from one province to another.

Both in theory and practice, municipal authority and local autonomy are important to Ecuadorean politics. Guayaquil and Quito officials play an important role, and this is further strengthened by the economic projects and fund-raising efforts of the many local entities – as, for example, the Guayaquil Port Authority. In the smaller regions as well, political chiefs and lieutenants play a major part in many aspects of everyday life. For the roughly 180 parishes officially designated as "rural," there is an elected five-member board which is concerned largely with local public works. Despite the appointive power of the president regarding such officials as governors, then, considerable responsibility remains in the hands of locally elected leaders. Experience varies too widely to permit ready generalization, but there are numerous municipalities and communities in which normal patterns of life and public affairs are regulated primarily by such individuals.

With occasional exceptions, the national president will not intervene directly unless there is a drastic deterioration of local leadership or a fundamental challenge to his ultimate authority. Provincial capitals have often launched major protests to demand more favorable treatment from the national government. During the first two years of the fifth *velasquista* administration, Riobamba, Ambato, Esmeraldas, and Loja all followed suit with locally led popular demonstrations to dramatize demands for action. Short of massive presidential intervention, such manifestations may well bring about policy changes from the national level. As discussed further in the final chapter, it is the independence and initiative of regional and municipal leadership which holds out promise for more progressive policies in the future. At the same time, however, the political system remains largely controlled by the political elites, and this stands as a political fact of life of primordial significance.

DYNAMICS OF POLITICAL ELITISM

Whether or not abiding by the constitutional structures of authority, political and socioeconomic groups do not necessarily conform to representational norms. Elitist in orientation and frequently divided over their own tactical and strategic objectives, they have been erratic in serving the needs and demands of their constituencies. The classic trinity of Church, armed forces, and economic interests continues to loom large in any discussion of Ecuadorean political behavior.

The Church. With the population at least nominally Roman Catholic, the influence of the Church has been traditionally strong. Its historical impact was suggested earlier, most intensively during the Conservative era of Gabriel García Moreno. The confiscation of Church lands by the Liberals under Eloy Alfaro at the century's turn by no means eradicated Church preeminence. Today it is a powerful institution, continuing to thrive as a social organism while exerting influence on political activities and attitudes. It is divided administratively into diocesan and missionary categories, with the former in the populated centers while the latter are officially designated as the *oriente*, the Galápagos, and the province of Esmeraldas. Quito, Cuenca, and Guayaquil are archdioceses, and the archbishop of Quito has been elevated to the College of Cardinals.

There are various indicators of Church vitality. For one, its priest-inhabitant ratio is higher than that of most other Latin American countries. By the mid-1960s there were some 1,200 priests, or roughly one per 4,000. Furthermore, the clergy has been growing in size as rapidly as the national population. While the Church feels itself in need of more priests, at least it is not losing ground. In addition, newly ordained priests have been predominantly Ecuadorean rather than foreign, and the seminaries continue to prepare and to train more local youths. Although a large contingent of foreign priests in the country remains (primarily from Italy, Spain, and the United States), the percentage has declined. Most are either in *oriente* outposts or along the coast, while *sierra* priests are for the most part Ecuadorean. The coastal-highland cleavage is also observable in the overwhelming numbers of *serranos* among new recruits to the clergy. The attraction of the religious calling is less strong with *costeños*.

This regional factor is evident, for Church influence has been historically greatest in the highlands. The nineteenth-century rise of the coast to challenge the traditional highland center of power exacerbated attacks upon the Church, deepening already existing cleavages. While the intensity of conflict has been dissipated more recently, basic differences endure. Conformity with religious attitudes and obligations in the highlands is greater than on the coast, where practices are less formal. In terms of distribution, nearly 70 percent of Ecuadorean priests are located in the highlands. While coastal attachment to the Church seems on the increase, the region's greater individual mobility and more varied community patterns all contribute to a political subculture in which attitudes toward the Church are less compliant and submissive.

Official church–state relations are based on a 1937 agreement with the Vatican in which the Church pledged its recognition of religious liberty in exchange for approval of its right to property ownership. These and comparable understandings have been constitutionally legitimized, and traditional issues of clericalism are less serious, although still present. Overt Church participation in public affairs may occur, although declared illegal by the 1937 pact. In 1951, for example, Cardinal de la Torre published a pastoral letter advising Catholic parents of the prohibition on enrolling their children in non-Catholic schools; the Liberal response was sharp. There have also been periodic disputes over government financial assistance to Church-operated schools, where politicians respond in keeping with their partisan affiliation.

Blatant intervention has been reduced but is not yet unknown. Especially in rural areas there has continued a tradition of clerical statements concerning presidential candidates. In 1956, for example, there was strong and open support for the rightist candidate Ponce, and four years later the archbishop of Cuenca threatened with excommunication any of his parishioners who voted for Galo Plaza, the Liberal candidate. Three years later the same cleric did excommunicate several members of his diocese who enrolled their children in an evangelical school. Certainly conservatism as a characteristic clerical attitude remains strong in the *sierra,* and there is sometimes little restraint on the part of rural priests. Liberals will rise to the attack occasionally, but the conflict is more often latent. Certainly the *sierra* clergy does indeed express political preferences during election campaigns. Such intervention in partisan politics, then, is by no means dead.

Church attitudes are also less monolithic than they once were, although the more conservative sector remains dominant. It was a harbinger of change when in May of 1963 the Ecuadorean hierarchy issued a pastoral letter from all its pulpits advocating support for land reform and an improved tax system. This encouragement of social and economic reforms advised landowners and businessmen to remember their human obligations to their less fortunate fellow beings. Further signs of social reformism within the Church occasionally appear. A few dioceses have undertaken developmental programs in addition to more orthodox works of charity. Clerical leadership has become increasingly social-minded in Imbabura, Bolívar, and especially in Chimborazo.

None of this represents a fundamental redefinition of Church attitudes, however. Historical ties with landowning interests in the highlands remain intact, and works of charity are more commonly regarded as the best means of aiding the dispossessed and the impoverished. On the coast the Church is less weak than it once was. In short, if less deeply involved in partisan politics than in the past, the Church is nonetheless a conservative force in Ecuadorean society and politics. Its social conscience has been stirred, but the responsive pattern is authoritarian and personalistic. As a component of Ecuadorean elitism, the Church reinforces existing traditions and stands resistant to popular demands for a just share in guiding the destinies of the country.

The Commercial and Entrepreneurial Sector. The socioeconomic isolation of businessmen, merchants, and large landowners from the impoverished and disenfranchised has important political manifestations. Given the rigidity of class structure and upper-class consciousness of its own social heritage, members of this elite have been influential far in excess of their numbers. Political leaders, frequently unable or unwilling to develop mass popular appeal or a broad political base, have therefore maintained and sometimes tightened their bonds with this socioeconomic elite. It is true that different subgroups exist with their own distinctive interests and attitudes. These tend to parallel the diverse economic activities which characterize coast and highlands.

Certainly the commercial, banking, and financial elite of the coast – or of Guayaquil, more properly – is the wealthiest in Ecuador. Even its oldest families, however, have difficulty in tracing back their ancestral riches or social prominence more than a few generations at the very most. This strikingly contrasts to the *quiteño* social elite, and in a sense the urban coastal elite comprises the *nouveau riche* in Ecuador. Its political ideas have been derived from Liberal ideas, and behavior suggests greater flexibility than is found among its *serrano* counterpart. Attitudes are less insular, less inwardly oriented than in the highlands. Certainly the business sector in Guayaquil is connected to international trade, commerce, and import-export activities. These provide it with interests unlike those of *serrano* landowners.

Coastal economic and business leaders are disinclined to adopt reforms or changes which might seriously intrude upon their own welfare. Yet their dependence upon the international market forces them toward a more modernizing stance, and Guayaquil's rapid population growth forces them to recognize the necessity of providing benefits for the urban poor. This coastal subsector of the commercial and business elite is further caught up in the rivalry with Quito. Such organizations as the Guayaquil Chamber of Commerce complain that the national capital drains off undue tax revenues created by the coastal economy, while unwilling to permit the repatriation of such funds through national services and programs. Concern over the national economy also abets a willingness to provide substantial financial backing to national parties and candidates. José María Velasco Ibarra has customarily received substantial financial backing from the coastal bankers and financiers, as have most of the liberal candidates with the exception of the populist *Concentración de Fuerzas Populares.*

Upper-class commercial interests in Quito contrast with those of Guayaquil. Traditional economic concerns are tied to land and property, with the large landowner the most typical member. While these individuals are generally less wealthy than members of the Guayaquil upper class, they also enjoy and esteem the prestige of family, ancestry, and alleged racial purity. As an avowedly "white" elite having descended from Spanish colonial leaders, this is the most socially privileged group in Ecuador. Such names as Flores, Larrea, and others will swiftly open doors throughout the republic. Generational accumulation of land ownership has not brought as rapid or dramatic an increase of wealth as with the Guayaquil *nouveau riche,* but it has supported aristocratic elitism on the highlands ever since the colonial period.

Often closely affiliated with the Conservative party, this aristocracy has been both swift and adept in moving to preserve its perquisites and powers. Although recognizing the existence of growing social pressures, the most common attitude advocates only minor and piecemeal reforms. Political ties with both the Church and the Conservative party have long been a feature which is brought to bear on important national issues. *Serrano* landowners away from Quito are especially reactionary. Lacking the subtlety or understanding of their more sophisticated *quiteño* counterparts, they reside in provincial capitals and are more rigid in their views. Their greatest prestige and authority is exercised in the southern highlands, especially in Loja, Azuay, and Cañar. Monopolizing regional instruments of power, they control local and provincial government while often dominating congressional representatives. With the authority of the central government somewhat diluted because of geographical remoteness, it is quite feasible for *hacendado* associations to overrule central authorities, as they did by repudiating the newly decreed agrarian reform law in 1964.

A relatively new business and entrepreneurial group has been added to the traditional landowning elite in the highlands. Quito, although not expanding with the drive of Guayaquil, has nonetheless been progressing. There is a rising group of modernizing businessmen and entrepreneurs, concerned about both social and economic problems in the country, which is increasing in importance. Thus the essentially antireformist bias of the upper-class elite is less monolithic, and there are at least long-range prospects that more enlightened and disinterested leadership will be produced.

In the meantime, however, old social customs and traditions die slowly, and the role of elitism continues to be filled by either highland or coastal upper-class leaders. Political power is often brought to bear through the chambers of commerce, agriculture, and industry. Not only do they provide the basis for election of functional senators, they also enjoy great economic influence. With the most important chambers naturally located in Quito and Guayaquil, they reflect these groups' respective economic interests and policy preferences. With origins traceable to the 1880s, these chambers have frequently collaborated with government officials, primarily through the pertinent ministry. Influence can be exerted through unofficial channels as well, including appeals to the president himself.

A recent indication of the chambers' importance came in May and June of 1970. Amid growing economic crisis, the Guayaquil Chamber of Commerce announced that President Velasco's proposed fiscal reforms would lead to 40 percent inflation within a short time. A critical exchange continued in the following weeks. Ultimately, following his seizure of dictatorial power in June, Velasco directed the arrest of "leftist agitators," including among this "dangerous" group the President of the Guayaquil Chamber of Commerce. Whatever else might be said, Velasco had no doubts as to the economic and political significance of this sector. Having long drawn electoral assistance of Guayaquil elites, he recognized the challenge in its outspoken opposition.[16]

Military and Security Forces. Although never far from the political center of power, Ecuador's military and security forces have frequently functioned in a defensive style. The tradition of the armed forces themselves has been that of defending the constitutional order.[17] Despite frequent interventions in political affairs, the military has preferred to remain in the back-

[16]For a broad overview which reflects agreement with much of the preceding section, see Eduardo Félix C., *Sociológia* (Quito: Editorial "La Union," 1971).

[17]A collection of essays and commentaries written over a forty-year period by an army officer which sheds light on traditional military attitudes and values is Rafael Astudillo, *Entre el pasado y el porvenir* (Quito: n.p., 1968).

ground unless public disorder or political turmoil become too extreme. In broad perspective the military involvement in politics gradually decreased in the first half of the twentieth century. Within the past twenty years, however, it has been rising, and seems likely to continue for the immediate future.

By the start of the twentieth century military ties with the Conservatives began to decline, and closer links were established with the Liberals. Thus a recent compilation of Ecuadorean presidents shows that nearly one-third of all presidents have been military and that, of these, the greater number appeared during the Liberal period from 1895 to 1944.[18] In most cases the period of military rule was brief and transitory, with the exception of such party activists as General Leónidas Plaza Lasso. Military presidents in this century have been concerned primarily with a defense of internal order, the preservation of national honor, and, of course, protection of the military's own corporate interests. Having generally assumed responsibility for protection of individual liberties and democratic institutions, the armed forces have only infrequently chosen to remain in power more than a short period of time. Here too, however, the pattern has been shifting more recently.

Throughout the independence period the military has mirrored the strong national preoccupation with the threat from Peru. Annual celebrations still commemorate the 1829 victory of Marshal Antonio José de Sucre and General Flores over Peruvian forces at the Battle of Tarqui. Despite long periods of quiescence along the Peruvian frontier, the potential threat from Ecuador's larger and more powerful neighbor has never been completely forgotten. The border war of 1941 remains etched indelibly on Ecuadorean memories. After a series of skirmishes along the border, Peruvian troops mobilized and invaded Ecuador in July of the year. Underequipped and outmanned Ecuadorean troops battled bravely in El Oro province but were unable to impede the Peruvian advance. The result, later legitimized hemispherically through the Rio de Janeiro Protocol, cost Ecuador approximately 278,000 square kilo-

[18]See Georg Maier, *The Ecuadorian Presidential Election of June 2, 1968* (Washington, D.C.: Institute for the Comparative Study of Political Systems, 1969), pp. 32-33.

meters of national territory. These events are still remembered unhappily, and even at Arroyo's death in 1969 there were unhappy recollections of his part in the humiliation.

For some years after 1941 the political role of the military was episodic, but since 1960 it has emerged as a major arbiter of political disputes. In that year the armed forces were initially supportive of President Velasco in the wake of his impressive electoral victory, but their attitudes soon changed. By April of 1961 Velasco found it necessary to arrest several officers on charges of conspiracy, while others were ordered into retirement. When popular protests against Velasco reached their climax in November of 1961, it was the military which tipped the scales and made possible Carlos Julio Arosemena Monroy's replacement of Velasco in the presidency. In April of 1962 military pressure forced Arosemena to break diplomatic relations with Cuba. By 1963 ranking officers were actively conspiring against their president. Decisive action was triggered in July of 1963 when Arosemena alcoholically insulted United States representatives during an official banquet.[19]

Members of the provisional military government included the functional senator for the armed forces, Col. Marcos Gándara Enríquez, as well as the three service chiefs, all of them Arosemena supporters and appointees. This second major political intervention in less than three years was marked by new self-perceptions on the part of the military leadership. After citing the threat of communist subversion in justification of the *golpe de estado,* the military assumed power within a context of widespread popular rejoicing over the fall of Arosemena. Its two initial manifestoes[20] pledged the junta to a return of constitutionality as soon as possible, but further noted "our firm intention to guarantee capital and labor in an atmosphere of reason and patriotism which answers to the exigencies . . . through which our Country is passing, in order to promote the advent of a better social structure, through a planned and comprehensive evolution, with benefits for all and for the supreme and sacred

[19]As noted earlier, an analysis which also examines several of the hypotheses now current regarding civil-military relations in Latin America is found in Martin C. Needler, *Anatomy of a Coup d'Etat: Ecuador 1963* (Washington, D.C.: Institute for the Comparative Study of Political Systems, 1964).

[20]A ready source of the texts is ibid., pp. 49-52.

interests of the Nation."[21] As Needler observed, there was an evident military belief that political leadership required the fulfillment of technical duties rather than the management of political complexities.

The junta remained in power until its voluntary withdrawal amid spreading opposition and domestic turmoil on March 29, 1966. Its record during some thirty-three months is revealing for an understanding of today's Ecuadorean military. In the political realm there had been reprisals and arrests against leftists, along with wholesale changes in government personnel. At the same time, new cabinet ministers and appointees at a subministerial level were drawn from the usual corps of figures who had occupied such posts in earlier years. Municipal changes were also decreed, especially in the case of Guayaquil, where the military removed Mayor Asaad Bucaram, a sturdy critic of the intervention. Considerable attention was also devoted to socioeconomic reforms, but performance was far outstripped by rhetorical manifestoes. Alleged "major" transformations were undertaken in the fields of agrarian reform, a new tax structure, the decreeing of a career civil service system, and a new penal code.

Although creating in the *Instituto Ecuatoriano de Reforma Agraria y Colonización* (IERAC) the first such agency in Ecuador, the military found itself unable or unwilling to commit the necessary political capital for effective implementation. Determined opposition by large landowners and the absence of strong civilian reformist elements soon gutted projected reforms. Tax revision attempted to tighten existing legislation, but made no basic alteration in the highly complex and generally discriminatory system already in existence. As for a career public administration, the junta's efforts were destined, like its predecessors', to ultimate failure. The penal code, which had actually been redrafted prior to the seizure of power, brought only a modicum of equity to a tortuously intricate system which was often ignored or rendered inoperable by private interests. In short, presumably well-intentioned military reforms were poorly conceived in detail and ineffectively administered in execution. With the collapse of the junta in March of 1966, little remained

[21] Ibid., p. 49.

as a memorial to its passing.

The moderate degree of popular support which the military establishment had previously enjoyed was sapped by the disappointment of early expectations and by the increasingly repressive actions adopted as a means of retaining political control. The suspension of university autonomy and denial of labor's right to strike added to the provocations of both military and police forces in combatting student and worker demonstrations. As a consequence, public opinion toward the military was at a low ebb by 1966. Indeed, Otto Arosemena Gómez was to note that when he became provisional president seven months later, one of his higher priorities was the restoration of public confidence in the military.[22] During the convening of the constituent assembly in 1966-67, moreover, Carlos Julio Arosemena Monroy used the legislative floor to launch his own embittered attacks, demanding public trials of junta members and of their major collaborators. Public sentiment died down after a time, but was not improved by rumors of fiscal scandal involving former air force officer Guillermo Freile Posso, an original member of the junta who had been retired by his colleagues after indications of ambitions for greater personal power.

In the immediate aftermath of the ill-fated experience of 1963-66, the armed forces withdrew from political activity. Under the fifth *velasquista* administration it gradually increased influence within the regime, abetted not only by favorable treatment from Velasco but also by close ties with his nephew, Minister of Defense Jaime Acosta Velasco. In the wake of the President's *autogolpe* in 1970 it appeared that his nephew and younger military officers had gained the ascendency. A reshuffling of the military hierarchy led to the retirement of several senior officers. However, the following year more traditionally oriented officers forced the resignation of the minister of defense, apparently reasserting the primacy of more establishmentarian elements.

Notwithstanding these transitory shifts of the balance of power among military officers, the traditional attitude remains that of its concern with constitutionality and domestic order.

[22]Interview with Dr. Otto Arosemena Gómez, July 1969.

Generally, the defense of internal stability is the responsibility of the national police, functioning under the jurisdiction of the minister of government. Despite efforts to modernize, the police are not well equipped to deal with massive street protests, student demonstrations, and the like; military troops have had to be called in to quell civil disturbances on several occasions. The necessity for such direct involvement of the military has heightened the preoccupation of the armed forces over questions of internal order.

The handling of common crime, in contrast to civil and political disturbances, is a matter which differs between rural and urban settings. For the former, rural police are customarily involved in handling civil crime. However, periodic mass uprisings create a more difficult situation. Characteristic of such political upheavals was the rioting of some 2,000 Indians in February of 1961 on a large *hacienda* in Chimborazo. And in August of 1964 a smaller band of Indians seized a landed estate in Cayambe, requiring the dispatch of police from nearby Quito. In urban centers the police are notoriously understaffed. Especially in Guayaquil, where the crime rate is high, it was estimated in 1965 that at least 3,000 police were required, yet only 700 were available. Given rising socioeconomic pressures in the cities, the activities of individual trade unions in Quito and Guayaquil, and especially the growing commitment to violent measures if necessary by student leaders, the magnitude of the problem has multiplied. With the continuing intransigence of many elitist elements, the likelihood of continuing manifestations of organized violence has grown apace. And when political protests are involved, the most common pattern will be military as well as police participation to curb the demonstrations.

Organized Labor. Ecuadorean labor is in a primitive stage of development, yet stands – however inadequately – as one of the major forces to protest the continuation of elitist domination. With Ecuadorean economic life historically based on primitive agricultural activities and the *latifundio,* it is understandable that effective trade unionism has been slow to emerge. Today's labor force is disunited and poorly organized; its evolution has been slow and tortuous. Early in the 1900s the Guayas Labor Confederation (*Confederación Obrera del Guayas*) was founded; before long a small group of workers in Quito formed the Artistic and Industrial Society of Pichincha (*Sociedad Artística e Industrial de Pichincha*). One of the earliest strikes was organized by railroad workers in 1908, and cacao workers soon followed when that market collapsed. There was further agitation during World War I, but not until 1922 did trade unionism begin to take shape.

The *Confederación de Sindicatos Obreros* (CSO), although essentially Quito-based, began to hold annual congresses, and contributed to the adoption of Ecuador's first true labor law in 1928. Young Socialist intellectuals were developing their own interest in the labor movement, and by the early 1930s the Marxist impact became more evident. Progress was slow; a series of reorganizations, "national" congresses, and regional conventions failed to secure meaningful benefits for the workers. In addition to Socialist and Communist efforts, the Catholic Church also entered the field in 1938 by convening the Congress of Catholic Workers in Quito, from which came the *Confederación Ecuatoriana de Obreros Catolicos* (CEDOS). By 1942 the Ecuadorean government reported 251 registered unions in the country, with a total of 22,778 members. Greater impetus came in 1944 when Velasco Ibarra, after riding to power on a wave of popular enthusiasm, pledged wholehearted approval to labor organizations. On July 4, 1944, slightly over 1,000 delegates formed a new national labor organization, the *Confederación Nacional de Trabajadores del Ecuador* (CTE). Its most influential leaders were socialists and communists, most notably Guayaquil communist Pedro Saad.

Elected first CTE secretary-general, Saad led it into affiliation with the *Confederación de Trabajadores de América Latina* (CTAL), the international communist labor organization. Although Saad and the communists were later ousted from the leadership, the general Marxist orientation persisted. By the 1960s the communists had recaptured internal control, although it was by no means monolithic. More recently the leadership has included both socialists and communists, with radical *fidelistas* occasionally present. Membership today is estimated at some 75,000, and the CTE remains the most important "national" confederation. Yet its internal rivalries, personal disagreements, and ideological conflicts have weakened its efforts to better the lot of the worker. Rival organizations have competed energetically, and their struggle has sapped the vitality and effectiveness of the national movement.

The Catholic CEDOC, six years senior to the CTE, has been relatively impotent until very recently, when it has been reinvigorated, in no small part as a result of the personal dynamism of Isabel Robalino Bolle, one of Ecuador's most active feminists. Serving officially as CEDOC legal adviser, she has helped to infuse it with a more progressive social consciousness. The growth of Christian Democracy in Latin America and its labor affiliates has also aided CEDOC. The hemispheric *Confederación Latinoamericana de Sindicalistas Cristianos* (CLASC) has thereby provided training through study programs, conferences, printed materials, and instruction at the CLASC school for labor studies in Santiago, Chile. CEDOC's leadership today is less characterized by social conservatism than it once was. However, it does not presently constitute an immediate challenge to the CTE; membership stands at roughly 25,000.

In addition to the CTE and CEDOC, a third self-professed national confederation is the *Confederación Ecuatoriana de Organizaciones Sindicales Libres* (CEOSL). Founded in early 1962 and claiming to represent an alternative to the communist- and Catholic-dominated confederations, it has enjoyed support and assistance from the North American AFL-CIO. The CEOSL has also affiliated with the pro-United States *Organización Regional Interamericana de Trabajadores* (ORIT). Many unaffiliated trade unions are complaining about the presence of alien influences in national organizations, citing the communists with the CTE, North Americans with CEOSL, and international Christian Democracy (especially West German support) with CEDOC. As for the CEOSL, its membership approaches 20,000, with recruitment efforts centered upon essentially white-collar associations.

The national confederations have expended considerable energy in competing for affiliates, and have generally given less attention to the winning of worker demands from management. Despite a small handful of capable labor organizers, the quality of leadership is spotty, further handicapping the growth of labor as an organized political force. For the urban workers, the most fortunate belong to local *sindicatos* or occupations groupings, some of which have been more successful in winning improved conditions from management. Probably the two most effective in providing for the welfare of their membership have been the *Federación Nacional de Chóferes del Ecuador* (FNCE – the cab drivers) and the *Federación Nacional Textil* (FNT – textile workers).

The former, including independent drivers, chauffeurs, and owner-operators, has issued and won important demands from management on several occasions. The textile workers' federation, one of the older labor groups in the country, has also succeeded in securing significant gains for its membership. Both the FNCE and the FNT have been affiliated with the CTE, but generally operate with considerable independence. Another strong occupational federation is the *Federación Ecuatoriana de Trabajadores de Embarques de Frutas y Anexos* (FETEF), first organized by Guayaquil fruitloaders in 1964. Serving as a kind of contracting agency, the FETEF itself, rather than the individual companies, pays members' salaries. It controls the bulk of its market, thereby ensuring favorable wages for its members, who number over 10,000. It has also provided considerable material support for CEDOC, with which it is affiliated.

As an interest group Ecuadorean labor has generally been ineffectual. The particularistic competition among the three self-proclaimed national confederations has mitigated against the growth of modern trade unionism. The successes of a few occupational groupings stand out as exceptions to the broader pattern. Moreover, both labor leaders and management have little mutual trust or confidence in bargaining and negotiation. For the employers, a traditionalistic paternalism is characteristic, and the behavior of labor leaders themselves has done little to dispel such an attitude. Seldom has labor been sufficiently united to apply meaningful pressure on the political leadership, which also projects a posture and attitude of condescension. Despite disruptive protests and strikes, labor has been largely unable to impose its policy preferences upon dominant economic or political forces. Weaker than either government or management, organized labor has therefore been somewhat marginal as a modernizing or unifying force.

Student Activism. The most eloquent, dramatic, and militant pressure group in Ecuador consists of its students. Idealistic, dedicated, and sometimes politically naive, the students have played a role which has been alternately functional and dysfunctional to the political system. The two major student organizations are the *Federación de Estudiantes Universitarios del Ecuador* (FEUE) at the university level and the *Federación de Estudiantes Secundarios del Ecuador* (FESE) for high school students. Membership in the FEUE is mandatory, although not in FESE; voting in student elections is also technically compulsory, although the requirement is not always observed. In university elections the rate of abstention often runs as high as one-third. Leadership is commonly, although not invariably, leftist; dominant student leaders are unwaveringly nationalistic, whatever their political orientation otherwise. Particularly since the rise of Fidel Castro in Cuba, there has been a strong leftist orientation. However, it must again be stressed that the exceptions have been readily identifiable among the student leadership.[23]

A 1962 UNESCO-sponsored study gives some measure of student political attitudes and participation.[24] A series of interviews with university students in Quito revealed that 89.7 percent did not belong to any political party; none of these organizations had a membership greater than 1.5 percent of the students interviewed. Asked to indicate their general assessment of political parties, 92.35 percent responded that political parties did not serve a positive function for Ecuador. Party leaders were judged in equally damning terms; 41.63 percent saw them as serving special interests, and another 40.77 percent believed that they were interested only in serving personal political ambitions. As a final measure of political attitudes, 70.15 percent did not participate actively in partisan politics.

This negative perception of political parties implied doubts as to their organizational efficacy, rather than a complacency with existing conditions. When asked to evaluate material living conditions, 50.54 percent termed them "bad," and only 4.9 percent saw them in a favorable light. Responding to an inquiry concerning national progress in the preceding decade, 47.56

[23]The Ecuadorean university structure is elaborated in Jacques M.P. Wilson, *The Development of Education in Ecuador* (Coral Gables, Florida: University of Miami Press, 1970), pp. 65-95.

[24]Gonzalo Rubio Orbe, *El pensamiento de la juventud universitaria de Quito* (Quito: Editorial Universitaria, 1966).

percent saw it as "normal" while 22.32 percent felt it was "deficient." Furthermore, 57.92 percent regarded political-administrative aspects as deficient. With such a set of attitudes existing even prior to the turmoil of the past decade, it is less than startling that the students represent a highly vocal group in criticizing existing conditions. This phenomenon has deep roots in the past as well.

Thus, the students have been involved in all but one nonconstitutional change of government since 1944. They participated in nationwide protests against Velasco in 1961, against the military regime of 1963-66, against Otto Arosemena's provisional government, and against Velasco once again since 1968. Certain of their grievances have been political, while others have related to questions of university policy and projected academic reforms. The conflict has been especially grave since 1969 in Guayaquil, where the issue of examination-free entrance into that university has divided administration and faculty as well as students. Protests were broken up only when paratroopers were dispatched to the campus, an action which terminated after the death of several students and injuries to scores more.

In the months following the initial outburst, the schism between students and administrators became complete. In early 1970 the president of the FEUE disappeared from Quito, and his body was later found; the killing was attributed by students to government authorities, and tensions heightened. By the close of 1970 there was a total breakdown of communications between the students and government, highlighted by the nocturnal destruction by explosion of the university printing press in Quito where the university paper *Orientación* was printed. After students had marched in protest to the presidential palace accompanied by their rector, Manuel Agustín Aguirre – a noted socialist educator and intellectual – the rupture contributed to Velasco's prompt suspension of the constitution and his closing of all universities and many secondary schools. Not until 1971 was there a partial reopening of university doors, and it was accompanied by a new and restrictive government-drafted decree on university education.

The politicization of pre-university students in Ecuador is striking, although most of the leadership comes from the universities. The most pronounced student radicalization exists in

Guayaquil. There many students have come from other coastal communities to study, are relatively unattached and rootless, and are more rapidly mobilized to action. In the highlands, the proportion of apathetic or uninvolved students seems somewhat greater, although student bodies to the far south at the Universities of Loja and Cuenca have long presented a nearly unbroken phalanx of opposition to national authority. At all five of the national universities, however, the tradition of major student involvement in administrative, curricular, and political affairs has further heightened the commitment of the student body. Even at the smaller Catholic University of Quito, where faculty control is strong, student activism is potent.

More than any other organized group in national politics, the students are disturbed by evident social and economic inequities. In concert with overtaxed facilities buckling under enrollment and budgetary pressures, this concern assures the continuing politicization of Ecuadorean students. Given the absence of a single political leader or party with which the students feel genuine affinity, their mobilization is likely to exert ever-expanding pressures upon the country's elitist forces. Yet the latter remain dominant, constituting a force to be reckoned with by those seeking progress and modernization in the country.

4
Political Parties and Popular Participation

Although Ecuador's many political parties generate intense and heated partisanship, more often than not they are obstructionist in nature. Characteristic opportunism leads to frequent shifts of existing alliances and coalitions, while the sheer number of parties makes such agreements necessary for the preservation of constitutional rule. Parties have grown accustomed to accommodations of convenience and to the intricacies of movement and maneuver, which are sometimes of byzantine complexity. Most parties are characterized by a strong element of personalism, with leadership exercised by a small handful of men. In most cases there is little semblance of organization at the grass roots, and lower level participation is minimal. Efforts to create mass parties are unusual. Only during elections is there concerted campaigning on a national basis. Between elections the organizations concentrate on relations with their counterparts at senior levels, and internal elitism negates effective participation by the rank and file.

If party organization is weak and ineffectively articulated, this is not to say that programmatic positions are avoided. However, attention is concentrated on the elaboration of broad philosophical statements couched in glittering generalities. In the swirling eddies of daily political bargaining, short-term gains will be prized over long-term ideological consistency. Personalistic domination of many parties permits major shifts and alterations in programs within a relatively short time span, and the adage about strange bedfellows in politics is amply demonstrated.

Notwithstanding all of this, the role of parties is by no means negligible; rather, it must be remembered that these organizations are elitist in leadership, receptive to alliance or coalition, and eager to capitalize on the slightest political opportunity. It is ironic that the representational element is minimal, given the constitutional ban on the illiterate vote and the concomitant restriction of the electorate. As Table 11 shows, in elections since 1948 the percentage of the population casting a vote has never reached 20 percent, and on occasion has dropped beneath 10 percent. With mass electoral participation so limited, there is consequently less direct pressure on the parties to make good their promises on socioeconomic progress and reform. So long as illiterates are denied the vote, party leaders will find it easy to maintain a basic commitment to the status quo rather than to work for the adoption of progressive reforms.

THE PROLIFERATION OF PARTIES

Typologies of political parties are not fully applicable in Ecuador. Organizational structures are impressive on paper but unimportant in practice; and while doctrinal statements may be precise, many parties shift position with such frequency as to discourage efforts at classification along the customary left–right spectrum. For the sake of simple presentation, we will first examine the long-established traditional parties and then turn to the most avowedly personalistic ones. Of the former, four will be included: the Radical Liberals (*Partido Liberal Radical* – PLR), the Conservatives (*Partido Conservador Ecuatoriano* – PCE), the Marxist parties (including communists, socialists, and splinter offshoots of both), and the Ecuadorean Nationalist Revolutionary Action (*Acción Revolucionaria Nacionalista Ecuatoriana* – ARNE). The first two represent the nineteenth-century political heritage, while the latter are creatures of the twentieth.

Traditional Parties. The long historical conflict between Conservatives and Liberals has been traced in chapter 2. The former, organized by Gabriel García Moreno in 1869, has long represented Roman Catholicism, church–state collaboration, and the traditional outlook of the highland aristocracy. Established as the champion of *serrano* landholders, it has maintained this posture through the years. Its political domination interrupted by Eloy Alfaro and the Liberals in 1895, the Conservative party was relegated to a secondary position through much of the present century. Its influence has sometimes flourished during periods of *velasquismo,* but Dr. Velasco's mercurial shifts have not permitted sustained growth. In 1956 Ecuadorean conservatism finally regained power through the disputed election of Camilo Ponce Enriquez, leader of his own personalistic and rightist mini-party.

Since that time the Conservatives, although denied the presidency, have wielded considerable influence. Their 1960 candidate, Gonzalo Cordero Crespo, was inundated by the triumphant *velasquista* electoral flood, but so was the Liberal candidate. The Conservatives later played a major part in the selection of Otto Arosemena Gómez as provisional president, and in 1968 their support of a second Ponce candidacy carried him to within 21,000 votes of the presidency. Broadening their electoral support that year, the Conservatives led the presidential balloting in seven of the ten *serrano* provinces, all four of the sparsely populated provinces of the *oriente,* and surprisingly polled some 22 percent of the vote on the coast. This latter was a marked improvement over the scant 9 percent polled by both Ponce in 1956 and Cordero Crespo in 1960.

Under the fifth *velasquista* administration the Conservatives continued to build their strength in anticipation of 1972 elections. Their congressional representation was better disciplined than most others. Moreover, a conscious effort to encourage younger leadership brought an increasing competence and vigor to the party. There was a growing conviction that Ecuadorean conservatism need not rely on the personality and acumen of non-party member Ponce in order to attract support. More than two years before scheduled June 1972 elections the Conservatives named Carlos Arízaga Vega from Cuenca as its standard-bearer. It was hoped that his early nomination might discourage the ambitions of ex-presidents Ponce and Arosemena Gómez, both of whom hoped to run with the support of the

Ecuadorean right.

Conservative party doctrine has also been modernized in an effort to broaden electoral appeals, especially among university youth. Jorge Salvador Lara, one of its more prominent figures, reflected this process in a speech to the party's general assembly in January of 1968. Calling upon his audience to "conserve" their heritage, he demanded at the same time that party members be "proponents of necessary change, of . . . a genuine policy of incessant improvement, progress and social advances." Urging the importance of modernization he further declared:

> If in Ecuador we democratic forces do not confront the urgent tasks of economic and social development to solve the hunger and the anguish of the great impoverished masses, it could well be that in a short time there might be produced a brutal and bloody outburst seeking the realization of that indispensable transformation under a Marxist banner.[1]

The Liberals – officially the Radical Liberal Party – were founded in 1878 by Gen. Ignacio de Veintimilla and consolidated their position with the *alfarista*-led "Glorious Revolution" in 1895. Representative of commercial and financial interests on the coast, the Liberals established a hegemony which was essentially uninterrupted until the ouster of Arroyo del Río in 1944. Since that time they have been frequently divided, and have won neither the presidency nor a congressional majority. There were party divisions during the elections of 1948, 1952, and 1956; only in the first of these were independent Liberals able to share in the victory of a candidate. Moreover, party disunity in the 1956 elections cost the Liberals what would otherwise have been a clear and indisputable victory for their candidate, Raúl Clemente Huerta.

In 1960 the PLR regrouped its forces and, in coalition with the *Partido Socialista Ecuatoriana,* backed Galo Plaza's bid for a second term, only to fall before Dr. Velasco. Faced again

[1] Jorge Salvador Lara, *Trayectoria y metas del Partido Conservador Ecuatoriano* (Quito: Editorial "Vida Católica," 1968), p. 15. For a description of Conservative organizational structure, see Partido Conservador Ecuatoriano, *Estatutos del Partido Conservador Ecuatoriano* (Quito: Editorial "La Unión," 1964). An updated mimeographed copy bearing the same title and dated January 16, 1970, was provided the author by party Secretary General Pío Oswaldo Cueva Puertas, in which somewhat greater attention is devoted to party structures and activities at the local level.

in 1968 with a Velasco candidacy, the two likeliest Liberal candidates declined, leaving the nomination for the party's senior statesman, seventy-six-year-old Andrés F. Córdova. Despite initial unenthusiasm within the party and a shortage of campaign funds, Córdova mounted an effective campaign which nearly carried him to victory. His margin on the coast was eaten into by the *velasquista* appeal, and he fell 16,000 votes short of victory. Minor consolation came from the election to the vice-presidency of Jorge Zavala Baquerizo, a ticket-balancing *costeño* from the left wing and a younger generation of the PLR, who led his nearest competitor by 15,000 votes.

Since 1968 the Liberals have again divided over political tactics. In the wake of elections the party directorate, under the leadership of the youthful nephew of Raúl Clemente Huerta, committed the party to collaboration with the Velasco administration "at the legislative level." In return for expected Liberal support in congress, the government offered appointments to several party members and backed Huerta himself for the presidency of the lower chamber. This drove a deep wedge into the party, with Córdova and his followers denouncing the decision as unbridled opportunism and a contradiction of party principles.[2] Córdova recalled that Velasco had been bitterly and adamantly critical of the PLR ever since his first rise to power in 1934. Endless debate and discussion centered about the precise meaning of congressional collaboration, resulting eventually in the formation of the Izquierda Democrática (Democratic Left) by opponents of the pact. In 1970 municipal elections this faction outpolled orthodox Liberals, further weakening prospects of success in 1972.

Owing largely to these recurrent schisms, the Liberals have altered their doctrinal posture little in recent years. Historic nineteenth-century positions concerning church–state separation, secular education, and a federal structure of government have become antiquated with the passing of generations. Despite calls for national progress and a rhetorical commitment to national development, specific proposals have in most cases been either imprecise or sources of internal party contention.

[2] For the statement of a rising young leader who shared Córdova's dismay at the 1968 pact and later joined in the founding of the Izquierda Democrática, see Rodrigo Borja, *Historia de una claudicación* (Quito: n.p., 1970).

An August 1965 declaration in conjunction with Chile's Radical party demanded a liquidation of remaining vestiges of feudalism and pledged a struggle as representatives of the working class in opposition to foreign interference.

The most recent declaration of party principles was approved at a National Assembly on December 14, 1969 (prior to the formation of the *Izquierda Democrática*). Claiming for itself a "leftist" orientation, the PLR proclaimed its belief that "the essence of political activity is realization of an authentic democracy, which is not possible unless all Ecuadoreans are truly equal and free." Advocating both urban and rural reform, promising revision of the tax system, and attacking the existence of privilege in society, the PLR declaration included language similar to that of other parties seeking identification with democratic reformism and modernization. Thus the party insisted:

> For an authentic democracy to exist rather than the fiction of the present democracy, it is necessary to achieve integral transformation of the existing socio-economic structure, democratizing private property so that it will only deserve protection when it neither impedes nor obstructs the development of the national economy and the egalitarian distribution of income.[3]

There is no denying the importance of the Liberals' historical role in the introduction of a wide range of past reforms and changes, but the PLR, notwithstanding its 1969 statement, has found it difficult to translate its ideals into terms meaningful for contemporary Ecuador.[4] It is in part the effort to revitalize the party which has motivated younger Liberals in the present conflict. Yet this newest division merely underlines the difficulties and frustrations of the past quarter-century. If the upstart *Izquierda Democrática* has demonstrated electoral appeal in the highlands, on the coast it has been orthodox Liberals under the leadership of Francisco Huerta Montalvo which has mobilized the voters. Thus its dilemmas seem no nearer to resolution than they were a decade ago.

[3] The text appeared in *El Comercio* (Quito), December 15, 1969.

[4] Although more recently superceded by such statements as that of December 1969, a representative statement of the major PLR precepts appears in J. Gonzalo Orellana, *Resumen histórico del Ecuador; apuntaciones cronológicas complementarias 1947-1957,* Vol. 3 (Quito: Editorial "Fray Jodoco Ricke," 1957), pp. 92-99.

Ecuador's Socialist party (*Partido Socialista Ecuatoriano* – PSE) dates back to 1926, when it was organized by a group headed by Dr. Ricardo Paredes, a communist.[5] Almost from the outset there were internal divisions, related in part to the question of affiliation and commitment to the Soviet Union and to international communism. The "Friends of Lenin" group headed by Paredes changed the name in 1931 to the *Partido Comunista* (PC), at which juncture the socialists left, creating in effect a new PSE in 1933. For a number of years the socialists and communists maintained cordial relations, although the former enjoyed greater public reputation. With the participation of such noted intellectuals as Manuel Agustín Aguirre and Juan Isaac Lovato, the PSE held cabinet ministries on several occasions, and in 1938 they narrowly missed the presidency at a time when they held one-third of the seats in a constituent assembly.

In 1951 the PSE agreed to collaborate with the Plaza administration, but at the 20th Party Congress in 1954 this provided the basis for expulsion of several prominent leaders.[6] Factionalism has become more pronounced in succeeding years, with the rise of Fidel Castro in Cuba further complicating matters. That revolution had wide repercussions, especially among Ecuador's Marxist intellectuals. Such figures as Jorge Icaza, Alfredo Vera, and Benjamin Carrión defended it, and the last wrote of the Revolution having "won over" Ecuadorean intellectuals.[7] Growing dissidence within the PSE led to a breakaway of its radical wing in 1962 to form the *Partido Socialista Revolucionario Ecuatoriano* (PSRE) under the leadership of Telmo Hidalgo. Strongly sympathetic to revolutionary Cuba, it is willing to accept the use of violence if necessary to achieve a truly socialist regime. Still another Marxist party came into existence in 1966 when the eminent *cuencano* educator Carlos Cueva Tamariz founded the *Partido Socialista Unificado* (PSU)

[5] Carlos Vela, *Las tácticas del comunismo* (Quito: Editorial Don Bosco, 1961), p. 25.

[6] For a detailed discussion by the man who resigned his leadership of the PSE over the dispute in July of 1952, see Luis Maldonado Estrada, *Una etapa histórica en la vida nacional* (Quito: Editorial "Rumiñahui," 1954).

[7] Benjamin Carrión, "Teoría y Plan de la II Independencia," *Cuadernos Americanos,* Vol. 20, No. 1 (enero/febrero 1961), p. 64.

in a vain and paradoxical hope of reuniting the socialists.

In the meantime the communists have been competing with the three separate socialist parties for domination of the Marxist left. Long headed by labor organizer Pedro Saad – himself a moderate within the party – the communists themselves have been divided over tactics. While the PCE is essentially pro-Moscow in orientation, its youth wing, the *Unión Revolucionaria de Juventud Ecuatoriana* (URJE) adopted a pro-Peking posture. Today those Marxists most consistently identified as pro-Peking are members or sympathizers of the PSRE, which is the most radical of the Marxist parties. The other groups are more moderate; the PCE has for all practical purposes accepted existing rules of the game as they emerged from the interplay of the traditional parties. The PSE is even more moderate, having accepted these rules years ago.

Since 1948 Marxist electoral strength has declined. In 1956 the PSE joined the Liberals and independents in support of Huerta, and four years later they joined in another losing electoral alliance by supporting Galo Plaza. In 1968 they joined in yet another so-called "democratic front" to back Andrés F. Córdova. The Revolutionary Socialists and the communists had supported a minor leftist candidate in 1960 and once again in 1968, but received only 6 percent of the vote in 1960 and 2 percent eight years later. Congressional representation has also been slim, although the presence of such men as Cueva Tamariz and Lovato has brought considerable talent to bear on legislative sessions. Despite the reputations of such individual figures, it is true that "in general Marxism, in all its hues, lacks electoral force but has political significance through the influence that it exercises in certain intellectual, student and labor elites. . ."[8]

The *Partido Socialista Ecuatoriano,* in some ways the major Marxist party today, has predictably stressed in its doctrine the class struggle of the oppressed against the national oligarchy. Among its "maximum aspirations" are the socialization of means of production, the obligatory right to work, a restructuring of the administrative services of the state, spiritual

[8] Oswaldo Hurtado (ed.), *Dos mundos superpuestos; ensayo de diagnostico de la realidad ecuatoriana* (Quito: Instituto Ecuatoriano de Planificación para el Desarrollo Social, 1969), p. 226.

emancipation of the masses, and liberation from the tutelage of imperialism.[9] The socialists have also long advocated the emancipation of the Indian. In keeping with Ecuadorean party tradition, however, the socialists, as well as the other Marxist organizations, have not been successful in forging a doctrinal message with broad electoral appeal. At this writing, in consequence, the Marxist left lacks significant popular support.

The *Acción Revolucionaria Nacionalista Ecuatoriana* (ARNE), although termed an ad hoc party by Blanksten in 1951,[10] now has three decades' tradition in national politics. ARNE was founded in the wake of the disastrous Peruvian war, proclaiming itself in February 1942 as CONDOR – *Compañías Orgánicas Nacionales de Ofensiva Revolucionaria.* Founded at this moment of high national tragedy and disillusionment, CONDOR soon changed its name to ARNE and expanded beyond its initial existence as an underground movement. Coming under the powerful influence of one-time Conservative Jorge Juna Yepes, ARNE developed a quasi-falangist philosophy which placed it ideologically at the extreme right of the political spectrum. Although far from a personalist party, ARNE has been molded by the leadership of Luna Yepes and, since 1959, also by Jorge Crespo Toral.

Concentrating on the formation of a party elite while devolving a secretive cellular organization, by the early 1950s ARNE had achieved influence well beyond its numbers. After supporting the successful Velasco candidacy in 1952, *arnistas* enjoyed a period of prestige and growth. Eventually *arnista* leaders broke with the president, however, and before 1956 elections the party was also riven by internal controversy. There followed a long political drought from which ARNE is only slowly emerging. Jorge Crespo Toral, its presidential candidate in 1968, is an incisive and vigorous politician. Yet he won but 4 percent of the vote, while *arnista* congressional candidates were also unsuccessful. Since the inauguration of the fifth *velasquista* government ARNE has dedicated its organizational efforts toward youth, and is attempting to build strength in rural areas.

[9] For a sampling of party principles and statutes see Orellana, *Resumen histórico,* pp. 106-16.

[10] George I. Blanksten, *Ecuador: Constitutions and Caudillos* (Berkeley: University of California Press, 1951), p. 70.

Its vocal leadership praises the military, defends preservation of order and discipline, and reiterates *arnista* ideology.

There is an aggressive nationalism to its thought, while the legacy of *Hispanidad* (see chapter 2) strongly colors its doctrine. Especially as expressed in the writings of Luna Yepes, there is strong identification with *Hispanidad* as an affirmation and vindication of the Spanish cultural heritage. There is a residual sympathy with Spain's Franco regime, although less widely advertised in recent years. Demanding structural changes in the organization of the Ecuadorean state, ARNE rejects notions of class struggle, repudiates capitalism and Marxism, enshrines the family as the basic social unity, and guarantees private property.[11] Responding to strong patriotic sentiments, ARNE applies such phrases as "historic destiny," "national discipline," and "authoritarian democracy." The *arnista* ideal of the Ecuadorean state is to have a "national, organic, democratic and authoritarian structure, more diverse than those which have been forged by defeated efforts of more than a century of pseudo-democratic life." Personal rectitude, the integrity of the guiding elite, and a national moral regeneration remain fundamental in party doctrine.

Personalistic Parties. There are a host of ad hoc groups which personify their individual leaders. Ranging widely across the political sphere, they exist primarily to forward the fortunes of their respective *caudillos.* Starting on the political right is the *Movimiento Social Cristiano* (MSC). One of the smallest of all personalistic organizations, the MSC is the private preserve of Camilo Ponce Enríquez, long the leading rightist politician in the country. Scion of a Conservative family, as a youth Ponce chose for private reasons to make his way individually. First coming to prominence under Velasco's second government, he founded the *Movimiento Social Cristiano* in 1951. Returning as a cabinet minister under Velasco in 1952, Ponce provided the political astuteness which aided the president in surviving that

[11]Jorge Luna Yepes' more ideological writings are cited in chapter 2. For more specifically party-oriented documents of recent years, see ARNE, *Proyecto de constitución para la república del Ecuador* (Quito: Talleres Gráficos Nacionales, 1964). Two other relevant statements are ARNE, *El pensamiento de ARNE, 1970* (Quito: Industriales Gráficas "CYMA," 1970), and ARNE, *Ideario de ARNE; ideas nuevas para una patria nueva* (Quito: Imp. Fernández, 1968).

term in office. Resigning before the 1956 election to stand as the candidate of the rightist coalition *Alianza Popular,* Ponce squeezed into office by a disputed 3,000-vote margin.

The first avowedly conservative president since 1895, Ponce survived his term despite a weak political base and an inheritance of *velasquista* economic mismanagement. From 1960 through 1968 Ponce remained acknowledged spokesman of the right, increasing his prestige by staunch opposition to the military junta. In 1968 his MSC and the Conservatives banded together once again under the *Alianza Popular* label, further supported by the regional *Federación Poncista* (FP) which he had established in Guayaquil in 1966. Despite continuing strength in the *sierra* and an improved showing on the coast, he ran a close third behind Velasco and Córdova. His public declarations since that time underline Ponce's continuing interest in another bid for a second presidency. However, the Conservatives' intention of running their own candidate in 1972, along with the presence of Otto Arosemena to the right of center, indicate the obstacles which Ponce may face.

His MSC advocates policies similar to those of the Conservatives. Critics have charged that the MSC actually stands to the right of the Conservatives. In 1964, attempting to capitalize upon rising sympathy for Latin American Christian Democrats following the victory of Eduardo Frei in Chile, Ponce changed his party's label to the *Partido Demócrata Cristiano.* However, there were denunciations of Ponce for misrepresenting his own views. By 1966 the official name of the party reverted back to the MSC, and Ecuador's true *Partido Demócrata Cristiano,* an official affiliate of the international Christian Democratic movement, has periodically issued reminders that *poncista* declarations about his "Christian" movement do not change the fundamentally conservative spots.

Also standing to the political right is the *Coalición Institucionalista Demócrata* (CID), founded on February 2, 1965, by former Liberal Otto Arosemena Gómez. A well-connected *guayaquileño* who had previously served as deputy and once as president of the lower chamber, Arosemena and two colleagues were elected to the 1966 constituent assembly, where he entered into a pact with the political right to secure the provisional presidency of the republic.[12] Following the inauguration of Velasco in 1968 he returned to the task of party organization. Although clearly available for another occupancy of the presidential palace, Arosemena stood in need of political allies; in 1970 municipal elections his CID drew little support in the Guayaquil contest.

Although rejecting in the very best tradition of an Ecuadorean rightist the label of either rightist or leftist,[13] Arosemena and his CID generally stand to the right of center. The party program includes a commitment to the private sector as bearing major responsibility for economic progress. In the words of the party manual, the aspiration of the CID is for "the rule of law over relations between labor and capital, guaranteeing to both that there be neither class struggle nor disturbance of national production with evil consequences." And again:

> The CID believes that the country should promote industry; but that the laws of industrial protection must be correlated with those protecting the artisans. . . . As the free importation of primary materials could give place to abuses, . . . the State will have to organize together with artisanal workers' systems of control. . .[14]

Committed to "economic and social transformation" but spelling out its proposals in cautious language, the CID also speaks of agrarian reform as a fundamental necessity; yet it stresses the colonization of unoccupied lands and warns against actions which might affect agricultural productivity. Terming itself "fundamentally Christian" and totally opposed to communism, the CID is more general than specific in its programmatic statements. The record of Arosemena's administration – even granting the constraints placed upon any such interim regime – suggests that development is envisioned within a context of major commercial and business interests.

Among the more recent personalistic groups is the *Partido*

[12]The accomplishments of his administration are set forth in *Plan de gobierno del doctor Otto Arosemena Gómez, presidente constitucional de la república* (Quito: Talleres Gráficos Nacionales, 1967).

[13]Dr. Arosemena was quite explicit in denying such means of identification during an interview with the author in August of 1969.

[14]Coalición Institucionalista Demócrata, *Manual para los militantes del nuevo partido* (Quito: n.p., 1969), p. 28.

Nacionalista Revolucionario (PNR) of former president Carlos Julio Aorsemena Monroy. A *velasquista* during the 1950s, Arosemena Monroy had led the opposition to the Ponce government from 1956 to 1960, becoming president of the *Federación Nacional Velasquista* before reaching the national vice-presidency in 1960. Soon turning against Velasco and helping to foment rebellion against the latter, he was himself forcibly removed from power in 1963 and went into exile.[15] Creating what was first termed the *Movimiento Nacionalista Arosemenista* as a vehicle for elections to the 1966 constituent assembly, Carlos Julio rapidly regained his earlier prominence and, despite the quarrels of 1960-61, threw his support to Velasco in the 1968 race. Since then he has been pointing toward 1972 elections and a possible return to the presidency, building upon his popularity in Guayaquil and seeking unobtrusively to assume the *velasquista* inheritance. He was publicly silent in the months following Velasco's suspension of the 1967 constitution, apparently hoping for eventual backing.

The PNR naturally follows the doctrinal inclinations of its leader, which are those of the reformist left. Party literature describes the PNR as having been born "as a necessary and unpostponable response to the crisis and misery which pitiless exploitation forces upon the masses." Furthermore, it denounces Ecuador's status as "a semi-colony at the mercy of foreign capitalist interests."[16] The party calls for the development of a nationalist conscience, that revolutionary criteria may be applied toward the realization of an economic and social transformation. Its program demands the renovation of existing structures, supported through the action of the "popular classes." A multiclass organization in intent, the PNR views itself as nationally representative, stressing its identification with rural and urban sectors, workers, students, educators, and professionals. War without quarter is to be waged against large landowners, "*criollo* oligarchs," and all those who would "impose imperialism" upon Ecuador.

[15]For his personal views on these turbulent events see the collection of Arosemena's letters in Movimiento Nacional Arosemenista, *Cartas para la historia* (Quito: Publicaciones del Movimiento Nacional Arosemenista, Editorial "Fray Jodoco Ricke," 1966).

[16]Partido Nacionalista Revolucionario, *Declaración de principios y estatutos del Partido Nacionalista Revolucionario* (Guayaquil: n.p., n.d.), p. 1.

Detailed proposals suggest a commitment to structural change which is absent from the doctrine of most Ecuadorean parties. Concerning agrarian reform, the PNR calls for the definitive end of *latifundismo* and the deliverance of the *campesino* from a state of servitude and misery, asserting that "land belongs to him who works it. The land of the State, moreover, will be delivered gratuitously to the peasant." Other PNR commitments promise the liquidation of such national monopolies as bananas and coffee, a systematically planned growth of agricultural and artisanal production, and the application of "radical" tax reform, which is described as taxation at rates appropriate to the income of the contributor.[17] PNR propaganda slogans include a promised 15 percent rebate on rentals, cheap housing, the free provision of government lands to the peasantry, and the inevitable phrase "1972 *al poder con* Carlos Julio Arosemena" – "to power with Carlos Julio Arosemena in 1972."

Of all the personalistic parties, none so resembles the archetypical ideal as much as that of the great civilian *caudillo* José María Velasco Ibarra. Although enjoying support from various sources during his earlier career, Velasco did not form an official organization until the occasion of 1952 elections, at which time he brought into being the *Federación Nacional Velasquista* (FNV). When out of office he has generally been in either forced or self-imposed exile, during which the organization withers on the vine. With the return of its champion to the campaign wars, however, the odd conglomeration of interests and individuals committed to *velasquismo* regroups its forces. During campaigns there are a variety of *velasquista* fringe groups which constitute themselves on behalf of his candidacy.[18] Although Velasco has occasionally enjoyed organizationally competent leadership in the FNV – as with Carlos Julio Arosemena Monroy, Jaime Nebot Velasco (no relation), and Galo Martínez Merchán – this has been largely transitory. The usual pattern is that of Velasco's own energetic, charismatic, and often demagogic campaigns through which, in a country the size

[17]For discussion of the leading programmatic commitments, see ibid., pp. 2-5.

[18]Thus in his most recent presidential campaign, there were such organizations as students for Velasco, the *velasquista* feminine movements, workers for Velasco, and a whole host of regional groupings – most of them weakly articulated and operationally removed from the FNV itself.

of Ecuador, he can personally reach a significant number of voters.

Both the FNV and the *velasquista* governments have attracted an exceptionally broad political and socioeconomic cross-section. Indeed, relatively few of the senior figures in Ecuadorean politics have not been *velasquistas* at some point in their careers. The disruptions and discontinuities which have so marked Velasco's many terms in office are often repeated within the FNV itself. Because of the disparate groups which are sometimes attracted to it, internal rifts and the clash of personal ambitions are pronounced; despite Velasco's disinclination at any point to designate a chosen successor, there have been many aspirants to the mantle of *velasquismo*. The *caudillo* has generally articulated reformist populism during his campaigns, but once in office this rhetoric is overcome by essentially conservative policies, generally ending in the turbulence surrounding the collapse of the *velasquista* administration.[19]

In addition to Velasco's personal repugnance for administrative and organizational structures, he has further hindered the creation of a broadly based and enduring party through his own vehement hatred of political parties. His writings and public declarations are liberally dotted with vitriolic denunciations of political parties, which he views as malevolent purveyors of corruption, moral turpitude, and self-seeking ambition.[20] During his fifth administration Velasco returned repeatedly and angrily to this theme, holding the parties responsible not only for congressional obstruction of his program but also for the fomenting of social division within the country. It was only the provisions of the 1967 election law which forced the FNV to be registered as an official "party," a fact which Velasco resented. His own preference has been to call *velasquismo* not a party but rather a "movement," allegedly transcending the pettiness of partisan interests by means of a populist, patriotic, multiclass mass structure.

Neither the FNV nor any other organized manifestations

[19]See the concluding chapter for a discussion of the fifth *velasquista* government.

[20]For a perceptive commentary by a noted Ecuadorean historian, see Alfredo Pareja Diezcanseco, "Teoría y práctica del conductor conducido," *Combate,* Vol. 20, No. 1 (enero y febrero 1962), 9-23.

of *velasquismo* have survived independent of the *caudillo's* own magnetism. His characteristic mistrust of his advisers – some of whom have indeed betrayed his confidence in the past – has prevented close or lasting association, further robbing his movement of continuity. Following his 1968 inauguration Dr. Velasco again saw a gradual erosion of his support, heightened by his usual unpredictable shifts in policy and dramatized by *velasquista* defeats in 1970 municipal elections. While such men as Galo Martínez Merchán, Jaime Acosta Velasco, and Carlos Cornejo Orbe hoped to receive Velasco's blessing in 1972, none could be certain of either his confidence or backing. The potential for political influence lay in Velasco's personality and in control of the organs of government rather than in concerted efficiency from the *Federación Nacional Velasquista.*[21]

Included among Velasco's supporters in 1968 was the tiny *Partido Demócrata Cristiano,* which stood slightly to the left of center. Since its 1965 founding the Christian Democrats have concentrated on attracting university students and young professional men to their ranks. It has largely eschewed electoral politics in the effort to erect an effective organizational apparatus. Ideological reformism has not attracted anticipated support from Ecuadorean youth, and PDC appeal was further impaired by its participation in the fifth *velasquista* administration. Despite the recognized ability of the party's Gil Barragán Romero in a ministerial post, there was a feeling that his participation was not consistent with progressive party principles. A subsequent rift within the PDC further weakened the movement, and it had little success in 1970 municipal elections. Its prospects for the immediate future appeared problematical at best.

The Concentración de Fuerzas Populares (CFP). The most striking of Ecuadorean parties, and one of the more unorthodox, is the *Concentración de Fuerzas Populares* (CFP), commonly termed simply the "*cefepe.*" Strongly personalistic leadership has been traditional, first under its founder Carlos Guevara Moreno and in the last decade under Asaad Bucaram.

[21]One of the most perceptive analyses of Velasco as a political leader is that of Agustín Cueva, "Interpretación sociológica del *velasquismo*," *Revista Mexicana de Sociología,* Vol. 32, No. 3 (mayo/junio 1970).

Each man in his turn has exercised party rule with an iron hand. Additionally, however, the *cefepe* is fundamentally a regional rather than a national party. Its domination of Guayaquil has endured, despite brief interruptions, for more than two decades, and it has also been influential elsewhere on the coast. Along with its personalistic and regionalistic traits has been the *cefepe's* striking success in reaching the popular classes. While neither Marxist nor radical, the party has strongly espoused the cause of Ecuador's dispossessed, and has drawn significant strength from it along the coast.

The CFP was founded in Guayaquil in 1947 by Carlos Guevara Moreno, a dynamic figure who had served as minister of government in the second *velasquista* government. The *Concentración de Fuerzas Populares* in its earliest years reflected Guevara's concern for socioeconomic reforms, as well as his sympathy for Velasco. In 1952 the *cefepe* supported Velasco, and many expected Guevara to prove his closest political associate. Having already brought Guayaquil under his political control, however, Guevara Moreno constituted a threat to Velasco, and before long he was driven from the government and into exile. He returned before the end of that administration, however, and in 1956 stood for the presidency of the republic.

At that juncture Guevara Moreno seemed to stand second only to Velasco as a leader with roots in the popular sectors. His weekly journal *Momento* reiterated attacks against the oligarchy, and Guevara championed the masses in speaking of the "*pueblo contra trincas*" – the people against political trickery. An expert political tactician who ran a tight operational organization, Guevara Moreno was unable in 1956 to make the leap from regional to national domination, yet his future and that of the party appeared bright. The impressive victory of his *cefepista* second-in-command, Luis Robles Plaza, in the Guayaquil mayoral race suggested further Guevara's prospects of future success. All indications pointed to his establishment of the CFP as a truly national party by the time of 1960 elections.[22]

[22]For a sympathetic and detailed review of the CFP during its years under the leadership of Guevara Moreno, see Rafael Galarza Arízaga, *Esquema político del Ecuador* (Guayaquil: Editorial Alborada, 1963), pp. 131-45.

However, a series of minor miscalculations began to erode his position, and growing corruption in the *cefepista*-dominated municipal administration of Guayaquil further tarnished Guevara Moreno's public image. He was defeated by a *velasquista* in his bid for another term as Guayaquil mayor in November of 1959 and, amid growing stories of scandal and corruption, he gradually withdrew from politics. When he gave party support to a minor Marxist presidential candidate in 1960, Guevara forfeited his remaining strength. By 1962, party leadership had been seized by Asaad Bucaram, who came to enjoy the unchallenged leadership which had once been Guevara's. In contrast to his predecessor, Bucaram had risen from humble origins as a Guayaquil street peddler. A man of large physique and striking features, he was well equipped to head a party which still advocated a restructuring of national society on behalf of the oppressed.

Acquiring great popularity as the *cefepe* regained strength, Bucaram won the mayorality of Guayaquil in June of 1962 with 43.2 percent of the vote in a thirteen-man race. Ousted and jailed following the July 1963 military *golpe de estado,* he later led his party to first place in 1966 elections to the constituent assembly. The CFP nearly doubled the total of its nearest competitors on the provincial level in winning 28 percent of the valid vote, thereby capturing four of the thirteen provincial delegates, with Bucaram heading the list. The following June Bucaram became mayor of Guayaquil for the second time, polling over half the valid vote in a five-man race. At the end of his term, desirous of remaining in political office as the 1972 campaign neared, he ran for provincial prefect on a coalition ticket with the Liberals. This resulted, in June of 1970, in a massive triumph despite a concerted anti-*cefepe* effort by several other parties.[23]

Asaad Bucaram, despite occasional heavy-handedness and a penchant for the expression of personal power, has been extremely effective in communicating with the poorer classes of Guayaquil. As a so-called "*turco*" of Middle Eastern origins, Bucaram has been one of the most popular leaders in recent

[23]For a discussion of his more recent political fortunes as well as his role in the *guayaquileño* effort to reshape national politics, see the concluding chapter.

memory. He also enjoys a reputation for impeccable personal honesty and administrative rectitude. Even his bitterest opponents, many of whom quail at the thought of his occupying the presidency, concede the effectiveness of his municipal administration in dealing with the boundless energy and massive problems of Guayaquil. Moreover, his evident commitment to major socioeconomic reforms is unquestioned, and follows in the *cefepista* tradition.

In the 1950s the CFP was a party which, although denying any personalist inclinations, at the same time gave Guevara Moreno the title of "Leader-Director" with virtually unlimited authority within the party hierarchy. In terms of doctrine, the CFP declared itself "democratic, progressive, anti-feudal, and opposed to *caciquismo.*" Referring frequently to the welfare of the masses, *cefepista* declarations have further stressed the need to break the power of the oligarchies, to incorporate the masses into the political system, and to dedicate the "Party of the Ecuadorean People" to transforming the "actions of the State into social action at the public service." The weakest human sectors have been identified as the rural laborer, children, women, the Indian, the coastal *montuvio,* and the urban worker.[24]

The original CFP ten-point statement of doctrine remains unchanged, and more detailed policy proposals have not altered the evident populistic tone. An introduction to the present edition of party doctrine is illustrative:

> We aspire to a deep and radical revolutionary transformation in the methods and goals of the Ecuadorean State. We look for the spiritualization of the people, their elevation in culture, their maturity with regard to political conscience and moral perspectives. We respect conscience and its intimate right to religious faith without accepting the Church as a political and electoral mechanism at the service of feudalism.[25]

Asaad Bucaram's *personalismo* remains central to the CFP. His official party title is "Supreme Director" or "Supreme Chief,"

[24]For the original ten-point statement of *cefepista* doctrine, see J. Gonzalo Orellana, *Resumen histórico,* pp. 116-19.

[25]Concentración de Fuerzas Populares, *Que es el CFP? doctrina, estatutos y programa de Concentración de Fuerzas Populares (partido del pueblo ecuatoriano)* (Guayaquil: Editorial Bermúdez, 1967), p. 3.

and although the party convention is officially the supreme authority, organizational provisions make clear Bucaram's individual domination.[26] When President Velasco deported Bucaram following the June 1970 *autogolpe, cefepista* activity became moribund in his absence. Thus the party's fate, notwithstanding its unquestionable hold on the allegiance of the majority of Guayaquil voters, rested on the fortunes and abilities of its *caudillo*. In this, the CFP is fully consistent with the traditions of Ecuadorean parties.

ELECTIONS AND PARTICIPATION, 1948-68

Multiplying party fragmentation reduces the effectiveness of the aggregative function, and this is further aggravated by the restrictive system of representation. Ecuador has always prohibited electoral participation by illiterates, and while the issue of broader suffrage has been frequently raised, the ban against illiterates has never been lifted. Article 4 of the 1967 election law was quite explicit: "The Ecuadorean over eighteen years of age who knows how to read and to write is obliged to obtain the Identity and Citizenship Card which permits him to participate in elections and plebiscites."[27] The law also disenfranchises those not registered in their local parish of residence, those whose political rights have been suspended, and members of the military or police serving on active duty (article 5). Not until 1968 was voting compulsory for women as well as for men, although female suffrage had been permitted on a voluntary basis since 1929.

The impact on electoral participation is depicted in Table 11, starkly underlining the discriminatory effects of the electoral law. In 1948 presidential elections, for example, only 14.3 percent of the total population was *eligible* to participate. After reaching 20 percent and going higher, it again dropped in 1966 when competition for the constituent assembly represented the first election in more than four years. Overall participation

[26]Provisions pertaining to the authority of the Supreme Director are found in articles 22-24 of the party statutes, in ibid., pp. 29-30.

[27]Congreso Nacional del Ecuador, *Ley de elecciones* (Quito: Talleres Gráficos Nacionales, January 1968), p. 143.

Table 11
ELECTORAL PARTICIPATION, 1948-1968

Year	Est. Popltn.	Registered Voters	Valid Votes	Reg. Voters as % of Popltn.	(6)	(7)
1948	3,196,693	458,021	281,895	14.3	61.5	9.1
1952	–	–	353,755	–	–	–
1956	3,804,559	779,837	604,332	20.5	79.5	15.8
1960	4,269,370	1,102,391	767,105	25.8	69.6	17.9
1966	5,585,000	1,013,698	615,073	18.1	60.7	11.0
1968	5,776,100	–	850,557	–	–	14.7

Sources: Electoral data were compiled from the *Tribunal Supreme Electoral,* with population figures from national censuses or official TSE estimates.
All are presidential elections excepting 1966, which was for the constituent assembly.
Column (6) reports the valid votes cast as a percentage of registered voters; column (7) reports the valid votes cast as a percentage of the population.

figures are even lower when the valid votes are tabulated. After eliminating those which were either blank or nullified through voter error, as well as inscribed voters who did not exercise their right, usually no more than 60 to 70 percent of the registered voters cast valid votes. Transferring this to the overall population, the true extent of electoral nonparticipation emerges vividly.

Thus in 1948 only 9.1 percent of the total population of Ecuador cast a valid vote; although this figure has risen in more recent years, in both 1966 and 1968 it was less than 15 percent. Thus in any given year the valid votes cast in an Ecuadorean election are but a small proportion of the total national population. The electoral process is clearly unrepresentative of the country. Even a populistic Velasco or Bucaram, campaigning intensively as a candidate of the masses, mingles with and speaks to many Ecuadoreans constitutionally forbidden to vote. The electoral system of representation thereby reinforces the elitist cast of Ecuadorean politics.

Presidential Elections.[28] In the past quarter-century Ecuadorean presidential elections have frequently been closely con-

[28]All electoral data presented in this chapter comes from the official figures at the Tribunal Supremo Electoral, with calculations performed by the author. It should be noted that the data are not precise; that is, data are not reported in uniform fashion by the TSE through the years; moreover, there are frequent inaccuracies, such as columns of figures whose totals are incorrect. Wherever it seemed defensible, these totals have been recalculated.

Table 12
PRESIDENTIAL VOTE BY REGION, 1948-68

1948	Plaza	Flor	Enríquez		
Sierra	38.0	49.3	12.7		
Costa	46.6	20.9	32.5		
NATL.	41.0	39.9	19.1		
1952	**Chiriboga**	**Alarcón**	**Larrea**	**Velasco**	
Sierra	18.9	45.9	5.1	30.1	
Costa	19.1	12.1	5.2	63.6	
NATL.	18.8	33.1	5.1	43.0	
1956	**Chiriboga**	**Ponce**	**Huerta**	**Guevara**	
Sierra	20.1	46.4	22.9	10.6	
Costa	12.6	9.3	36.3	41.8	
NATL.	16.7	29.5	29.0	24.8	
1960	**Plaza**	**Cordero**	**Parra**	**Velasco**	
Sierra	22.4	32.9	3.4	41.3	
Costa	24.9	9.5	9.7	55.9	
NATL.	23.4	22.4	6.1	48.1	
1968	**Córdova**	**Ponce**	**Gallegos**	**Velasco**	**Crespo**
Sierra	31.1	35.3	1.9	26.9	4.7
Costa	31.0	22.8	2.2	41.6	2.4
NATL.	31.0	30.4	2.0	32.8	3.8

Here, as in the charts appearing in this chapter, regional totals have excluded the *oriente* and the Galápagos Islands, where the electorate is far too small to be meaningful.

tested, with outcomes hotly disputed among a kaleidoscopic variety of candidates, parties, and coalitions. Before examining trends over time, a brief account of individual contests will be helpful. The 1948 race seemingly marked the beginning of a transition toward more progressive electoral politics; certainly it introduced a twelve-year period of constitutional stability unparalled since the nineteenth century. The Conservatives ran party stalwart Manuel Elicio Flor, a prominent lawyer and constitutional authority. The PLR, still sensitive to the humiliation of 1941 and deeply divided over responsibility for the debacle, joined with the socialists behind General Alberto Enríquez. In the meantime, however, independent Liberals and progressives knit together an electoral coalition backing former ambassador to the United States Galo Plaza. This so-called *Movimiento*

Cívico Democrática Nacional (MCDN) gathered together a group of young professional people who hoped to depart from more traditional politics.

The MCDN and Plaza waged a vigorous campaign while demanding renewed attention to economic development and a streamlining of government structures. The Conservatives were handicapped by their traditional weakness on the coast, while Enriquez was an ineffective campaigner. An observer of that campaign recorded that the poorly financed contest reached but a small proportion of the citizenry.

> Lack of party resources precluded the printing on any large scale of campaign leaflets and posters; and campaign propaganda, such as it was, appeared largely in the form of brief slogans painted on walls and buildings. Plaza, the only presidential candidate with substantial financial resources, introduced a few United States campaign methods, such as radio addresses and a nationwide campaign tour. His advisers, however, considered it prudent that he hold these activities to a minimum in view of the economic inability of other contestants to duplicate them.[29]

In a close race which was not officially decided until three weeks after election day, Plaza squeezed into office with a 3,000-vote margin out of some 281,000. With 41 percent of the vote he led Flor with 39.9, while Enríquez trailed distantly. With two candidates standing for the center-left, Flor might have won but for the lack of Conservative strength on the coast, where he received but 20.9 percent of the vote. As Chart 1 shows, the Conservatives polled nearly half of the *sierra* vote. Had the center-left united behind a single candidate, its domination of the coastal vote would have been more than enough to offset Conservative strength in the highlands.

Four years later the center-left remained divided, the Conservative situation was unchanged, but the "Great Absentee" Velasco returned to Ecuador seeking his third term. While representatives of the traditional forces marked time and engaged in internecine dispute, Velasco was off and running in a characteristically intensive personal campaign.[30] The Conservatives even-

[29]Blanksten, *Ecuador,* pp. 79-80.

[30]Among his other contributions to national politics, Dr. Velasco was the first political leader to undertake nationwide campaigns, a practice which had become widespread by the 1960s.

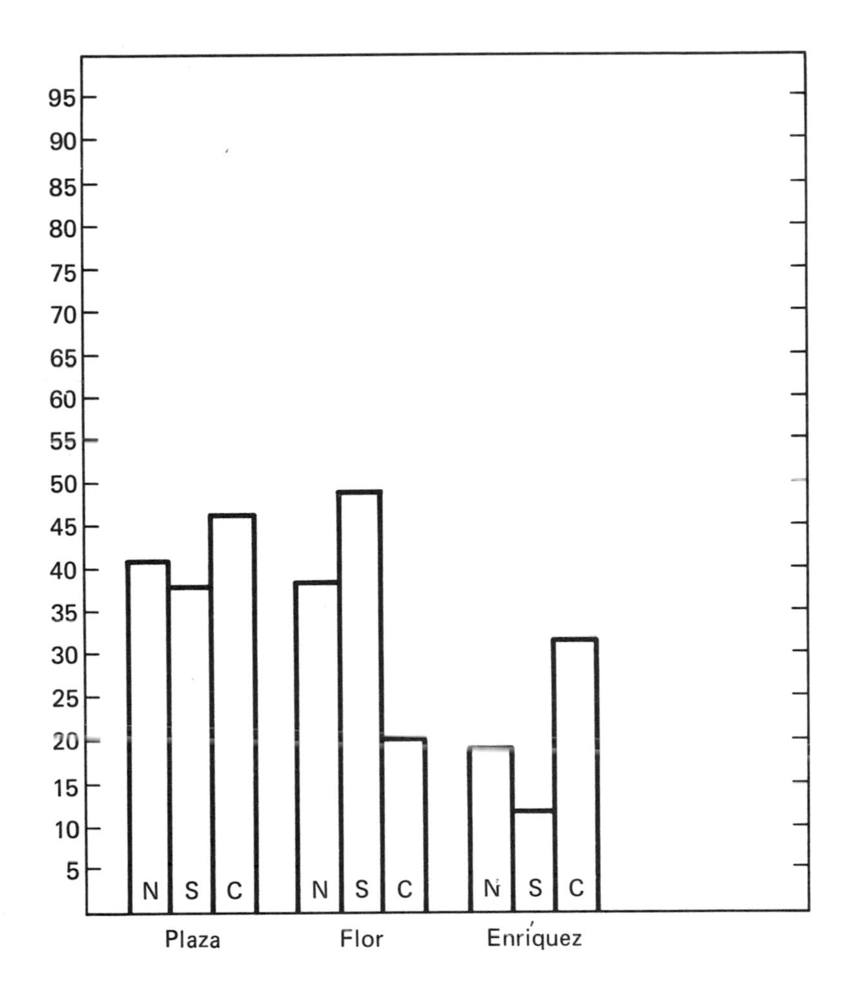

CHART 1. PRESIDENTIAL VOTE BY REGION, 1948.

In this as in charts for later elections, N = national, S = *sierra,* and C = *costa* percentages of the vote.

tually ran Ruperto Alarcón Falconí, whose virtual seizure of the nomination in the face of fierce opposition later denied him much needed financial and organizational support. The center-left was scarcely better off; the PLR remained divided, and only with difficulty named the popular mayor of Quito, José Ri-

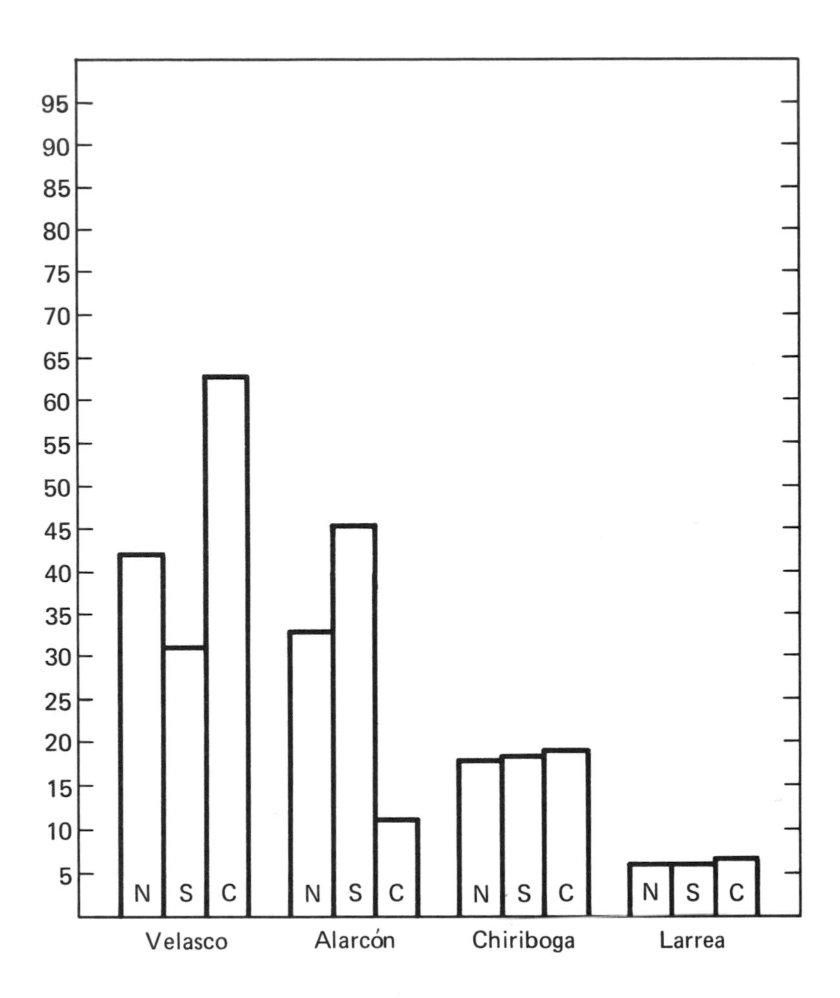

CHART 2. PRESIDENTIAL VOTE BY REGION, 1952.

cardo Chiriboga Villagómez. Others, including many supporters of President Plaza, banded behind José Larrea in another informal coalition. Disunity was so evident, however, that Plaza himself withheld the backing which Larrea had first expected.

Despite reports from an anti-*velasquista* press that Alarcón was the front-runner, and in defiance of a rumored coalition between Chiriboga Villagómez and Larrea, José María Velasco Ibarra forged ahead and never faltered. His characteristic eloquence, driving energy, and tireless public appearances soon made him the center of attention. Having been outside the country since 1947, moreover, he could attack with impunity the errors of intervening years. Having seized the initiative, Velasco never relinquished it; the close of the campaign saw his opponents striving in vain to capture the offensive.

On election day Velasco polled 43 percent of the vote, a comfortable 10 percent lead ahead of Alarcón Falconí. Chiriboga Villagómez trailed with 18.8 percent of the vote and Larrea with but 5.1. Velasco showed expected strength on the coast, polling nearly two-thirds of the valid votes and thereby denying the center-left what it might otherwise have expected. In the *sierra* Velasco won a creditable 30.1 percent, compared with Alarcón's 45.9. Chiriboga's only real source of strength was Quito, where his success as mayor enabled him to win the province of Pichincha with some 20,000 votes, nearly one-third of his national total. Although Alarcón had won seven of the ten highland provinces, Velasco won two and was second in most others, while the president-elect also led in four of the five coastal provinces.

The 1956 competition was not complicated by a *velasquista* candidacy, but nonetheless was compounded by an array of candidates and coalitions. Camilo Ponce and his MSC joined with the Conservatives in the *Alianza Popular,* thus presenting a solid front. In contrast, the Liberals were once again divided over the candidacy. When Galo Plaza, eligible for another term, spurned party overtures, the PLR turned to Raúl Clemente Huerta, a young Guayaquil lawyer. The party's 1952 standard bearer, José Ricardo Chiriboga Villagómez, determined to make another bid and, optimistic of backing from President Velasco, entered with the support of dissident Liberals and independents. In Guayaquil, *cefepista caudillo* Carlos Guevara Moreno announced his intention of expanding his movement to the national scene; hopefully his coastal strength, combined with some highland votes, might carry him to victory in the four-way contest.

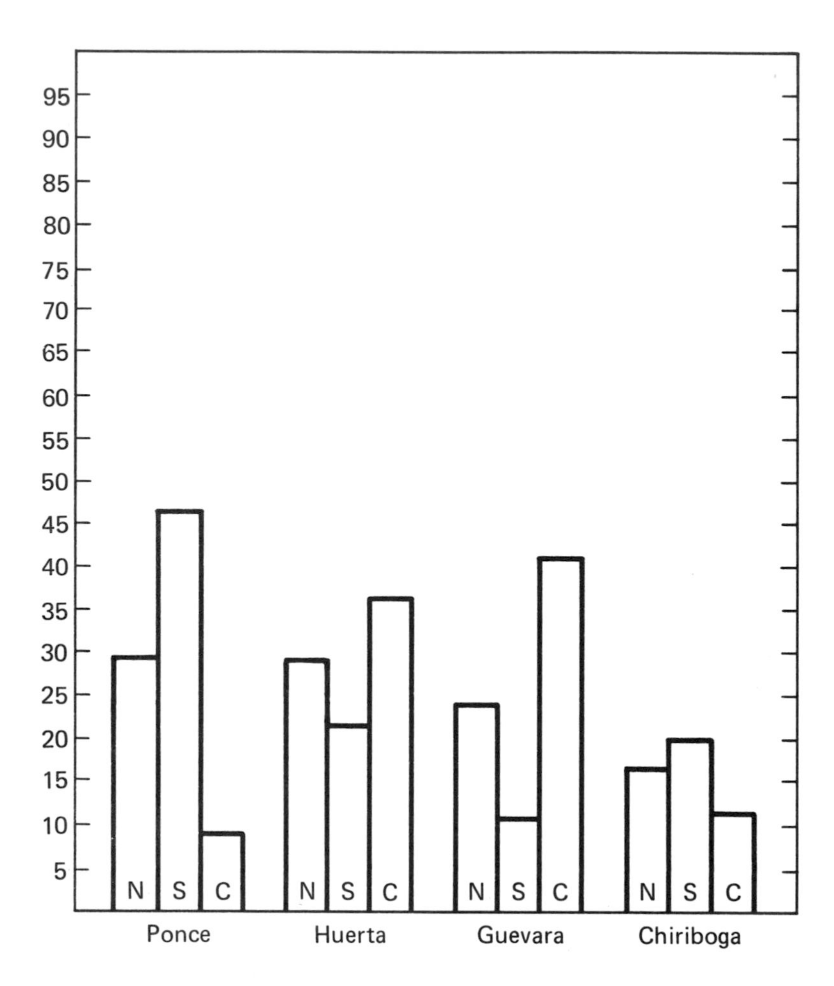

CHART 3. PRESIDENTIAL VOTE BY REGION, 1956.

In one of Ecuador's most intensive campaigns, the four candidates waged mutually recriminatory attacks. Center-left criticisms of Velasco resulted in his unofficial but extensive support for Ponce. By the close of the campaign the outgoing president was speaking publicly against the Liberals. Early returns were extremely close, and the Supreme Electoral Tribunal decreed a thirty-day moratorium on electoral announcements pending completion of the tally. Nearly two months passed before proclamation of Camilo Ponce's 3,000-vote margin over Huerta. For the first time since 1895 an avowed representative of the right had won the national presidency.

Opposition forces claimed fraud, and even today cite the suspicious circumstances in the vote counting. The results were not overturned, however; examination showed that Ponce's thin margin had been possible as a result of Liberal division and the *cefepista* candidacy, for these three men together had won 70 percent of the valid vote. Ponce's percentage on the coast was lower than that of the two previous Conservative candidates, although his showing in the highlands was consistent with the Conservative pattern. Huerta had suffered directly from the Guevara Moreno candidacy, for the latter swept Guayas province while collecting 41.8 percent of the *costeño* vote, in contrast to Huerta's 36.3. Yet Guevara had won but 10.6 percent of the *serrano* vote, demonstrating *cefepista* regionalism. Chiriboga Villagómez ran weakly except for Quito, where he received a clear margin over his competitors. To sum up, only through several fortuitous circumstances – importantly including official support from the government – had Ponce won power for the political right after more than half a century's absence.

In the next four years Ponce deftly maneuvered through treacherous political shoals, moderating to some degree the 1956 electoral bitterness while proving that a government of the right could indeed survive in Ecuador. In 1960 Conservative Gonzalo Cordero Crespo, an experienced lawyer and politician from Cuenca, was named by his party to replace Ponce. The center-left, badly singed by past divisions, united behind former president Galo Plaza; the PLR, PSE, and independent Liberals supported his coalition, the *Frente Nacional Democrático*. However, the FND was also confronted by Velasco Ibarra, in quest of an unprecedented fourth term. Bringing together the newest model of the *Federación Nacional Velasquista,* he returned to the political fray with undiminished energy. Velasco had quite literally opened his 1960 campaign on the day he left office,

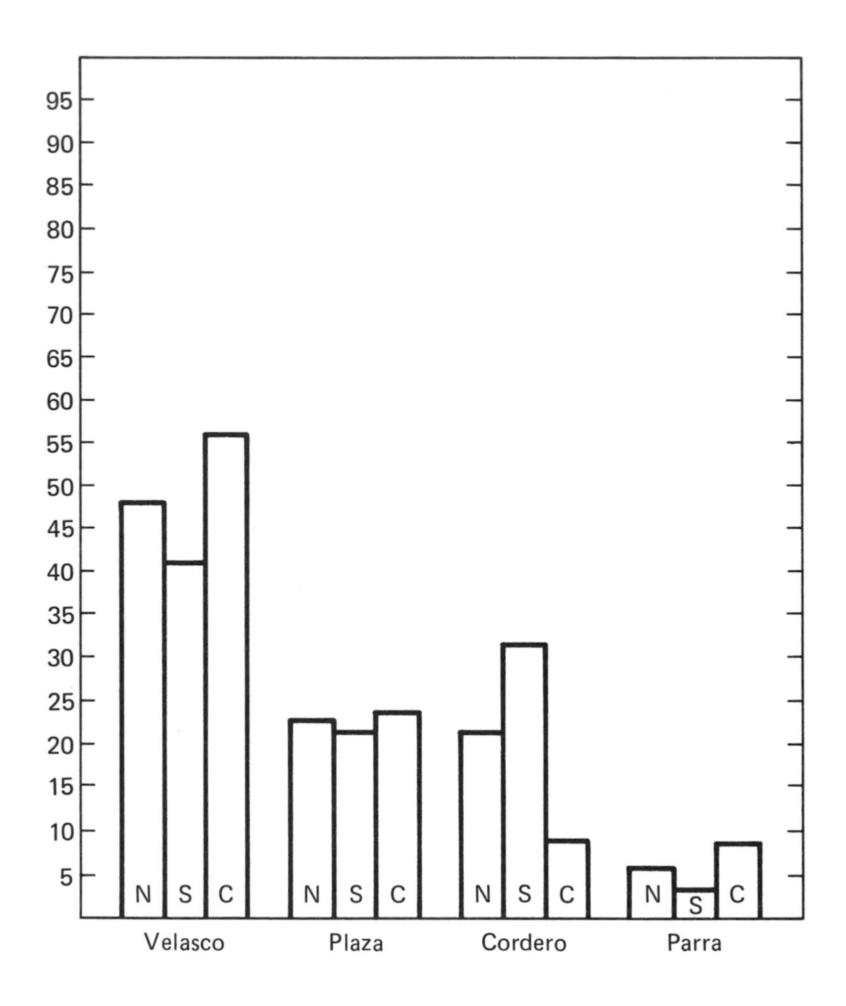

CHART 4. PRESIDENTIAL VOTE BY REGION, 1960.

with a vitriolic attack on Ponce, whose candidacy he had so significantly aided. Considerable momentum had been generated when the campaign began to unfold in early 1960. A fourth candidate, Antonio Parra, was named by a Marxist alliance of the communists and the Revolutionary Socialists; it also unexpectedly drew the endorsement of Guevara Moreno, now badly tainted by municipal corruption and scandal in Guayaquil. Parra, officially the candidate of the *Unión Democrática Nacional* (UDNA) although not a communist himself, was the closest to a communist-supported presidential candidate Ecuador had experienced.

The campaign, like so many others, turned largely on the impact of personality. Velasco stressed his qualities of energy, dedication, and commitment, although the oratorical tone was more reformist than in earlier campaigns. Responding to hemispheric winds of change, he promised the redemption of society's dispossessed. Plaza's campaign, well-financed but less aggressive than that of Velasco, was placed on the defensive by charges of support from private and public North American interests. His long years of friendship and sympathy for the United States opened him to charges of *entreguismo* – of selling his country's resources to North American capitalist interests. Such charges were quite damaging to Plaza's prospects. Gonzalo Cordero Crespo was forced to stand on the record of outgoing President Ponce, promising to continue existing policies while accelerating their implementation.

Once again, then, Velasco had begun the campaign on a positive note and steadily increased his drive to election. Amassing the largest plurality in many years, he won a fourth term with nearly 49 percent of the vote, leaving Plaza and Cordero Crespo far in arrears with 23.4 and 22.4 percent respectively. Velasco swept the coast with 55.9 percent of the vote, winning four of the five provinces and becoming the first ever to poll 100,000 from Guayas. His improvement over 1952 showed up in the *sierra,* where he led Cordero Crespo by nearly 9 percent and Plaza by 19 percent. Of his two major competitors, Cordero Crespo ran far ahead of Plaza in the highlands while the situation was reversed on the coast. Leftist candidate Parra polled less than 6 percent of the vote. For the victor, he won an unprecedented twelve of the twenty provinces (including Galápagos); his capture of both Quito and Guayaquil was also an electoral first. In short, his victory was the most truly national achieved in modern times, and he reentered the presidency with an unprecedented national mandate.

Eight years were to pass before another presidential contest, although there were congressional contests in 1962 and 1967, along with the race for the constituent assembly in 1966. In 1968 there was a five-way race, with three ex-presidents seeking another term in office. In a classically balanced contest, Camilo Ponce and Andrés F. Córdova led the traditional forces of center-right and center-left, while Velasco defied age and past reverses to run again.[31] Moreover, polar extremes were also included, the ARNE's Jorge Crespo Toral representing the far right while an ad hoc *Unión Democrática Popular* (UDP) consisting of assorted Marxists backed an independent, Elías Gallegos Anda. Velasco eventually won by a small margin; never before, however, had three presidential candidates been so closely bunched, with less than 2.5 percent separating Velasco from the third-place finisher, Ponce. Of the two minor candidates, Crespo ran ahead of Gallegos while the two men together totaled barely 6 percent of the vote.[32]

Electoral Trends. The five presidential races from 1948 on do not provide great analytical treasures, owing to the erratic and changing nature of competition. Three factors complicate meaningful interpretation: (a) the participation of José María Velasco Ibarra in three of the five elections; (b) the frequent division of center-left strength through internal dissension and, in 1956, the additional involvement of the regionally powerful but nationally weak CFP; and (c) the role played by some outgoing presidents in the selection of their successor. In the first case, Velasco's clearly reformist campaign appeals in 1960 and 1968 so contrasted with the more conservative outline of his administrative policies as to drain doctrinal meaning from electoral support.

Secondly, the PLR fragmentation, the personalistic elements of two Plaza candidacies, and the Quito popularity of its

[31]Unlike Ponce and Velasco, Córdova's stint in the presidency (1939-40) had been of an interim nature, the result of congressional action rather than national elections.

[32]See the concluding chapter for a detailed discussion of the 1968 campaign.

former mayor Chiriboga Villagómez are all complicating factors. And thirdly, while Plaza kept hands off the 1952 campaign

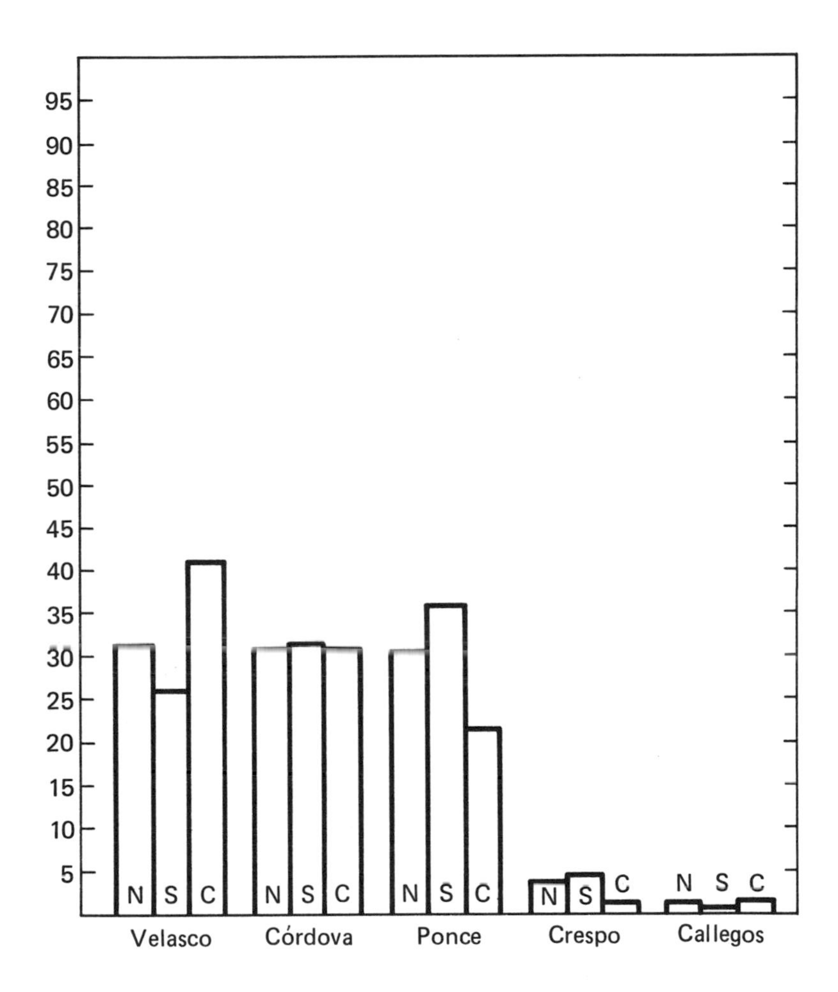

CHART 5. PRESIDENTIAL VOTE BY REGION, 1968.

despite his antipathy toward Velasco, the latter in 1956 hinted at possible support for Chiriboga Villagómez, flirted briefly with Guevara Moreno, and then in effect more than provided the margin of victory for Ponce. Later, prior to the 1968 elections, the understanding between provisional president Arosemena Gómez and the Conservatives worked on behalf on Ponce, although less explicit than anti-*poncistas* charged.

Looking at sectoral or party trends over time, then, permits only limited generalization. Perhaps the sharpest picture comes from inspection of the Conservative vote. Without exception the so-called center-right entered the fray with but a single candidate. Conservatives Flor in 1948 and Alarcón in 1952, Cordero Crespo in 1960, and rightist Ponce in 1956 and 1968 stood alone (although in 1968 the *arnista* candidacy of Jorge Crespo Toral also represented a rightist vote). Chart 6 reflects the major characteristics of this center-right vote. Nationally the percentages dropped progressively from 1948 through 1960, notwithstanding Ponce's circumstantial win in 1956 – before rising again in 1968. Only in 1948 did the conservative candidate receive more than one-third of the valid votes, while the mean for the five elections stands at 31.1 percent. In 1968 Camilo Ponce was within one percentage point of that mean.

Conservative regional strengths and weaknesses have persisted over time, despite some fluctuations. The *serrano* vote is consistently above the national total, while for the coast it is lower. For these five elections the mean percentage for the center-right candidate in the highlands is 41.9 percent, although lower in 1960 and 1968 than earlier. On the coast, support ranged from a low of 9.3 percent in 1956 to a high of 22.8 percent in 1968. The mean was 14.9 percent. Their substantial coastal vote in 1968 suggested a possible breakdown of traditional patterns. One view explained this by *poncista* personalism more than genuine sympathy for the Conservative party, although the latter understandably cited the results as proof of growing support beyond the highlands.

The center-left vote is less easily analyzed, given the disparity of its sectors, factions, and electoral coalitions through the years. The figures in Chart 7 are based on the combined Plaza-Enríquez vote in 1948, Chiriboga Villagómez-Larrea in 1952, and Huerta-Chiriboga Villagómez in 1956; the Guevara Moreno candidacy of 1956 is omitted, although this is rather perilous to the analysis. Only with Plaza in 1960 and Córdova in

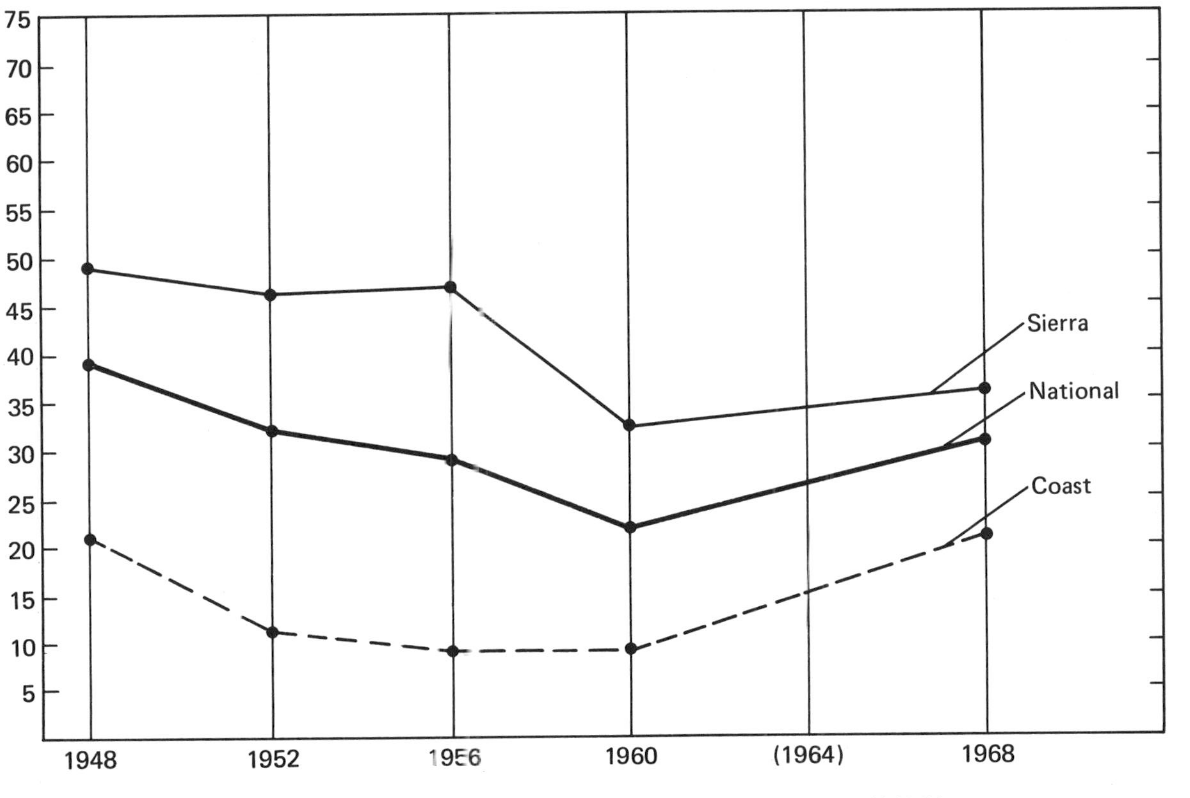

CHART 6. CONSERVATIVE PARTY VOTE FOR PRESIDENT, 1948-68.

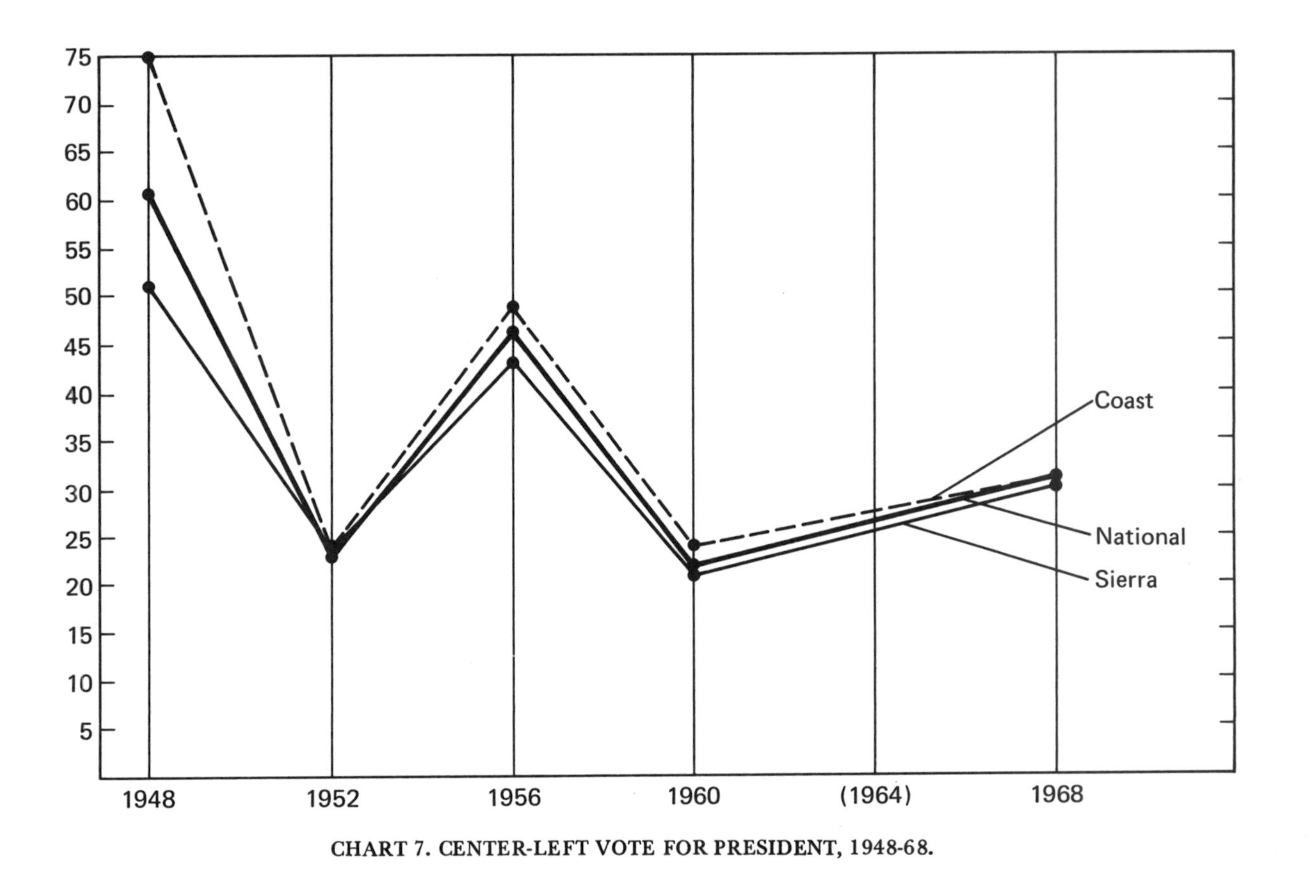

CHART 7. CENTER-LEFT VOTE FOR PRESIDENT, 1948-68.

1968 has there been a clear case of a single center-left candidate. Having accepted such arbitrary conditions, one then finds two striking characteristics: first, a highly varying support from one election to the next; and in any single election, close correspondence between regional and national totals. In the first instance, national support was greatest in 1948, reaching 60.1 percent; since then the highest figure is that of 45.7 percent in 1956. In the two most recent presidential contests, the center-left has polled less than one-third of the valid vote. The three poorest showings of the center-left – 1952, 1960, and 1968 – were all those in which Velasco was a candidate. This suggests, as discussed below, that a considerable portion of the *velasquista* support has been drawn from voters who would otherwise back PLR candidates. At least one of the factors explaining the wide fluctuations of center-left strength across the years would seem to be the impact of *velasquismo*.

On a regional level, the *costeño-serrano* dichotomy is much less pronounced than it was for the center-right. Since 1952 the coastal and highland totals have generally coincided with one another, and also with national totals. In the last two contests this has been remarkable – extraordinarily so for Andrés F. Córdova. Center-left strength would seem almost equally divided between coast and highland were it not for the competition from Velasco's several candidacies. Moreover, for 1956 this center-left data does not include the 41.8 percent attracted to the *cefepista* candidacy; with the CFP to the left of the Liberals, certainly its votes would more likely have gone to the PLR than to the center-right. And finally, it should be recalled that 1952 and 1956 center-left support in the highlands was increased because of the candidacy of Quito mayor Chiriboga Villagómez. He drew enthusiastic support from *quiteño* voters on both occasions, presumably from identification with his municipal administration rather than party affiliation. Such local or regional candidate identification may well have assisted in 1968 as well, since candidate Córdova was himself a *serrano*.

In addition to the preceding, one can also examine the *velasquista* experience over time. The national patterns naturally reflect the national scope of his 1960 victory, as well as the relatively "soft" result in 1968. As seen in Chart 8, *velasquista* regional strength is primarily on the coast, although since 1952

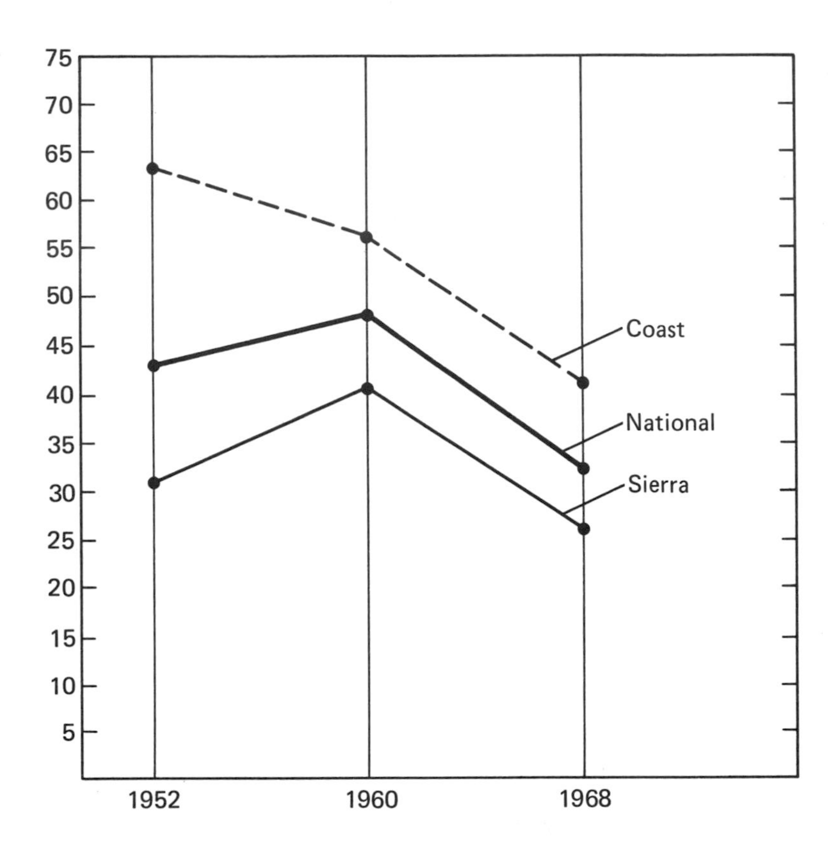

CHART 8. VELASQUISTA VOTE FOR PRESIDENT, 1952, 1960, 1968.

it has declined; despite the massive national victory in 1960, Velasco's strength on the coast has dropped well below that of 1952. Yet in the highlands, his vote has ranged between 26.9 percent in 1968 and a 1960 high of 41.3 percent. These voting patterns testify to the contention that Velasco has come closer than any other leader in bridging the gap between the two regions. More popular on the coast than the highlands, he has nonetheless drawn significant support from both regions.

As had occurred with his previous administrations, Velasco in his fifth administration was soon to find himself once again on rough waters, with popular support diminishing, policies uncoordinated or contradictory, and opposition rife. The course of political events since 1968 suggests both the enduring qualities of Ecuadorean party affairs and the possibility of forthcoming transition into a post-Velasco era.

5
The Clash of Tradition and Modernization

The myriad developmental problems confronting Ecuador as it enters the 1970s reflect both economic imbalance and social inequities. Pressures for rapid and lasting transformation are often in conflict with the vested interests of elitist groups, requiring responsive reforms from the political leadership. Despite unmistakable indications of a growing commitment to the goals of national modernization, the political system retains an attitudinal commitment and operational style heavily encrusted with tradition. It is the accelerating clash between tradition and modernization which best characterizes contemporary Ecuadorean affairs, and which contributes to both immediate and long-range uncertainties. This is vividly illustrated by the events and policies surrounding the administration inaugurated in September of 1968. Certainly the fifth *velasquista* administration well represented many of the enduring aspects of the political system. Moreover, major domestic policies also exemplified both traditional patterns and newly emergent modernizing perspectives, especially regarding the potential impact of the growing petroleum industry.

One of the major forces for change is also emanating from regional and subregional centers. The Ecuadorean history of such local and provincial initiative and energy underlies the varied activities in diverse sections of the country, nowhere more dramatically than in Guayaquil. While the extent of such subnational pressures cannot be fully calculated at this juncture, there are indications that local demands and needs will contribute powerfully to the mobilization of modernizing forces. Moreover, this is taking place within a context of rising nationalism. Dissatisfaction with existing conditions and political responses is colored by a growing recognition of both internal and external colonialism and dependency. The colonialist inequities of Ecuadorean sociopolitical life are even more deeply etched as a consequence of international influences, particularly those of the United States. As will be seen, political leaders in recent years have become increasingly strident in their criticism of external pressures, and have found growing popular support in nationalistic pronouncements and policies. Again, the impact of petroleum production has illustrated the nature of international colonialism, and this will be highly significant as the drive for modernization heightens.

VELASQUISMO *AND ENDURING POLITICAL TRADITION*

Contrary to the preceding twelve years, the decade of the 1960s marked a turning away from constitutionality. Not only was the inherent fragility of public affairs from 1948 to 1960 underlined, but, even more importantly, the recrudescence of instability testified to the inadequacy of government and its failure to mobilize the country for necessary and fundamental reforms. Thus the tortuous struggle toward a restoration of constitutional succession and legitimacy was almost incidental to the restructuring of a political leadership with the capacity and commitment for developmental progress. The immediate result, of course, was the fifth presidency of Velasco, which began to evolve following the collapse of the military junta in 1966. The road back to constitutional, elected government began with elections on October 16, 1966, for a constituent assembly.

José María Velasco Ibarra: Return of the "National Personification." Lists of candidates and new "mini-parties" proliferated in advance of the elections for the constituent assembly, especially in Quito and Guayaquil. In the capital 128,918 votes were cast for fourteen separate lists; the Conservatives led with 37,249, followed by the Liberals with 27,872. Conservatives also headed the field for Pichincha province, with the delegation composed of three Conservatives, two Liberals, and representatives of three other tickets. In Guayaquil fifteen slates competed. A resurgent CFP won 40,033 votes of the 121,479 cast, while none of its rivals topped the 20,000 mark. The CFP also led in Guayas province with 45,862 of 161,420 valid votes, thereby winning four of the thirteen seats.

When the constituent assembly convened in November, the division between so-called center-right and center-left was nearly equal. The former strongly favored the selection of Camilo Ponce as president, but anti-*poncista* elements strongly resisted. Conservatives therefore sought a candidate who might attract uncommitted votes. The first contest came over the choice of a presiding officer, with former Conservative presidential nominee Gonzalo Cordero Crespo opposing Liberal senior statesman Andrés F. Córdova. The seventy-nine-man assembly chose the former by a 41-34 margin, with the decisive votes coming from the small delegation of Otto Arosemena's *Coalición Institucionalista Demócrata* and from a Liberal representative of Esmeraldas.[1] A similar division led to Arosemena's election as provisional president over center-left candidate Raúl Clemente Huerta by 40-35. It was rumored that a secret pact had been signed between Arosemena and the Conservatives, an agreement which was acknowledged by Arosemena in March of 1968 following denunciations by Dr. Velasco.[2]

The narrowness of the division clearly left the 1968 national contest wide open, and 1967 municipal elections did little to alter the general uncertainty. In Guayaquil, an electoral coalition between the CFP and the Liberals resulted in a decisive victory by Asaad Bucaram as city mayor, while the joint slate won six of the eleven city *concejales*. *Velasquistas* and supporters of Carlos Julio Arosemena Monroy each won two,

[1] Dr. Julio C. Plaza Ledesma was subsequently expelled from the Liberal party for his vote. For discussions of both the popular and the Assembly elections, see *El Año Ecuatoriano, 1966* (Quito: Talleres Gráficos de Editorial Santo Domingo, 1967), pp. 42-60.

[2] For the text and a brief discussion, see *El Año Ecuatoriano, 1968-69* (Quito: Talleres Gráficos de Editorial Santo Domingo, 1969), pp. 53-55.

and the last went to a *poncista*. In Quito, locally popular Jaime del Castillo, running with *velasquista* backing, won the mayoralty with 35,692 votes, followed by a Conservative with 31,739 and a Liberal with 31,203. In the other provincial centers, the even division between Conservatives and Liberals persisted. As the 1968 presidential campaign approached, Ecuadoreans began to realize that they had yet to hear the last of José María Velasco Ibarra.

National political characteristics of personalism, paternalism, and opportunism are all personified by Dr. Velasco, the archetype of the Latin American civilian *caudillo*.[3] Like his country, possessed of deeply felt and strongly contradictory traits, Velasco is an unadulterated patriot whose vision includes the conviction that only he has the wisdom and capacity to lead his people from the wilderness. Two decades ago he was described in the Ecuadorean press thusly:

> Velasco Ibarra is the permanent *caudillo* which the country has had during the last decades. His figure stands out lean and ascetic, inflamed by vehemence, his accusing index finger eagerly extended. . . . Dr. Velasco is doubtlessly the man nearest the masses. Like them, he acts emotionally, in fits and starts. This is the secret of his success, apart from his extraordinary personal magnetism. On two occasions he has been the Man of Providence for the country. Both times he failed . . . caught in the net of his own contradictions.[4]

Author of nearly twoscore books on political and philosophical matters,[5] on which he is well-read, impeccably honest in financial matters, and concerned deeply over the future of his country, Velasco has so dominated the political life of Ecuador for the past four decades that an appropriate understanding of his temperament, style, and orientation helps in a comprehension of the political system.

Years before the third of his five terms in office, Velasco was viewed by an astute observer as having fallen before the

[3] See Agustín Cueva, "Interpretación Sociológica del Velasquismo," *Revista mexicana de sociología*, Vol. 32, No. 3 (mayo-junio 1970), 709-35.

[4] *El Comercio* (Quito), June 8, 1952, as quoted in Lilo Linke, *Ecuador*, 2nd ed. (London: Royal Institute of International Affairs, 1955), p. 30.

[5] One of his more recent and characteristic works is José María Velasco Ibarra, *Servidumre y liberación; del imperialismo atómico a la claridad del espíritu* (Buenos Aires: Americalee, 1965).

dilemma of many other Latin American leaders: that, although opposed to state intervention, he "had to embark upon a program of state intervention of unprecedented proportions in order to establish an environment conducive to liberty."[6] By the time of his 1960 election, moreover, hemispheric winds of change had strengthened his belief in the centrality of state intervention. During his abbreviated fourth term his administration advocated extensive reforms of existing institutions, although most commonly articulated by more leftist advisers than by Velasco himself. As before, administrative ineptitude, misplaced trust in his lieutenants, an ignorance of economics, and an inability to delegate authority led to a morass of policy inconsistencies. Subjected to bitter attack, he had typically responded with fierce denunciations of all who opposed him, and an ultimate breakdown in order had led to his ouster.

What have his goals been? His dedication to the populace – which has customarily excluded the problems of the Indian – is suggested by the following:

> The most important thing that I have tried to do is to create in the Ecuadorean people a pride in being an autonomous, sovereign nation, free and with its banner tested in the forge of battle and ready to endow a collective national entity with its own soul, with its own personality, with dignity and with its own ideas. The most important thing I have done is to try to awaken national optimism, to try to awaken the civic spirit of the nation, to try to convince the Ecuadorean people that they are masters of their own destiny in internal politics and that they are autonomous and sovereign in the realm of international politics; . . .[7]

While his administrative failures have receded swiftly into the shadows, the omnipresence of his personality has continued to attract Ecuador's masses. Here too a national paradox is personified in the man, for his patriotism is mixed with an elitist certainty that only he has the capacity for disinterested, enlightened leadership.

Velasco's rhetorical brilliance has unfailingly convinced the masses of his sincerity in seeking to realize their goals, and

[6] George I. Blanksten, *Ecuador: Constitutions and Caudillos* (Berkeley: University of California Press, 1951), p. 49.

[7] José María Velasco Ibarra, *Obra doctrinaria y práctica del gobierno ecuatoriano* (Quito: Talleres Gráficos Nacionales, 1956), Vol. 2, p. 477.

personal charisma has evinced an emotional faith in his ability. The bonds between Velasco and the masses have been renewed in campaign after campaign, and will not disappear so long as he is among them. In 1962 an Ecuadorean historian attempted to characterize Velasco's hold on his audience:

> Velasco possesses the technique of a fighting preacher, with sober movements of the body, mobility in the hands, accusing right index finger, admonishing, penetrating, of brusque movements, a large mouth, his head erect and inclined backwards. . . When there is great exaltation, he ends up moving around in a flood of words, from which he emerges with difficulty, amid a multiplication of insults at times, but at other times recovering with slow sentences, sudden acceleration, or with triumphal exclamations.[8]

In March of 1968 Velasco returned home from Argentina to take up the electoral cudgels once again. An earlier call from exile for a boycott of 1966 elections had failed and, when his initial reception in Guayaquil was unimpressive, there was a wishful tendency by his opponents to underestimate his prospects. By the end of the month, however, the newest edition of the *Federación Nacional Velasquista* had stirred to action, and a strenuous personal campaign belied the septagenarian's age. The announcement of support from Carlos Julio Arosemena Monroy had further improved Velasco's prospects. In the meantime Camilo Ponce's bid for a second term had been endorsed by the Conservative party, although personal conflict with Cordero Crespo later led to his departure from the party. Further rightist support was denied when ARNE chose to enter its own candidate, while a small splinter of the Conservative party ran a separate list headed by the 1952 candidate, Ruperto Alarcón Falconí. Offsetting these handicaps was the clear if tacit sympathy of provisional president Arosemena Gómez, ample financial backing, the eminence of the Ponce name, and recent growth of the *Federación Poncista* in Guayaquil.

While *velasquistas* and rightists had obvious nominees, the Liberals were in a quandry. Raúl Clemente Huerta, perhaps their most logical choice, was reluctant to run, as was Julio Moreno Espinosa, another strong possibility. Both eventually

[8] Alfredo Pareja Diezcanseco, "Teoria y practica del conductor conducido," *Combate* (San Jose), Vol. 4, No. 20 (enero-febrero 1962), p. 21.

demurred – possibly intimidated by Velasco's candidacy – and the choice finally narrowed to Andrés F. Córdova or Abdón Calderón Muñoz, the latter a young economist and rising party leader in Guayaquil. At the Liberal convention the choice was both generational and regional; *serrano* Córdova was seventy-six, while *costeño* Calderón Muñoz was in his forties. The former was eventually chosen and the party closed ranks behind him. Unlike the candidate himself, the PLR was extremely pessimistic about his chances.[9]

In accord with election laws the campaign officially began only sixty days before elections, although supporters of Velasco and Ponce had been mobilizing well before that time.[10] Velasco sought the initiative as usual, launching bitter attacks in all directions. Córdova was charged with having rigged the 1940 elections to assure the victory of fellow Liberal Arroyo del Río over Velasco.[11] He was scarcely more gentle with the Conservatives, angrily denouncing what he called a devil's pact between Arosemena Gómez and Ponce (see above) to assure their continuity in power. Velasco reiterated these charges incessantly, as well as offering long and detailed criticism of the new system of voter registration being implemented by officials of the Arosemena administration. He also unleashed attacks on large landowners, commercial interests, and the "Guayaquil oligarchs" which were reminiscent of earlier years' oratory.

Camilo Ponce's programmatic appeals emerged in bits and pieces, although finally being published as a campaign platform. Córdova elaborated his policy positions in more detail, yet he too placed considerable emphasis on personal style. Starting far

[9] This is necessarily a simplified review of a rather complicated set of events leading to Cordova's candidacy. Among a number of Liberals, I am especially indebted to interviews during June and July of 1969 with Andrés F. Córdova; Raúl Clemente Huerta; Rodrigo Borja; Francisco Huerta Montalvo; and Abdón Calderón Muñoz.

[10] The author observed the 1966 but not the 1968 campaign. In addition to information and analyses by many observers and participants, he is also appreciative to Professor Freeman Wright for the opportunity to read in draft form his manuscript on the 1968 campaign. To my knowledge this has not, unfortunately, been published.

[11] Typical of the *velasquista* style was the contention that Liberal provisional president Córdova had delivered 48,000 false votes to Arroyo del Río from the province of Manabí in 1940. As Córdova retorted, Arroyo received fewer than 48,000 votes in the entire nation! This did not in the least deter Velasco from later repeating his allegation.

behind his better-known opponents and with limited financial backing, Córdova stressed his personal integrity, sincerity, and openness. Like his competitors, Córdova also toured the country extensively. For all three major candidates, organizational preparations were at best erratic, and campaign efforts fell heavily upon the candidates' shoulders. True to tradition, personalism loomed large, especially given the generality of most platforms.[12] Velasco was, as always, eloquent, charismatic, angry, bitterly vitriolic toward his opposition, and unreserved in sweeping populistic pronouncements. Ponce, cooly reserved, was the conservative aristocrat; ever the unbending, self-disciplined patrician, he spoke self-assuredly of national unity and a rebirth of progress within an orderly system. Córdova, a stubby, pink-cheeked, fatherly figure, contrasted to Velasco's fire and Ponce's aloofness his own personal warmth, generating an image of sound experience, reliability, and paternal trustworthiness.

Election day, the first June Sunday in 1968, was relatively calm. Velasco soon appeared the unofficial victor by a narrow margin, but there were alleged irregularities in Guayaquil, where Velasco had gained more than his margin of victory. Following stormy outbursts during hearings before the *Tribunal Supremo Electoral* later in the month, the official recount validated most of the Guayaquil ballots. On July 17, 1968, the TSE presented the official returns to congress. Unlike 1960, Velasco's victory was not impressive, with nearly two-thirds of the votes cast for other candidates. His position in congress was tenuous, for the FNV was far short of a working majority in both chambers. Only twenty of the eighty deputies were *velasquistas,* while in the senate there were but nine of his followers. It was within this context that Velasco and the Liberals negotiated a controversial pact "at the legislative level," that the president might command a majority. This soon proved a chimera, however, for many Liberals, including Córdova, balked at the agreement. Thus the new president soon found himself stymied by congress; choosing not to compromise, he vilified its members as irresponsible, incompetent, and worse. The executive–legislative impasse swiftly broadened as a result.

[12]Velasco himself scorned the adornment of a platform, haughtily denouncing such commitments as part and parcel of the selfish evils of political parties.

From Constitutionality to Dictatorship. Inaugurated on September 1, 1968, Velasco was enmeshed in difficulties even before the close of the year. The legislative pact with the Liberals effectively dissolved, as *velasquistas* themselves fell to internal bickering while many Liberals rejected the pact. Moreover, national Vice-President Jorge Zavala Baquerizo, a *guayaquileño* Liberal, widened the breech with impassioned attacks on the president. In June of 1969 he denounced Velasco for initiating "subversive activities" and acting in dictatorial fashion, and the president stepped up the tempo of blanket indictments of congress. His administration, reminiscent of earlier periods in power, soon fell once more into a state of disarray. *Velasquista* cabinet ministers came and went through a veritable revolving door. By 1970 there had been substitutions in two-thirds of the ministries, and in several cases at least three men had entered and left the government. Ministers also shifted at times from one cabinet position to another.

Four individuals stood out as enjoying some degree of personal prestige and a degree of autonomy from Velasco: Jaime Acosta Velasco, Pedro Menéndez Gil, Galo Martínez Merchán, and Jaime Nebot Velasco (no relation). The first, nephew of the president, was the powerful minister of defense until his ouster in 1971 (see below); the other three were in and out of favor with the president. Menéndez Gil had occupied three different ministries before being appointed governor of Guayas province shortly before his unexpected death in May 1971. Martínez Merchan, a prime mover in organizing the FNV for the 1968 campaign, also served in different ministries, on one occasion holding two cabinet positions simultaneously. Longtime *velasquista* Nebot Velasco belatedly joined the government in 1971 as minister of interior. That same year a fifth man had also emerged as a power in the regime – Dr. Luis Robles Plaza, a decade earlier the right-hand aide to *cefepista caudillo* Carlos Guevara Moreno, and after the ouster of Acosta Velasco, the minister of defense.

Perhaps more important than ministerial instability was its impact on the direction of fiscal and economic policy. Thus, while economic problems mounted, leadership was diffuse and transitory; by June of 1971 there had been five different *velasquista* ministers of finance. It was, in fact, the economic decline which contributed most significantly to the rise of political opposition, as well as deepening the chasm between the executive and legislative branches. Less than a year after Velasco took office, falling exports and rising imports had reduced the foreign reserves by two-thirds, to a scant 15 million dollars. The budget deficit also grew by leaps and bounds. By January of 1970 it was estimated at some 1,200,000 *sucres,*[13] with the government unable to pay its employees fully or to provide many essential services. The public investment program was virtually abandoned, and a foreign bond issue of $70 million was necessary to finance the budget. Official spokesmen estimated that the government would be forced to commit 40 percent of its income to service the public debt, in addition to another 22 percent for the foreign debt.

Expenditures for 1969 could be covered only by expending 1970 revenue in advance. Although Velasco managed to obtain necessary congressional authorization, there were numerous restrictions on future expenditures. When Velasco's fourth finance minister took office in early 1970, the administration proposed a severe austerity program to brake the deteriorating fiscal situation and to avoid the rising spectre of rampant inflation. By the time congress had reconvened in March, however, the crisis was even more severe. The president announced in a message to the congressional finance commission that the 1970 budget deficit was in excess of 2,800,000 *sucres,* more than double that of the previous year. Moreover, virtually half of the sum was required for services rather than for investment in developmental programs. Velasco therefore proposed three measures: increased taxes to raise an additional 600 million *sucres;* a 905 million *sucre* reduction in expenditures; and a reconsolidation of the government debt of 636 million *sucres* with the *Banco Central.* These actions would reduce the deficit to only 400 million *sucres.*

Despite the urgency of the situation, congress occupied itself with minor legislation and anti-*velasquista* diversions, adjourning on May 4 without having acted on the recommenda-

[13]While the exchange rate fluctuated during this period, it averaged roughly 19 *sucres* per dollar. With the subsequent official devaluation of the *sucre* on August 17, 1970, a dual exchange rate system was abolished and the rate fell from 18 to 25 *sucres* per dollar.

tions. A wrathful Velasco promptly retaliated. Ten days after the adjournment of the legislature, charging that congressional irresponsibility left him no choice, the president issued four emergency economic decrees. He eliminated major tax exemptions, including those covered by the laws of industrial development, agricultural and livestock development, and tourism; a capital gains tax was applied to properties which had benefited by public works projects; and a variety of new consumer and sales taxes were levied. The most controversial of his decrees, however, called for a drastic increase in stabilization surcharges on imports, with increases ranging as high as 55 percent on selected items. The outpouring of criticism was immediate and profound.

Rafael Dillon Velásquez, president of the powerful Guayaquil Chamber of Commerce, protested that the emergency decrees would raise the cost of living 40 percent, driving small businesses into bankruptcy and aggravating unemployment. The "Guayaquil oligarchs" so often castigated by Velasco rapidly undertook an expensive public relations campaign against the measures while seeking support from congressional sympathizers. The finance minister explained that government budget experts had already carefully studied the measures, and he brandished the threat of rent controls and additional austerity measures. The administration further announced that the international reserves of the *Banco Central* had fallen from $39 million to $23.7 million in the first five months of 1970, while the unfavorable balance of trade was nearly 50 percent greater for 1970 than for a comparable period in 1969. Velasco rained vituperation on Guayaquil bankers and industrialists, denouncing what he termed an unprincipled betrayal of the Ecuadorean masses. It was amid this inflammatory fiscal and political situation that nationwide municipal elections were held.

Already frayed *velasquista* hopes of improving their status through elections were dashed to shreds. In Quito, the architect Sixto Durán Ballén won the mayoralty with 62,431 votes, some one-third of the total; he was followed by a son of Andrés F. Córdova, who drew over 50,000 as candidate of the dissident Liberals (*Izquierda Democrática*), while a Conservative was third. The *Federación Nacional Velasquista* failed to win a vacancy on the city council, and placed but one representative on the ten-man provincial delegation. In Guayaquil the continuing CFP-PLR coalition won a tremendous popular victory. Asaad Bucaram, unable to succeed himself as mayor, won 63 percent of the vote in a four-man race for prefect of Guayas province, while his Liberal running mate, Francisco (Pancho) Huerta Montalvo, swept to the mayoralty with the same 63 percent against four opponents. The coalition also won nine of the sixteen-man provincial delegation. Throughout the country, the *velasquista* candidates were generally outdistanced by their opponents.

In the wake of elections, predictable postmortems examined the returns for possible harbingers of the 1972 race, and the smashing CFP-Liberal triumph in Guayas received the greatest attention. President Velasco, however, was undeterred by the apparent rebuff to his policies, and commenced with implementation of his recent economic decrees. Opposition continued to mount apace; the Supreme Court shortly ruled his tax proposals unconstitutional by a vote of 22-15. Student rioting broke loose, first in Guayaquil and then in several other cities. Protests culminated in a massive demonstration in Quito, where the rector of the Central University led a march to the presidential palace. Vice-President Zavala issued one last attack on Velasco and soon disappeared into hiding, while newspapers editorially condemned presidential action. Blocked at every turn, yet determined to brook no further opposition, the embattled *caudillo* took the final, perhaps inevitable step and assumed dictatorial powers on Monday, June 22, 1970.

Broadcasting over radio and television, Velasco charged that "nihilistic revolution" threatened Ecuador; his assumption of dictatorial powers was therefore necessary to save the country from internationally inspired anarchy. Congress was dissolved, the universities were shuttered, and tank-supported troops occupied school grounds. Student-dominated demonstrations led to repeated clashes the day of Velasco's seizure of total power, with tear gas and sporadic firing employed to disperse the crowds. A wave of arrest orders included Central University rector Manuel Agustín Aguirre; its law school dean, José Santos Rodríguez; Carlos Julio Arosemena Monroy; and Rafael Dillon Velásquez. A new wave of executive decrees imposed travel bans, halted currency exchanges, and blocked foreign currency accounts. The president also announced that most of the semiautonomous state corporations would be eliminated. Velasco further justified his actions as the manifestation of popular will, pledging the eventual organization of a national plebiscite to legitimize his rule and to replace the 1966 constitution.

The critical political variable lay in support of the armed forces, and military leaders, many of them beholden to Defense Minister Acosta Velasco, pledged their unqualified support for the president. Having received these assurances, Velasco's so-called *autogolpe,* or self-seizure of power, was complete. He was Ecuador's civilian dictator. Yet his decision to rule by decree did little to cool the long-simmering feud between Velasco and Guayaquil's wealthy merchants. The latter initially feared a government swing in the direction of state socialism as a means of coping with the fiscal crisis. Velasco charged that the country's worst enemies were in reality the "monopolists of money," while his influential nephew spoke approvingly of the reformist military regime in neighboring Peru as achieving social justice through the eradication of "absurd privileges." Another *velasquista* bellwether, Galo Martínez Merchán, told the Cuban news agency *Prensa Latina* that privilege in Ecuador should be abolished, and that the road to socialization might well be the course to pursue.

Such official statements spread near-panic in Guayaquil, especially when yet another executive decree restricted foreign exchange matters to the Central Bank, requiring all foreign currency to be turned in by July 5. Commercial banks were overwhelmed by customers withdrawing their savings before possible bank nationalization, and some 55 million *sucres* were withdrawn in a single day. Moving swiftly to deter further action, Velasco and key ministers flew to Guayaquil for extended discussions. The climate was little improved, however, and hostility between the government and coastal economic interests continued. In August of 1970 came the announcement of devaluation, the first such action since 1961. By that time the year's imports had risen markedly ($127 million as compared to $97 million for the first six months of 1969) while exports had fallen sharply.

The trade deficit stood above $50 million, the budget deficit persisted, and a one-month drop in international reserves from $33 million to $16 million all had combined to force the decision for devaluation. The value of the *sucre* was therefore officially reduced from eighteen to twenty-five to the dollar. This 28 percent devaluation benefited certain exporters, but also assured a sharp increase in prices. Added to a 4 percent sales tax imposed a few weeks earlier, it put a severe squeeze on precisely those middle and lower classes whose support Velasco had continued to court. In addition to the obvious political implications, devaluation also provided but temporary hope for a slackening in the fiscal crisis. In the same month the newest minister of finance estimated that by year's end the budget deficit would be 1,068 million *sucres*.

Velasquista efforts to eliminate semiautonomous agencies or to bring them under centralized control hoped to reduce expenditures significantly, since these organs had been consuming nearly two-thirds of ordinary government revenue. At the close of August a more realistic and vastly simplified exchange rate was also adopted. In September the awarding of three loans from the Inter-American Development Bank (IADB) provided an additional $29.7 million for transportation and public works projects. By the close of the year the situation had improved; moreover, Velasco had largely placed responsibility for fiscal and economic policy in the hands of the *Banco Central* and the *Junta Monetaria*. The official view held that short-run adjustments would carry the country through at least two years of transition, by which time oil revenues would presumably lead to a major economic transformation.

Despite continuing fiscal fragility, 1971 saw a few glimmers of sunlight. At the start of the year exchange reserves had risen to $58 million, while an increase of over 50 percent in the value of banana exports further strengthened the economy. In March of 1971 Velasco's sixth minister of finance announced a balanced budget for the year. Of some 5,100 million *sucres*, 70 percent was allocated to administrative expenses and nearly 25 percent for servicing the public debt, leaving merely 5 percent for investment in development. Revenue from the collection of income tax had increased by 25 percent over the preceding years, further easing the situation.[14] The major concern by mid-1971 was the renewed threat of inflation and a possible rise in unemployment. Consumer prices in Guayaquil had risen nearly 10 percent in less than a year, while the money supply was reaching record heights. Appreciative of the political implications, Velasco decreed a minimum wage increase from 600 to 750 *sucres* monthly, but the measure was generally received as inadequate.

In addition to attacks from commercial interests on fiscal reforms and growing popular resentment at the rising cost of living, Velasco was also faced with continuing political opposition in the wake of his *autogolpe.* His primary weapon in the political conflict was reiterated support for the national plebiscite in August of 1971.[15] As he first announced in June of 1970, Velasco foresaw the vote as involving approval of a new constitution. While the basic intention was to seek a demonstration of broad popular support, the plebiscite was to revolve about the proposed adoption of a new constitutional order. The president had two major criticisms of the 1967 charter: (1) congressional powers were so broad as to render ineffective the executive branch; (2) the continuing independence of semi-autonomous agencies caused excessive budgetary pressures while prohibiting meaningful developmental planning by the government.

The president advocated a return to the 1946 constitution, thereby reducing the power of the legislature and strengthening the presidential system. A commission of jurists was named to draft a new document, and its discussions for months were shrouded in mystery. The president had indicated that he would remain in office until the completion of his four-year term in 1972, whatever the outcome of the referendum. The political parties were initially uncertain in their response, although in

[14]A special commission on tax evasion found that only 418 of Ecuador's 873 medical doctors and 444 of its 1062 lawyers submitted tax returns. Among those found to be avoiding taxes was a property owner whose worth was over 100 million *sucres.* It was also estimated that 800 million *sucres* annually were lost through falsification of customs records in Guayaquil.

[15]This would have been Ecuador's first plebiscite, although there had been a referendum on July 11, 1869, to approve the García Moreno constitution, the so-called "Carta Negra" or "Black Charter." For a discussion, see *El Universo* (Guayaquil), October 14, 1970.

time most came to oppose its provisions. However, in June of 1971 he suddenly announced that the plebiscite would not be held; Velasco briefly declared that he would consider the possibility of adopting a revised version of the 1946 constitution by executive decree. Despite a year's announcements about the importance of the plebiscite, he said little in justifying its cancellation.

At that juncture his nationwide popularity appeared to be waning, but Velasco nonetheless had at least temporarily gained the upper hand over the organized opposition. From the time of the June 1970 *autogolpe* the regime had persistently harassed its opponents. Liberal, Conservative, and other party leaders were arrested and jailed; many were held overnight in retaliation for public criticism of the government, then released the following morning. Such unanticipated and sporadic detentions helped to restrain the opposition, as well as disrupting any effective organizational plans. The most sustained persecution had been directed at the Guayaquil leadership, especially the recently elected Bucaram and Huerta. Both men were arrested in September 1970. The youthful new mayor was soon released although prohibited from resuming his office. Bucaram, whose presidential potential had blossomed following his overwhelming triumph, received less gentle treatment. After brief imprisonment he was unceremoniously flown into Panamanian exile.

That Velasco was able to retain power while largely cowing his opponents testified to continuing military support. In three of his four previous administrations he had ultimately been toppled with either participation or tacit concurrence of the armed forces. Always generous in his treatment of the armed forces, Velasco went even further upon his return to office in 1968. Owing largely to the political acumen of his nephew as minister of defense, the president succeeded in maneuvering sympathetic officers into key posts. With Acosta Velasco encouraging moderate reformist officers, the president came to rely substantially upon their backing. At the time of the 1970 *autogolpe,* he initially threatened to resign until urged by the armed forces to seize power for himself. In subsequent months he actively sought to maintain this support; at the close of September he retired some twenty senior officers, replacing them with younger men of his own choosing.

A bizarre episode in late 1970 underlined the internal fissures of the military itself. General César Rohn Sandoval had been recently promoted ahead of several more senior officers to the post of air force chief of staff. On October 27 Rohn was kidnapped in Quito; the government first arrested rightist elements, but then swung in the direction of the left as well. A week after his disappearance Rohn reappeared in the capital, having reportedly escaped his abductors. Charges were lodged against a son of Andrés F. Córdova who had been passed over by Rohn's promotion. There were also rumors that Rohn himself had been involved in improper business dealings. Two months after the abduction, already relieved of his post, General Rohn was assigned to Washington as Ecuadorean representative to the Inter-American Defense Board.

The decisive nature of military support for Velasco was further dramatized in April 1971, when yet another upheaval rocked the government. The outcome left the president more vulnerable than ever. Difficulties began when Minister of Defense Acosta Velasco, ever shuffling the officer corps with skillful zeal, overstepped himself by removing General Luis Jacome Chávez, commandant of the military academy in Quito. Jacome Chávez refused the order and demanded the dismissal of both the Minister and General Julio Sacoto Montero, the army commander. Jacome Chávez failed to win backing sufficient to enforce his demands, and instead was placed under arrest. A few days later, however, Acosta Velasco was called to the military academy and was summarily detained. He promptly submitted his resignation, took refuge in the Peruvian embassy, and later in the month was dispatched to Madrid as ambassador. General Sacoto Montero was also a casualty; recently advanced from the rank of colonel over a host of senior officers, he was forced to resign as commander of the army.

Although the president had ridden out the storm, it was at heavy cost. He had in effect yielded to a military ultimatum in order to remain in office. Within the military, senior traditionalist elements had regained the upper hand over more reformist-oriented younger officers. In the process Velasco's most trusted confidante – his nephew – had been removed from authority. Coming within a few months of the death of Menéndez and the resignation following an internal disagreement of

Martínez Merchán, the president was stripped of his most powerful lieutenants. The ouster of Acosta Velasco apparently removed the man most likely to carry forward the banner of *velasquismo*. By 1972 the new minister of interior, Jaime Nebot Velasco, seemed the president's only remaining source of personal strength and support. It was transparently evident that the president entered the final year of his term on the sufferance of senior military officers. Clearly his prospects of survival until September of 1972, and the ultimate fate of the fifth *velasquista* government, lay in the hands of the armed forces.

In early 1972, the return of Asaad Bucaram from a brief exile to campaign for the presidency stirred the concern of traditional elites. Ranking military officers also mistrusted the populist leader and, fearful of a possible Bucaram victory in June elections, pressured Velasco to postpone elections and continue in power. The president resisted all such suggestions and, consequently, was sent into exile as the result of a bloodless *golpe de estado* on the night of February 15. A three-man junta headed by General Guillermo Rodríguez Lara, the army chief of staff, suspended elections and reintroduced military rule. At the outset General Rodríguez announced the intention of restoring the 1945 constitution, which had been strongly reformist in orientation. A program was outlined which suggested broad parallels to the progressive attitudes of the military regime in neighboring Peru. Rodríguez, however, was known for his connections with traditional business elites, and the true inclinations of the new regime were not immediately clear.

DOMESTIC POLICY AND MODERNIZING PERSPECTIVES

The preparation, formulation, and implementation of domestic policy in Ecuador has customarily received verbal acceptance, but there has been a large gap between word and deed. Until recent times, political emphases were less commonly socioeconomic than they were constitutional or legal. In the post-World War II era, greater attention has been directed toward policy outputs, although without question the level of rhetoric has continued to outstrip practical achievement. As pressures for change and reform have heightened, the clash of tradition and modernization has become increasingly evident. Two major policy areas amply illustrate these conflicting forces: agricultural and industrial development. The former is tied to sporadic efforts at agrarian reform and increased productivity, while the latter strongly reflects the anticipated potential of petroleum as an economic bonanza. To place these within a broader perspective, a brief overview of developmental trends is necessary.

The Politics of Growth. Ecuador's real gross domestic product grew from 1965 to 1969 at an annual rate of 4.8 percent.[16] With the population increase estimated at 3.4 percent, this left a per capita rise of only 1.4 percent annually, far below the 3.3 per capita growth projected as the target of the 1964-1973 national plan.[17] Public utilities, governmental expenditures, and construction were the sectors showing the most significant improvement, although a mild construction boom had leveled off by 1970. Neither agriculture nor industry showed rapid growth. After having accounted for a combined 51.2 percent of gross domestic product in 1965, by 1969 they had dropped to 47.8 percent. As suggested by the discussion in chapter 1, the underlying factors involved "low-technology farming heavily dependent on a few traditional export crops with limited growth potential, such as bananas, coffee and cocoa, and a manufacturing sector which is approaching the limit of feasible import substitution."[18]

The imbalance of exports and imports had already become substantial before the initiation of the Velasco administration

[16]Unless otherwise indicated, data in this section are derived from the Social Progress Trust Fund Annual Reports issued by the Inter-American Development Bank under the title *Socio-Economic Progress in Latin America.*

[17]For a study contracted by the military government with projections which have largely been unrealized, see Ralph J. Watkins, *Expanding Ecuador's Exports; A Commodity-by-Commodity Study with Projections to 1973* (New York: Frederick A. Praeger, 1967). As has been argued at several junctures, failures to meet major goals have been a testimony to political instability and erratic leadership.

For a more recent study from the Junta Nacional de Planificación y Coordinación, see César Raúl Robalino Gonzaga, *El desarrollo económico del Ecuador* (Quito: Talleres Gráficos Nacionales [1969 or 1970]).

[18]Inter-American Development Bank, *Socio-Economic Progress in Latin America; Tenth Annual Report, 1970* (Washington: Social Progress Trust Fund, 1970), p. 203.

(see preceding section). For the period from 1965 to 1969, imports averaged an annual growth rate of 9.1 percent, while exports expanded annually at only 1.6 percent. Consequently, where there had been a trade surplus of $25.5 million in 1965, by 1969 there was a deficit of $31.9 million. The increase of consumer goods imports in 1968 and 1969 continued into the 1970s, despite a noticeable slowing in the growth of capital goods and industrial raw materials. As already noted, a combination of economic and fiscal stresses led to the 28 percent devaluation of the *sucre* on August 17, 1970. Despite fears of inflation and the threat of an uncontrolled wage and price spiral, the country's reserves climbed dramatically, reaching a record high of $61.3 million by October 1970.

One of the systemic obstacles to the formulation of rational socioeconomic policies was the dearth of adequate development planning. The institutionalization of planning had come in 1954 with the establishment of the *Junta Nacional de Planificación y Coordinación Económica.* It was responsible for the formulation of sectoral plans for the ten-year developmental program (1964-1973) required by terms of the Alliance for Progress, and subsequently drew up a revised plan for 1969-73. Targets were largely unrealistic and unrealizable; by 1969 not a single economic indicator had approached its stated goal. The planning process itself has been hampered by the proliferation of organs and agencies – Velasco was by no means the first political leader to find himself hamstrung by the multiplicity of overlapping bodies. Whether his dissolution and reconsolidation of various planning bodies following the 1970 *autogolpe* will encourage more rational developmental planning remains an unanswered question.

Such problems have contributed to a generalized inability to meet the growing pressures of social conditions which, as outlined in the first chapter, have become more urgent with the population expansion and migration from countryside to city. Social welfare policies have been of a short-run, ameliorative nature, and have not been effectively designed to mount a systematic assault on underlying problems. The turbulence of the political system has also served to undermine its capacity to develop meaningful policy in such areas as education, health, and housing. In relative terms, greater progress has been shown in education than in other fields of social policy. Thus, the past decade has shown progress on several important educational indicators. Notwithstanding the fact that the average Ecuadorean can still expect a mere three years of formal education, the literacy rate is now estimated at about 70 percent, the highest figure in history.

During the provisional government of Arosemena Gómez in 1967 a National Literacy Training Program was established, committed to the eradication of illiteracy within five years. While this goal was overly ambitious, nonetheless there has been a serious effort through adult education, for which students, teachers, and professionals have been recruited to staff the campaign. By the close of the decade some 3,000 centers had been founded through the country, and the program in its early years seemed relatively immune to the vicissitudes of national politics. UNESCO support helped to systematize the effort in its initial stages. Besides the literacy campaign, the number of teachers and classroom facilities have grown, although barely managing to keep pace with increased enrollment. The ministry of education reported, for instance, that there was a primary school enrollment of approximately 600,000 in 1960-61, with a teaching staff of 15,300. By 1968-69, enrollment had swollen to some 925,000, while there were 24,400 teachers. A further breakdown of primary school figures showed that enrollment in rural areas was nearly twice that of urban centers.

At a higher level, however, the pattern was different; such was the paucity of rural secondary education that the bulk of students for these grades were found in urban regions. Overall, the greatest progress during the 1960s lay in the secondary schools, where enrollment tripled, reaching a total in 1968-69 of 204,254 students. On the university plane, in no small part because of the political and politicizing elements discussed in chapter 3, the quality of education has not been improved measurably. Several loans from the Inter-American Development Bank have encouraged curricular reorganization and expansion, but the basic condition of university education continues in the same pattern.

The shortage of adequate housing is in some ways even more critical, and slum conditions in the urban centers are becoming rapidly more pronounced. Despite the 1961 creation of a national housing bank (*Banco Ecuatoriano de Vivienda* – BEV) to assist in financing for the lower income sectors, too little has been accomplished. From 1965 to 1969 the BEV invested capital in programs resulting in the construction of 6,915 units. Both then and now efforts are severely handicapped by a shortage of funds. In December of 1970 the Velasco government, in one of its major policy efforts, enacted an urban reform law. Through a combination of tax incentives, provision for unused urban property, and long-term payment arrangements for potential homeowners, the administration vowed to alter existing conditions. However, funds were still limited, administration was inexperienced in such matters, and continuing migration aggravated the situation. Substandard construction, property deterioration, and extreme overcrowding still remain typical of the urban areas. The misery of such conditions is pronounced.

Gross inequities and shortcomings also continue to characterize the realm of health and sanitation. In 1970 the ministry of public health reported infant mortality at 86.1 per 1,000 live births, and from 1966 to 1970 the general mortality rate was steady at some 10.8 per 1,000. Life expectancy was also constant throughout the decade, at fifty-five years of age. Tuberculosis, pneumonia, and a variety of gastro-intestinal and respiratory diseases have been the most common causes of death. The inadequacy of existing facilities is indicated by Ecuador's total of only 12,500 beds, a ratio of 2.3 per 1,000 inhabitants, among the lowest in all of Latin America. The ministry of public health, which was established only in 1964, has recently undertaken medical extension programs and is stressing the improvement of health services in rural areas. Moreover, a national health code was drawn up at the close of 1970. Once again, however, prospects for significant improvement of facilities are not good for the immediate future.

Municipal services have also been severely taxed by the growing urban population. By the start of 1970, only one-quarter of all Ecuadoreans were served by water systems; 62.1 percent of the urban residents had potable water, and only 6.3 percent in rural areas. Furthermore, only one-fifth of the population had sewerage service, 55 percent of the urban and less than 1 percent of the rural residents. Several water projects, as well as urban sewerage programs, were initiated in 1969, and improvements were undertaken in the cities of Riobamba, Loja, Esmeraldas, and Ibarra. By the close of 1970 several additional projects were underway in provincial urban centers, and the government was soliciting aid from other international agencies. In this social policy area as with others, the magnitude of environmental conditions further aggravated the difficulties of administrative weaknesses, political interference, and an absence of continuity. A lack of funds was also striking, and the possibility of funding programs adequately was dependent upon the modernization of the agricultural and industrial sectors.

Agricultural Realities and Reforms. The broad outlines of traditional rural life and agricultural practices were sketched in the opening chapter.[19] Again in the words of the Inter-American Development Bank, "lack of capital, backward technology, and traditional and institutional rigidities in the Ecuadorean agricultural sector explain in part why the country's land tenure system . . . has been dominated by a small number of owners, while the majority of rural people farm fragmented, small, uneconomical plots."[20] In 1968, the percentage of the work force engaged in agriculture stood at 53.7. Virtually three-fourths of the land holdings that year were under 12.3 acres in size, totaling but 15 percent of the cultivated area. At the other extreme, 45 percent of all cultivated farmland was in units larger than 1,235 acres, constituting but 0.2 percent of all such holdings. It was estimated that the agricultural contribution to gross domestic product that year was 31.6 percent, and per capita production had increased a scant 1.8 percent. For 1966-69, it had actually declined by 1.1 percent.

A closer inspection also shows that from 1962 through 1968 yields actually dropped in seven of the ten most important crops. Given an increase in the amount of land under cultivation during these years, it is evident that the very modest overall increase in productivity was not the result of technological improvement, agricultural modernization, or a more efficient and equitable land tenure system. At the close of the

[19] A careful and thoughtful treatment, although its data are no longer current, is José Ignacio Albuja Punina, *Estructura agraria y estructura social* (Quito: "Editorial Ecuatoriana," 1964).

[20] Inter-American Development Bank, *Socio-Economic Progress,* p. 211.

decade two of the three major export crops showed a decline in productivity. Both coffee and cocoa fell from 25 to 30 percent, and international market conditions also affected banana exports adversely. The only improvement was recorded for sugar, which in 1969 rose 17.8 percent over the previous year. Among products for domestic consumption, rice and barley provided bright spots, rising in 1969 by 85 percent and 45 percent respectively.

The future of banana exports in particular was increasingly uncertain as Ecuador entered the 1970s. As noted earlier, bananas bore limited economic importance to the country until 1948. In the next six years, however, acreage multiplied tenfold, from 37,000 to 370,000 acres. The easy availability of unoccupied government lands on favorable credit terms played a major role, as did concerted attention from international banana interests seeking a new source to supplement or supplant their Central American holdings. By 1957 bananas had become Ecuador's most valuable export crop, and they have retained this position ever since. Produced primarily by small landholders, three-fourths of whom own lands smaller than 250 acres, bananas by 1970 directly supported at least 75,000 families. Roughly two-thirds of Ecuador's foreign exchange is now earned by banana exports. By the close of the 1960s world consumption was nearly 15 million tons, almost one-quarter of which was produced in Ecuador. The government's heaviest direct tax – over 20 percent – was being levied on banana exports, contributing mightily to the degree of fiscal soundness which existed.

Despite the high productivity of past years, however, long-range prospects are increasingly uncertain. The predominant strain of bananas grown in Ecuador is the large Gros Michel banana, while a smaller variety – the Cavendish – has become more popular on many markets, especially the United States. North American housewives, lured by the advertising blandishments of "Chiquita Banana," have been buying the Cavendish with growing frequency. This strain, developed through United States technical assistance in Central America during the 1960s, now brings nearly twice the price as does the Gros Michel. Experts contend that barring a major switch to the Cavendish, Ecuador is doomed to a decreasing share of the international market. Yet at present there are some 5,000 producers of the Gros Michel variety and only around 200 raising the low, densely planted Cavendish.

Ecuadorean producers have argued that the Cavendish is far more expensive to produce. In addition, it requires more complex and technical cultivation and harvesting than does the Gros Michel. Necessary credit, technical assistance, and expert advice could not readily be extended to the many small banana producers. The government has taken no significant action as yet, and heavy concentration on the Gros Michel continues. Sales declined sharply during the early period of the fifth *velasquista* administration, dropping some 15 percent in 1969 from the previous year. In 1970 government emissaries sought to expand Ecuador's share of the British market, which until that time had been controlled in favor of Commonwealth producers. Sales rose slightly in 1971, but the feud between Velasco and a growing number of exporters boded ill for the immediate future. More importantly, however, the pressures from the Cavendish are ominous unless Ecuador basically reorients its production patterns.

Sugar cane has been perhaps the most promising agricultural commodity over the past decade, although very far indeed from matching the earnings of bananas. Traditionally grown for domestic consumption, sugar even at the start of the 1960s was barely able to meet internal needs. However, the 50,000 acres on the coast have become increasingly productive since that time. Cane is being grown on large plantations and is then processed in nearby refineries. New varieties of cane have been developed, and production has risen by nearly 50 percent. Improved methods of cultivation and the introduction of mechanization have been largely responsible for its emergence as an export commodity; the actual acreage being harvested has not grown significantly. Government policy has done little to encourage sugar, and export taxes have been levied more recently. A heavy tax on sugar exports in 1969 produced sharp criticism from the industry, and it remains the private sector which is working for further expansion of the sugar economy.

In terms of sources of revenue, then, the picture is mixed. Bananas earn considerable income, but its producers face the threat of the Cavendish; only sugar of the other export crops is thriving, and its share of the market is still essentially small. Recognition of such agricultural realities has led to the raising of agrarian reform as a potential means of increased productivity, higher earnings, and a sound agricultural structure in general. Efforts to alter the system of land tenure can be traced back many years, although frequently abortive in execution. At the close of the 1950s a special commission was named to draft a comprehensive document, and it was being readied when Velasco was ousted in 1961. Not until 1964 was a formal, comprehensive program finally inaugurated. On July 11 of that year the *Junta Militar* officially proclaimed the Agrarian Reform and Colonization Decree (no. 1480). With this act all previous legislation was superseded, and responsibility was vested in the *Instituto Ecuatoriano de Reforma Agraria y Colonización* (IERAC).

An autonomous organ, IERAC was assigned the following objectives: elimination of such land tenure abuses as *huasipungo,* improvement of agricultural wages, provision of credit and technical services, legalization of land titles; curtailment of absentee ownership, and colonization. The law provided for means of reversion of lands to the government, for expropriation under specific circumstances, and for empowering IERAC to intervene directly if justified by population and social conditions. Ceilings were established on the size of land holdings, varying among geographic regions and types of agricultural activity. At its inception IERAC sallied forth amid a blaze of publicity, and the military regime heavily propagandized its commitment to agrarian reform. Yet the early record proved most disappointing, owing in no small part to the succession of provisional governments which followed.[21]

Colonization projects received top priority, for their implementation did not strike directly at the interests of large landowners. Programs were centered primarily on the eastern slopes of the Andes and along the coastal plains. From 1965 through June 1970, almost 12,000 families received title to 415,000

[21]For an enthusiastic official report on the first year's accomplishments, see IERAC, *Síntesis de las labores realizadas por el I.E.R.A.C.* (Quito: IERAC, Oficina de Relaciones Públicas, 1965). A similarly effusive report on early accomplishments is Lincoln Larrea Benalcázar, *La comunicación en el proceso de la reforma agraria* (Quito: IERAC, 1966 [?]).

hectares of land (see Table 13). In the first six months of 1970, 1,491 families received 50,128 hectares of land, the vast majority of which resulted from the colonization program (1,186 families with 47,162 hectares). Overall, during its initial five years IERAC had benefitted 40,000 families; this included final land titles for 15,821 families; provisional titles to 1,088 families; and the settling of 20,073 families through the removal of disputed tenure. IERAC also aided in the development of agricultural cooperatives, which numbered 930 by the start of 1970 with a membership of some 25,000.

As the six-month figures suggest, the emphasis on colonization was much greater in 1970 than before; this came in part from growing political controversy swirling about IERAC. President Velasco had set his sights on the agency soon after his inauguration, maintaining a steady stream of criticism and invective. Resentful of his inability to control IERAC, he early determined that it was foremost among the agencies over which executive control was required. As originally organized, the IERAC Board of Directors was a nine-man body, only three of whose members were cabinet ministers. The remaining six were beyond the reach of the president, including four directors elected by the *sierra* and *costa* chambers of agriculture. Thus the administration held minority representation in the directorate, which exercised overall responsibility for agrarian policy.

Velasco himself was typically vague as to his own policy preferences in the agricultural sphere. Whatever his intentions toward IERAC as an instrument for reform and modernization, Velasco's hands were tied by the agricultural pressure groups which dominated its directorate. In late 1969 the president pressed for organizational revisions, and ultimately secured authorization from the legislative branch. As decreed on February of 1970, the IERAC directorate was reconstituted, with five of its nine members government appointees. Moreover, the agency was stripped of its autonomous status and was made directly responsible to the minister of agriculture.[22] Thus the executive for the first time had gained control of IERAC, and Velasco soon moved to establish even more firmly his personal dominion.

In September of 1970 during an unannounced personal visit to IERAC offices, the president excoriated its bureaucrats

Table 13
AGRARIAN REFORM AND COLONIZATION

Year	*AGRARIAN REFORM* Families	Land	*COLONIZATION* Families	Land
1964	831	2,194	728	17,614
1965	12,617	56,614	2,686	97,821
1966	4,712	26,795	2,708	92,123
1967	4,452	25,154	1,567	58,416
1968	1,884	20,983	1,408	43,043
1969	3,463	20,736	1,525	59,623
1970*	305	2,966	1,186	47,162
TOTALS	28,264	155,442	11,808	415,802

Source: Official IERAC report, November 1970.
Land area is listed in hectares. Asterisk (*) for 1970 indicates these figures cover only the first six months of the year.

and announced further internal reorganization. Three days later, on the 12th, no fewer than 770 functionaries presented their forced resignations, and Velasco announced that few would be replaced. With the economic pressures and political troubles which had accumulated at this point, the president's attention was soon diverted. By 1971 activity had nearly ground to a halt, with little likelihood that significant policy output would be forthcoming in the agricultural sector for the remainder of the *velasquista* administration. The history of agrarian reform in Ecuador therefore stood as one of effusive public pronouncements but limited accomplishment. It had done little for the vast majority of the rural populace, land tenure practices were not greatly changed, and overall agricultural productivity had not grown significantly. For the moment, it remained the industrial sector which promised the greatest likelihood of revising fundamentally the traditional economic structure.

Industrial Growth and Subsoil Resources. The contributions of industry to the national economy through the years have been consistently small. Given the essentially agricultural pattern of economic history, the industrial sector has constituted a smaller element in Ecuador. In 1955 industry accounted for 21.6 percent, of the gross domestic product; by 1962 it was only slightly higher at 23 percent, and in the period from 1965 to 1969 the average annual real growth rate for industry was 3.8 percent, lower than the figure for the economy at large. The proportion of the labor force actively engaged in industry is lower today than it was twenty years ago, and for the years 1966-69 Ecuador's growth rate in manufacturing production was well beneath the 7.2 percent average for all of Latin America. Regional comparisons also showed that in total manufacturing output for Latin America from 1966 to 1969, Ecuador's share was less than 1 percent.

Such unimpressive figures, however, misleadingly shroud renewed activity within the industrial sector. The opening of textile and other plants has brought a marked shift to factory production from artisans and cottage industry, and the average productivity per worker has consequently increased significantly. The textile industry now ranks second only to foodstuffs in productive value. Concentrated in the highlands, where they originated with individual and family weaving, textile plants have increased in number and size. Nonetheless, much of this production remains in small shops employing only a dozen or fewer workers. There has been some additional expansion in the production of foodstuffs and in such other items as beverages, cigarettes, and wood products. With the rate of imports on the rise for several years, there has been a concomitant shift in the structure of manufacturing, as consumer goods are being displaced in part by intermediate and capital goods.

Such manufactured goods as fish products, processed sugar, and pharmaceuticals are assuming greater importance for the export trade. From 1961 through 1967 the export of manufactured goods trebled in comparison with total exports, constituting 12.5 percent of that total in 1967 as compared with 6.8 percent in 1961. The development of light industry is now seen in moderately optimistic terms, and the rising *quiteño* modernizing business elite has joined with coastal interests in reinforcing such trends. Despite glowing government statements about industrial development, however, little real impetus has come from official sources. Although industrial development laws in 1957, 1962, 1964, and 1967 announced extensions of tariff protection and tax incentives to new and incipient industries, there has been a shortage of both expertise and capital. To a considerable degree the energy and activity which does exist has come from the private sector in Guayaquil, Quito, and Cuenca.

Support has come from the Inter-American Development

Bank for several developmental projects. Three loans in late 1969 totaled $7.5 million; $6 million were for credits to finance industrial, fishing, and tourist development, while an additional $1.5 million was destined for the so-called "pre-investment" fund. Channeled through the *Comisión de Valores – Corporación Financiera Nacional* (CV-CFN), these funds represented 53 percent of the government's developmental program of $14.1 million. Emphasis was to be placed on the expansion of chemical, lumber, food, nonmetallic minerals, and machine metal industries. The obvious hope was for the providing of seed-money which would impel industrial development and diversification. However, this was unlikely to alter the economy fundamentally, and the rapid transformation which is now greatly anticipated rests upon the discovery of subsoil deposits of petroleum and copper.

Prior to 1964, exploitable quantities of petroleum were limited. Anglo-Ecuadorian Oilfields, Ltd., had arrived in 1917 and became the major exploiter of existing holdings, accounting for some 85 percent of crude oil production by 1963. Although exploration of the *oriente* had begun in 1937, the initial search was unrewarding, and most exploitable resources were presumably centered on the coast, largely on the Santa Elena Peninsula. The number of wells in production declined by more than 20 percent from 1955 to 1963, at which time 1,135 wells had a daily average of 6,750 barrels, or only 5.9 barrels daily per well.[22] National consumption of petroleum products had increased substantially but production continued to drop, while a decreasing number of workers were employed in petroleum. The limited development had been largely the result of foreign capital, with private Ecuadorean sources having participated only marginally. However, the entire picture was radically changed with the discovery of extensive subsoil deposits in the *oriente* in the 1960s.

In March of 1964 the *Junta Militar* signed a five-year exploration contract with the Gulf-Texaco Oil Company. In the original concession this consortium received rights to 3.6 mil-

[22]Alianza para el Progreso, Comite de los Nueve, *Evaluación del plan general de desarrollo económico y social del Ecuador* (Washington: Alianza para el Progreso, 1964), p. 305.

lion acres in the Napo region of northeastern Ecuador, and an estimated $44 million was invested in the five years. Fourteen of the fifteen wells drilled produced commercially marketable petroleum, and the company estimated that once transportation facilities were improved, production would reach at least 14,000 barrels daily. The agreement included an automatic three-year renewal option, and Gulf-Texaco announced its readiness to invest an additional $200 million during that time. It further proposed that the oil be shipped abroad through a fourteen-mile feeder line costing $2 million, which would connect with the larger trans-Andean pipeline at the Colombia frontier. By this time, however, the *Junta Militar* had long since disappeared, and as the renewal date approached, President Velasco announced that major contractual revisions would be required.

In addition to a renegotiated contract stipulating higher royalty payments, the government also demanded the construction of a pipeline directly from the *oriente* to the Ecuadorean coast, which the consortium retorted would cost $100 million and ten years to complete. Following intensive negotiations during which Velasco sought to drive a hard and vocally nationalistic bargain, a new agreement was signed in July of 1969. To begin with, two-thirds of the original concession reverted to the government; Gulf-Texaco was left with 1.2 million of the original 3.6 million acres for exploitation. Royalty payments were increased from 6 to 11.5 percent; the company also paid an advance of $6 million on royalties and another $5 million for rights to the concession. Included in the revised contract was a commitment by the consortium to spend approximately $35 million for a network of roads and a jungle airport. For the long run, it was estimated that as much as $300 million would be spent or invested in Ecuador by the close of the century.

A point of major dispute revolved about the pipeline issue.[23] For the government, it was a matter of national pride that the oil be pumped across Ecuador and exported directly from the coast. More than nationalistic sentiment alone was involved, however, for the most logical coastal outlet, Esmer-

[23]For a brief discussion of alternatives for the pipeline, see Juan E. Rassmus, "Oil Development Starts in Ecuador's Amazon Basin," *World Petroleum*, Vol. 39, No. 1 (January 1968), 50-52.

aldas, would obviously be a major beneficiary of any such pipeline and necessary port facilities. At the same time, the conflict was compounded by the concern of *guayaquileños* that the result would be the creation of a possible future rival to its coastal supremacy. Gulf-Texaco, in contrast, preferred the much cheaper and more readily available feeder line connecting with Colombia. Eventually a compromise was reached. The consortium agreed to construct a pipeline from the *oriente* to Esmeraldas, with a minimum capacity of 250,000 barrels daily. Completion was scheduled for the close of 1972; in the meantime, the spur line with a 30,000-barrel daily capacity would provide a link to the trans-Andean line at the border with Colombia.

Early success has been substantial. At the outset, Gulf-Texaco estimated that exploitable reserves might be in excess of 1 billion barrels, with a realistic capacity of 200,000 barrels daily.[24] Moreover, much of the oil appeared to be largely sulphur-free, unlike Venezuelan petroleum. Given the magnitude of reserves, other foreign oil companies have been attracted to Ecuador. The government, having reclaimed much of the territory originally ceded to the consortium, has been eager to proceed. Within a year of the renewal with Gulf-Texaco an additional eight agreements were signed, and there was a scramble for exploitative rights in an area estimated at no less than 5 million acres. A contract was also signed for rights in Manabí and Esmeraldas, while off-shore drilling along the Guayas coast searched for deposits of natural gas.

For Ecuadoreans, these developments seemed to herald the coming of a new era in national life. Income from the initial investment rapidly infused a shot of adrenalin into the economy, and the mood of the early 1970s reflected expectations of an impending bonanza, one which would provide a magical panacea to socioeconomic development and national modernization. While the potential of some 200,000 barrels daily was dwarfed by Venezuela's daily average of 3.7 million barrels, it nonetheless promised a great boon. Following scheduled completion of the pipeline to Esmeraldas in December of 1972, some $70 million annually in foreign exchange was underway in

[24]By way of comparison, in the first half of 1969 Mexico averaged a daily production of some 455,000 barrels.

1970, with the final cost calculated at $140 million. More than a thousand men were engaged in the task, which required the crossing of terrain as high as 13,000 feet.

Even prior to the opening of the pipeline, increased foreign investment was entering the country. By the close of 1970 more than thirty wells had been drilled by Gulf-Texaco alone, with a daily output of 32,000 barrels. The following year the Ministry of Natural Resources announced that a total of fifty-seven wells had been drilled in the *oriente,* and daily production had reached 47,471 barrels. The Ministry also indicated the government's intention of building a state oil refinery which would process up to 32,000 barrels. A trade mission from Czechoslovakia in early 1971 also arrived to investigate the possibility of installing oil refineries. At the same time the International Bank for Reconstruction and Development (IBRD) estimated that the development of petroleum would assist the balance of payments by more than $25 million annually from 1970 to 1972.[25]

There were, to be sure, warnings about the utilization of petroleum revenue. The same IBRD report contended that if government expenditure grew more than 6 to 7 percent annually, public investments would diminish and the inflow of capital would fall. Nonetheless, the Velasco administration spoke frequently of an economic transformation before the middle of the 1970s, and official planning increasingly made assumptions based on anticipated oil revenues.[26] Both economic and political ramifications were underlined even more vividly with news of copper deposits in the southwestern Andes not far from Cuenca. Although a concession for copper production had been issued in 1937 for a site in Cotopaxi province, the enterprise had not proven profitable, and copper mining had virtually disappeared after World War II. However, a team of United Nations geologists uncovered potentially vast quantities in Chaucha, and estimates ran as high as 100 million tons of copper.

This led to the signing in June 1970 of a four-year contract for mining rights between the government and the Over-

[25]Bank of London & South America, *Review,* Vol. 5, No. 53 (May 1971), p. 293.

[26]A sober if generally optimistic assessment of both the promise and peril of oil revenues for Ecuadorean life appears in Blasco Peñaherrera, "Ecuador petrolero; esperanzas y peligros en una nueva era de la economía nacional," *Vistazo* (Guayaquil), Vol. 14, No. 165 (febrero 1971), 10-14.

seas Mineral Development Company, a Japanese firm composed of both public and private interests. The company received rights to 76,500 acres, with the copper to be smelted in Ecuador and marketed in Japan. The Japanese firm agreed to invest $5 million during the life of the contract. Following an initial survey, the company expected to construct the roads necessary for transporting the copper to the sea. Under the agreement, the government will participate in administrative operations. In addition to receiving 55 percent of the net profit, it will receive royalties of some 7.5 percent of gross production, based on a sliding price scale derived from the ore content. Initially unnoticed in the heady excitement over petroleum income, it is now recognized that the impact from copper is also potentially lucrative. Should both petroleum and copper production meet early expectations, the implications for Ecuador's future would be far-reaching. Furthermore, the political ramifications of massive foreign investment would presage a degree of dependency on external forces which carries with it unforeseen, and possible untoward, consequences.

6
Dependency, Nationalism, and Regionalism

In their rising demands for socioeconomic progress and a better life, the people of Ecuador are becoming increasingly imbued with the spirit of nationalism endemic to the developing areas. The growing middle class constitutes a sector with growing potential for political involvement, while the uneducated and impoverished masses as well would provide a powerful force were they to be mobilized. Nationalistic desires for independence, progress, and modernization are such that even the most internationally oriented economic elites may well find themselves caught up in a tide of assertive national pride. The developmental process in Ecuador may also assume more explosive proportions than are now visible, especially in view of growing concern over economic dependency. The reliance on external agents, particularly the United States, represents a source for both resentment and animosity. Moreover, the vistas opening up through the exploitation of petroleum and possibly copper may well serve to exaggerate existing nationalistic attitudes.

A growing school of writers in both Latin and North America is articulating views on both external and internal dependency. In terms of international relations and the developmental process, proponents of the dependency thesis hold that underdevelopment is the result of colonialist relations with the developed countries of the world. For Ecuador the nature of such relations with the United States is substantial, for the impact of North American policy on Ecuadorean society and politics – whatever the reasons or justifications – can only grow in the immediate future. Economic penetration by United States interests may well support a strengthening of the domestic colonialism of Ecuadorean elites; thus so-called local oligarchs may themselves contribute to the maintenance of both external and domestic dependency relationships.

A North American political scientist recently described at length a dependency model for the hemisphere as one in which Latin American domestic development has been limited or conditioned by the needs of dominant economies within the world market. Consequently, "growth in the dependent nations occurs as a reflex of the expansion of the dominant nations, and is geared toward the needs of the dominant economies – i.e., foreign rather than national needs."[1] Dependency means, moreover, that the developmental alternatives open to a dependent nation are defined by the degree of integration into the world market. For Ecuador, such arguments bear considerable persuasiveness, first when bananas became the major economic support for the national economy, and now with the anticipated income from oil and copper. Discovery of the latter natural resources has therefore brought forth dramatically the harbingers of a future in which Ecuador's relations with the United States may be even more central to domestic affairs as well as international politics.

FOREIGN POLICY AND NATIONALISM

Until recent times Ecuador's foreign policy has followed traditional patterns of a state militarily and economically weaker than its surrounding neighbors. Historically Ecuador's major concern has therefore been its defense of territorial integrity against Latin American neighbors. This cornerstone of foreign policy was long maintained through a succession of confrontations with Colombia, Brazil, and Peru. Each of these neighbors has imposed its greater power on Ecuador, and a

[1] Susanne Bodenheimer, "Dependency and Imperialism: The Roots of Latin American Underdevelopment," *Politics and Society*, Vol. 1, No. 3 (May 1971), 331-32.

series of disputes have been concluded by Ecuador's loss of territory. In the last few years the major focus of Ecuadorean foreign policy has shifted in the direction of the United States. Even so, however, traditional relationships with Latin America continue to provide the backdrop for an understanding of the country's foreign policy.[2]

Relations with Latin America. Within the context of history, Ecuadorean foreign policy has hinged until recently on a festering dispute with Peru. A military invasion by the Peruvians in July 1941 and the subsequent acquisition of territory in southern Ecuador created a state of acrimony which only today appears to be receding. In the wake of that military action a Protocol of Peace, Friendship, and Boundaries was signed with Peru. Popularly known as the Rio Protocol, it was guaranteed by Argentina, Brazil, Chile, and the United States. The Protocol was signed under considerable duress by the Arroyo government, but its validity was explicitly accepted in 1944 by the Velasco administration which followed. Subsequently, the mapping of the revised border revealed the nonexistence of a river demarcation which complicated the terms of the boundary demarcation. Ecuador, reiterating its determined claims of remaining an "Amazonian country," pressed with renewed vigor for a reopening of the entire issue.

In August of 1951 President Plaza announced his refusal to accept a conclusive boundary settlement with Peru unless Ecuador received an outlet to the Marañón–Amazon river network. Velasco further stoked the fires of controversy during his 1952 presidential campaign, and soon after taking office broke diplomatic relations with Peru. The issue abated somewhat during the Ponce administration but flared anew after Velasco's 1960 reelection. On September 28, 1960, his foreign minister announced Ecuador's official nullification of the Protocol before the United Nations General Assembly. Shortly thereafter the Supreme Court of Justice declared:

[2] A review of territorial questions coming up to 1940 appears in Jorge Pérez Concha, *Ensays histórico-crítico de las relaciones diplomáticas del Ecuador con los estados limitrofes,* 2 vols. (Quito: Editorial Casa de la Cultural Ecuatoriana, 1961 and 1964).

A compendium of diplomatic agreements through 1960 is Antonio Bustamante Munoz, *Lista de los instrumentos internacionales concluídos por el Ecuador* (Quito: Editorial Casa de la Cultura Ecuatoriana, 1960).

. . . the absolute nullity of the Rio Protocol is an incontrovertible thesis of a scientific and juridical value and a matter which originates a problem of life and death for Ecuadorean nationhood. . . . The hour has arrived to determine whether enlightened international opinion will tolerate triumphs of force, whether Pan-Americanism is only an empty and fantastic dream, or if it is, in reality, a body of principles, flesh of our flesh and blood of our American blood for the reign of justice and morality in the life of nations.

Since 1960 Ecuador has fervently maintained the thesis of nullity. Arguing fundamentally that its territory was seized by dint of armed aggression and that acceptance of the Protocol of 1942 reflected hemispheric pressure on a government which by then had lost its right to legitimacy, Ecuador has demanded a reopening of the entire question. The Peruvian response has been reiteration of the Protocol as a valid international agreement, and governments in Lima have refused to reopen the matter. This impasse helped to block the convening of the Eleventh Inter-American Conference scheduled for Quito in 1960 but never held. Despite a general hemispheric unwillingness to reconsider the matter, Ecuadorean governments insisted upon the thesis of nullity. A characteristic declaration was issued by the Constituent Assembly during 1966 which affirmed the nullity of the Protocol. Thus the agreement,

. . . being an instrument in violation of the norms of American International Law and of the most elemental conditions of international coexistence, is indisputably a null institute. . . Ecuador proclaims its respect for treaties freely arrived at, but it cannot accept an instrument in violation of law, whose very clauses leave standing the illegitimate occupation of the territory of a State through the use of military force. . . .[3]

By the close of the decade, however, the dispute became less central to Ecuadorean foreign policy. Politicians even today pay lip service to the thesis of nullity, but it no longer receives the attention it once did, and there is greater concern with other matters. Moreover, there is an awareness that as a practical matter little can be done. Peru is not about to accept a renegotiation of the entire dispute, and other Latin American countries prefer to forget the controversy, whatever the injus-

[3] *El Año Ecuatoriano 1966* (Quito: Editorial Santo Domingo, 1967), p. 103.

tice committed three decades ago. Relations between the two neighbors are presently more cordial than they have been in many years. Should there be a fresh dispute, the Protocol would doubtless be raised again. Otherwise, the likelihood is decreasing attention to the dispute by Ecuadorean leaders. Rather, interest in economic progress has drawn greater attention to the burgeoning Andean Pact. The possible economic benefits are clearly more salient than the futility of the nullity argument over territory which is largely uninhabited and does not have any readily apparent economic value.

The Andean Subregional Integration Agreement (Andean Pact) was signed at Cartagena, Colombia, on May 25, 1969, by Ecuador, Colombia, Peru, Bolivia, and Chile.[4] Its major objectives were delineated as: (a) the polling of resources and coordination of subregional economic development; (b) promotion of accelerated growth by means of economic integration; (c) facilitation of intraregional trade; and (d) improvement of subregional participation in the broader Latin American Free Trade Association (LAFTA). Creation of the Andean Pact sought to increase the tempo of economic cooperation among member states in the face of only modest LAFTA progress, as well as helping to provide a counterweight against such dominant countries as Argentina, Brazil, and Chile. During its present formative period the Pact has concentrated on trade liberalization and foreign investment policy.

A special commission was created as the institutional framework for trade liberalization. In April 1970 the five member states agreed on removal of all tariffs and other import restrictions among one another for a long list of products, especially a host of agricultural goods. Chile, Columbia, and Peru were to meet the commitment at once, while the more underdeveloped economies of Ecuador and Bolivia had until the close of 1973 to comply. As for investment policy, the membership agreed on a set of common rules affecting foreign investment in a document considered during a December 1970 meeting. At

[4] It was intended that Venezuela would also join, and a variety of measures have been adopted to make this possible. The question has been debated in Venezuela since the 1968 presidential campaign, at which time the subsequent victor, Rafael Caldera, endorsed Venezuelan membership. The reluctance of influential business interests, however, is such that as of late 1971 the Venezuelans remained outside the Andean Pact.

the outset the left-of-center governments of Chile, Peru, and Bolivia maintained a strongly nationalistic posture, while Ecuador and Colombia preferred a more traditional attitude toward foreign capital. The potential impasse was ultimately circumvented, with Colombia accepting the principle that foreign companies should ultimately revert to local ownership, a position to which Ecuador also acceded.

Members of the Pact defined foreign-owned companies as those with more than 50 percent foreign shareholding. These enterprises were prohibited from employing local sources of credit except under critical circumstances. New firms seeking entry into the subregion would be required to sign agreements within three years establishing *compañías mixtas,* or joint ventures. These would require investors to deliver at least 51 percent of their share capital to nationals within fifteen years in Chile, Peru, and Colombia; twenty years would be permitted to Ecuador and Bolivia. Moreover, new foreign companies could be established before 1980 in the mining and petroleum sectors, but no concessions could be granted for longer than twenty years. Ecuador's economic elite, initially somewhat distrustful of the implications of membership, has grown more enthusiastic about developmental prospects, and it is the private sector more than the government which has taken the initiative. In 1971 the trade among the five member states was but 5 percent of the total subregional export trade; thus the potential for expansion is substantial.

Relations with the United States. Where Ecuador's dealings with its immediate neighbors has been marked by greater cordiality, the relationship with the United States has grown somewhat unsettled. Popular resentment of North American policy has become more evident, ranging from Quito street demonstrations in 1960 – when the United States joined other guarantors of the Rio Protocol to deny Ecuador's claims for the thesis of nullity – to Esmeraldas street graffiti in 1969 charging a local Peace Corps volunteer with being an agent of the Central Intelligence Agency. Moreover, the political leadership has not been immune to the instrumental values of nationalism, and has shown a growing proclivity to intersperse public statements with criticisms of U.S. positions. The issues have varied, but criticisms have been explicit.

It was under Presidents Velasco and Arosemena Monroy in the early 1960s that the present trend became manifest, owing in no small part to Ecuadorean interest in the Cuban revolution and disapproval of United States policy toward the Castro government. Tensions were exacerbated during the provisional administration of Otto Arosemena Gómez, and first drew wide attention with the 1967 conference of hemispheric presidents in Punta del Este, Uruguay. Arosemena, the youngest chief of state in attendance, was also the only one who refused to sign its final declaration. In his speech at Punta del Este on April 13 the president cited a host of reasons for not signing; privately he also indicated dismay that, instead of a presidential dialogue at the conference, a virtual ratification of already-drafted North American proposals was expected.[5] Arosemena said in part:

> We Ecuadoreans believe and know that 300,000 Latin Americans share in what we have expressed. That will suffice. If the sentiment and thinking of those men, women, aged people and children is not heard today, there will be resounding consequences one day. My faith, the faith and hope of my people is that of arriving at the heart and the conscience of those who today lead the world in order that they fully recognize the deep sense of those who cry, with reason and with justice, for the reclamation of the advent of a more human life, dignified by the full exercise of law, in an atmosphere of peace and harmony.[6]

Arosemena's refusal to sign the final document caused North American consternation, but provoked a wave of popular approval in much of Latin America, not to mention Ecuador itself.[7] Without questioning the honesty of Arosemena's motives, it is also unlikely that he was unaware of the enthusiasm engendered by his action. In tweaking the whiskers of Uncle Sam, he assured himself greater and more favorable recognition among Ecuadoreans. This was further heightened later in the year by his expulsion of the North American ambassador to

[5] Interviewed by the author in July 1969, Dr. Arosemena reiterated his admiration for the people of the United States and his respect for Lyndon B. Johnson, but also decried Washington's consistent unwillingness to discuss socioeconomic needs of Latin America on a basis of equality, particularly at the Punta del Este meeting.

[6] Otto Arosemena Gómez, *Discurso de Punta del Este* (Quito: n.d.), p. 3.

[7] The author, traveling in the region at the time, read enthusiastic editorial approval of Arosemena's position in Santiago and Lima, as well as in the Ecuadorean press.

Quito. In the months following Punta del Este, Arosemena had been increasingly critical of the Alliance for Progress, while North American officials were increasingly irritated. In Ecuador U.S. Ambassador Wymberley Coerr, a career foreign service officer, protested both privately and publicly.

In early October the president had attacked the functioning of the Alliance in a speech, charging additionally that U.S. aid to Ecuador was customarily subject to interminable negotiations, and that Ecuador was obligated to buy materials from the United States at inflated prices. Speaking shortly thereafter at the *Colegio Americano* in Guayaquil, Ambassador Coerr responded by calling such criticisms "destructive." The president immediately retaliated by ordering Coerr's expulsion within forty-eight hours, virtually unprecedented in U.S.–Latin American relations. Ecuadorean public opinion was largely approving, sharing Arosemena's view that Coerr had been imprudently overstepping diplomatic bounds in what was regarded as interference in internal affairs. While the cynical view again held that Arosemena was motivated by strengthening his visibility before leaving the provisional presidency, there is little doubt that he was genuinely angered by statements he viewed as uncalled-for.

With the inauguration of Velasco in 1968 there was a temporary hiatus in diplomatic tensions, but this was short-lived as a consequence of growing controversy over a question of hard economic importance — the undersea resources of offshore waters. Conflict had been mounting for some time between the United States and Pacific maritime countries over fishing rights and the two-hundred-mile limit. Ecuador's oceanic waters have abundant resources as far west as the Galápagos Islands, including tuna, mackerel, sailfish, sea bass, shrimp, sardines, and anchovies. A few large commercial enterprises operate out of Ecuadorean ports, while an estimated 10,000 small fishermen also ply the coast close to the beaches. With activity on the upswing, the total catch has more than doubled in the last ten years. Ecuador, along with several of its neighbors, claims territorial jurisdiction a distance of two hundred miles from shore. Vessels with foreign registration are permitted to fish these waters once a licensing fee is paid, and an annual renewal is required. Non-Ecuadorean fishing fleets have often ignored these requirements, however, and have been supported by official U.S. insistence on a twelve-mile limit to territorial waters.

The controversy had already worsened relations between Peru and the United States when Ecuador became seriously involved in 1970. A few months earlier a conference in Buenos Aires including Ecuador, Peru, Chile, and the United States had failed to reach a solution on territorial waters. The conferees had skirted the issue while discussing collaboration on the conservation of marine resources. Then in January of 1970 the three Latin American countries renewed their claims of jurisdiction for two hundred miles; diplomatic exchanges were inconclusive and the Ecuadorean navy began to arrest and fine foreign-owned tuna fishing boats. Ten boats sailing out of southern California were taken into custody in early January of 1971 and, after brief protest, Washington announced the suspension of arms sales to Ecuador for one year, amounting to some $800,000. A wave of anger swept Ecuador immediately, and President Velasco announced that arrests would continue until the principle of two-hundred-mile jurisdiction was accepted.

Nationalistic ire was strong, as suggested by the following editorial – one of many – which appeared in Quito's *El Comercio.*

> By denouncing Ecuador, the Pentagon (military headquarters of the United States) as well as the Soviet Union – both with powerful navy fleets – consider the 200-mile claim by several American countries, and possibly nations of other continents, a military danger.
>
> Great naval, political and economic interests are at play and are functioning not only in the form of the fishing companies' plans and ambitions, but also in the plans and proposals involved in hegemony and universal domination, so that the powers carelessly have a dispute in territorial sovereignty with the smaller countries.[8]

Tempers flared in the United States as well where, despite efforts by the State Department, the union of fishermen called for a boycott of Ecuadorean products if the fishing dispute were not resolved in favor of its constituency. As Ecuador assumed its role as defender of hemispheric claims on the dispute, Latin American support was staunch. *El Mercurio* of Santiago, Chile, denounced the suspension of U.S. military aid as

[8] As quoted in *The Times of the Americas* (Washington), February 10, 1971, p. 6.

unjust economic pressure, while *El Espectador* of Bogotá, Colombia, denounced the California ships as "pirates" disrespectful of small states. In Quito, President Velasco decried the international moral crisis "in which the rights of small countries are not respected, in which the strong believe they are authorized to impose on the weak all the caprices they can imagine."

Ecuador was unwavering in its policy of arresting and fining violators; somewhat ironically, their naval fleet included ships previously received on loan from the United States. From January to May of 1971 twenty-six United States vessels were seized, and North American tuna boat owners had paid $1.3 million in fines (all refunded by Washington).[9] Positions hardened in both Washington and in Latin American capitals, as parties to the dispute insisted upon essentially irreconcilable positions. United States policy preferred to set aside the legal question over a two-hundred-mile sea, vainly hopeful that an international conference on the law of the seas in 1973 might resolve the question. The Latin American states, including Ecuador, regarded the fish as a natural resource and, consequently, as requiring regulation and acceptance of the two-hundred-mile limit.

For Ecuador, the tuna catch in particular was becoming increasingly lucrative. Tuna, a migratory fish appearing off the Ecuadorean coast from January to April, was valued up to $10 million annually by the start of the 1970s, with a potential factory value of $50 million. Ecuador also hoped that with the addition of modern, refrigerated ships which could go further than the customary twenty-five to thirty miles, income from fishing would be increasingly profitable. By mid-1971 the controversy continued unabated, while the verbal debate shifted toward ecological and conservationist concerns. Ecuador's ambassador to the United States, Carlos Mantilla Ortega,[10] undertook to explain his country's position. Holding that the two-hundred-mile limit constituted the "biological boundary" of the offshore Humboldt Current, Mantilla explained that the purse-seining method of fishing was wasteful and destructive of

[9] According to U.S. law, the government is to recover the cost of reimbursement by deducting the amount from foreign aid to the country involved.

[10] The ambassador is a scion of the Mantilla family, which founded Quito's leading daily *El Comercio* in 1906 and has published it ever since.

undersea life. In using massive nets which sweep through the ocean, a wide variety of marine life is caught, with the tuna retained and the remainder — often dead — returned to the seas. This affront to conservation, in his view, was fundamental to the controversy, although North American opponents denied his charges.

An additional argument used by Ecuador and other Latin Americans has held that in a literal sense the bounties of the sea are indeed national resources within the two-hundred-mile limit. Minerals wash into the ocean from mountain streams; these nourish the plankton; and from there the food chain extends all the way to the tuna itself. Thus, as Mantilla argued repeatedly before North American audiences, reasons for defending the two-hundred mile limit were "scientific and technological. We have been doing research into fishing for many years. We know that if the wasteful methods used by [North] American fishermen are allowed to go on, the fish will eventually disappear."[11] Thus the controversy has continued, with battle lines drawn out on grounds of conservation as well as of national interest, international law, and economic reward. Despite the possibility of occasional quiescence, the dispute will unquestionably continue; whether heated or muted, it is unlikely to be resolved soon, even notwithstanding the 1973 conference to discuss precisely such matters. Thus the issue stands as divisive between Ecuador and the United States, and legitimate nationalistic interests as well as self-serving political propagandizing can be expected to capitalize on the disagreement.

A recent development which may further provide an augury of future trends is the growing willingness to deal with the communist world, a phenomenon also found in other Latin American countries. Growing nationalism and a sense of the necessity of asserting independence in the face of the sometimes smothering North American presence, along with the possibility of unalloyed economic benefit, have all merged into a willingness to deal with the communist countries. Ecuador had maintained an explicitly anticommunist stance in its postwar foreign policy; this first shifted perceptibly in 1960 when Velasco pursued proper if not unsympathetic exchanges with the Castro

[11]As quoted in *The Times of the Americas* (Washington), May 12, 1971, p. 5.

regime. Moreover, his vice-president had visited Moscow and, following Velasco's ouster and his own assumption of the presidency, encouraged contacts with both Cuba and Eastern Europe until military pressure forced its suspension. Yet the virulent anticommunism of past years, supported by a nervously defensive military establishment, has diminished in more recent years.

When Velasco returned to office in 1968, he indicated a renewed willingness to open relations with the communist world. In May 1970 he accepted Ivan Ivanovich Wartchaik as Soviet ambassador to Ecuador, while sending socialist intellectual and educator Juan Isaac Lovato to Moscow. Within the year a pair of Ecuadorean-Soviet Friendship Institutes were opened, one in Quito and another in Guayaquil, while scholarships for study in communist countries were made available. The Velasco government was amenable to the possibility of economic exchanges and watched with interest the Peruvian "opening to the left" toward Eastern European governments. Receptive to ties which might prove economically beneficial, Ecuador is aware that such moves not only run contrary to North American policy preferences but, even more importantly, represent a clear manifestation of national independence and sovereignty.

DOMESTIC COLONIALISM AND REGIONALISM

In contrasting views of internal colonialism with those of external dependency, an eminent Mexican educator and political sociologist has observed that "there exists, in effect, a monopoly in exploiting natural resources, work, the import-export trade, and fiscal revenues. . . . The dominant country monopolizes the colony, and prevents other countries from exploiting its natural and human resources. This monopolization is extended to mass culture and to the sources of information."[12] Consequently, there is a form of internal dependency also characterized by a relationship of domination and exploitation.

[12]Pablo Gonzalez-Casanova, "Internal Colonialism and National Development," in Irving Louis Horowitz, Josué de Castro, and John Gerassi (eds.), *Latin American Radicalism; A Documentary Report on Left and Nationalist Movements* (New York: Random House, Inc., 1969), p. 125.

Customarily this is structured about a rural-urban dichotomy; thus there will be exploitation of the colonized rural sector by the colonial urban elite. This condition of domestic dependency parallels that of external relationships, providing additional undergirding for extremely uneven development. "The laws of the market and the scarce political participation and organization in subdeveloped zones simultaneously serve to maintain a 'dynamic of inequality' and prevent the processes of egalitarianism characteristic of development from emerging."[13]

Regionalism – Disruptive or Modernizing? Within the Ecuadorean context there are manifest signs of such domestic dependency. At present the relative domination of Quito and Guayaquil retains overriding importance, with at least 75 percent of industrial enterprises and the greatest proportion of business and modern services. The economic elites, perhaps best represented in a corporate sense by the chambers of commerce and industry, continue to control those potentially modernizing elements introduced – especially in Guayaquil – early in the twentieth century. Moreover, they have continued to play a central role in political life, operating where possible behind the scenes but emerging publicly at times of crisis. Such groups represent a clientele insofar as it is tied to the international system, acting as junior partners of external exploitation while remaining the dominant elite within Ecuadorean society. In a recent interpretation,

> The economic groups are characterized by their efficiency of action. This is due to the small number of their members, giving them great mobility; to the social and economic relations which permit them to apply pressure directly on the government, to the influence that they exercise over other pressure groups, especially the press, and to the quality of adhesion of their members, owing to the struggles that they maintain for the defense of their economic interests.[14]

Furthermore, internal colonialism is tied in no small part to regional and subregional distinctions. The complexities in Ecuador are great for, instead of a single dominant center set

[13]Ibid., p. 136.

[14]Oswaldo Hurtado (ed.), *Dos mundos superpuestos; ensayo de diagnóstico de la realidad ecuatoriana* (Quito: Instituto Ecuatoriano de Planificación para el Desarrollo Social, 1969), p. 231.

apart from isolated rural natives, there are the twin regional cities of Quito and Guayaquil. Moreover, such centers as Cuenca, Riobamba, Ambato, Esmeraldas, and Machala also impose a subregional monopoly of commerce and trade upon surrounding territory. Economic production and social life remain manifest in such conditions as exploitation of the Andean Indian and the coastal *montuvio*; historical traditions reinforcing existing exploitative practices; and a wide array of discriminatory policies ranging through such dimensions as law, politics, trade, credit, barter, language, and ethnicity.

Only if these manifestations of traditionalism and conformity are broken down can true modernization of life and society come to Ecuador. Perhaps the strongest force which might lead to a constructive reorientation of existing patterns is that of regionalism. Itself a long-established fact of Ecuadorean history, regionalism and subsidiary subregional development might well provide the motivating force in any significant transformation of national life. The writing of Hugo Burgos (see chapter 2) is suggestive of ways in which this might come to pass. In his study of Riobamba and environs, Burgos dealt with the concept of marginality and the extent to which it is breaking down, as the disconnection between traditionally isolated Indians and the broader society has become less absolute. Observing the specifics of a growing relationship between Riobamba and Guayaquil, he has written that

> . . . the symbol of the new generation is expressed in the young *cholo*-fied Indian, drifting between two cultural universes, two economies, carrying a transistor radio in his hand, without having lost his affiliation to the traditional community. The pre-industrial metropolis of Riobamba is the point of departure from which this new generation believes that it is going to find new horizons.[15]

Couching much of his analysis in terms of the internal dependency thesis, Burgos argues that there must eventually be a change for the dispossessed from customary colonized status. Both politically and economically it must enter into the decisions now controlled by the small and powerful elites. *Mestizos,*

[15]Hugo Burgos Guevara, *Relaciones interétnicas en Riobamba; dominio y dependencia en una región indígena ecuatoriana* (México: Instituto Indigenista Interamericano, Ediciones Especiales 55, 1970), p. 162.

cholos, and Indians alike "have to be treated and to participate equally in the taking of decisions concerning their future, but the present economic system that is changing so slowly from paternalism to competition does not provide nor will it soon provide important changes to this present structure of unbalanced relations."[16] Existing subregional groupings, he contends, are in the early stages of what must necessarily become a new form of geographically horizontal interaction. He foresees as a viable subregionalization five new groupings, extending across the republic from east to west, thereby embracing *costa, sierra,* and *oriente.*

Burgos identifies these as: (a) Esmeraldas – Carchi/Imbabura – Napo; (b) Manabí/Esmeraldas – Pichincha; (c) Manabí – Cotopaxi/Tungurahua – Pastaza; (d) Guayas/Los Ríos – Chimborazo/Bolívar; and (e) El Oro – Azuay/Cañar/Loja. A somewhat fragmented subregionalization, derived more from analysis of economic complementarity than from Burgos' socioeconomic-demographic interpretation, has been proposed by Hans Linnemann of the United Nations for the *Junta Nacional de Planificación y Coordinación Económica.* The result, he concludes, would be a fully integrated national economy permitting balanced subregional development. He advocates an explicit governmental commitment to a regional policy understood to enhance broad national planning and the achievement of developmental progress extending throughout the entire republic.[17]

Whatever the precise configurations of such proposals or their realistic prospects for restructuring the subregions as a means of national integration, they are suggestive of the latent force of such cleavages for contemporary Ecuador as have already been described (see especially chapter 1). In order to achieve socioeconomic modernization for the country, political elites must provide the leadership which will facilitate structural and institutional change. The extent to which local and subregional activity is constructive or dysfunctional to the national system remains uncertain. In the past, notwithstanding the

[16]Ibid., p. 379.

[17]Hans Linnemann, *Regiones económicas del Ecuador, su integración y desarrollo; estudio preliminar* (Quito: Junta Nacional de Planificación y Coordinación Económica, Sección Publicaciones, 1965). A description and accompanying maps for Linnemann's recommended subregions appear on pp. 88-94, 99, and 101.

degree of local autonomy which has existed, actions have largely centered on the mobilization of sentiment against an allegedly unresponsive national government. Often such local action has been a means of protesting a lack of national support for promised funds and public works. Other times it has been a denial of unacceptable tax burdens imposed from Quito.

Examples of such episodes remain common in Ecuador, and there have been several cases during the most recent *velasquista* government. Moreover, they epitomize the continuing personalism of Ecuadorean politics. One such instance took place in March of 1970 in Riobamba with the proclamation of a general strike to dramatize the city's charges that promised public works had not been forthcoming. In addition to an effective municipal work stoppage, three army officers were taken into custody. President Velasco himself flew to the city, delivered a harangue from the balcony of the municipal building, and privately agreed to many of the local demands. Later in the week his Minister of Public Works signed a contract for construction of a road to Baños, and the situation returned to normality. Two months later there was also a general strike in Loja, designed to secure a national allocation of additional funds for educational and economic developmental projects. One of Velasco's ministers went to the city, and again there was a favorable reaction to local demands.

Somewhat more disruptive, if equally consistent with traditional patterns of regionalism, was an outburst at Tulcán in June of 1971. Situated as it is next to the Colombian border, Tulcán has long been a center of illegal trade and unabashed smuggling. Moreover, legitimate trade with neighboring Ipiales in Colombia is common, and the inhabitants cross the frontier frequently as a part of their normal routine. However, the Velasco government instituted a toll tax of 8 cents on such traffic, and local leaders requested exemption from Quito. The president promptly – and illegally – deposed Tulcán's municipal officials, dispatched military troops to the city, and demanded adherence to the new tax. Disorganized popular demonstrations resulted, a strike was announced, and the local bishop protested the imposition of force. Before the situation was stabilized, more than two dozen Ecuadoreans had been injured and six killed. The central government eventually relented by abolishing the border tax, releasing its prisoners, and reinstating the town's elected authorities.

The recurrence of such episodes is likely to continue, whatever the political hues of the national government. To be sure, such actions are scarcely envisioned as providing meaningful impetus for a reform policy. However, such disruptive events – whatever the possible justification – testify to the strength of local and subregional loyalties, as well as to the relative absence of any firm commitment to central authority. There is a powerful if largely unrealized potential which might well be brought to bear on the articulation and implementation of national policy. Inevitably this will come most tellingly from Quito, Guayaquil, and, to a lesser extent, Riobamba and Cuenca. For Riobamba, the major influence presently emanates from the local bishop, Monseñor Proaño, the most progressive member of the higher clergy in Ecuador. Elected officials there seem unlikely to influence national policy significantly in the immediate future. Similarly, the prospects for modernizing impetus from conservative Cuenca are not overwhelming.[18] However, municipal leadership in Quito and Guayaquil constitutes a possible source for modernization, and this has been underlined in recent years. Indeed, political leadership in both municipal governments may provide an antidote to the traditional narrowness which one Ecuadorean has termed the hypertrophy of the political system.[19]

In Quito the presence of the national government inevitably overshadows the functioning of municipal officials. The mayor has tended to be more the administrator and technician than an active political partisan. While frequently enjoying both political visibility and influence, his effectiveness as mayor has demanded some aloofness from party politics during his incumbency. The configuration of party allegiance in both Quito and Pichincha has been subject to considerable fluctuation. Conservative party strength in the *sierra* has not been automatically transferred to the capital; neither has any other party succeeded

[18]This is not to deny a strong commitment to municipal development. However, for an informative exchange with Cuenca's last elected mayor, Alejandro Serrano Aguilar, see Alberto Borges, "La moral administrativa, clave del progreso cuencano," *Vistazo* (Guayaquil), Vol. 14, No. 162 (noviembre 1970), 56-58. A series of articles recreating the history and growth of Cuenca also appear in the same issue.

[19]Hurtado (ed.), *Dos mundos superpuestos,* p. 239.

in placing its stamp on the *quiteño* electorate for more than a brief period. And as would be expected, the partisan cast of Quito politics is not unrelated to the proclivities of the occupant of the presidential palace.

For the past two decades the Quito mayoralty has most frequently been held by representatives of broadly liberal coalitions. José Ricardo Chiriboga Villagómez won two consecutive terms from 1949 to 1953 as the head of a center-left alliance, polling massive victories with 72.4 and 85.4 percent. Benefiting at least indirectly from the ad hoc grouping which had helped to elect Galo Plaza in 1948, he concentrated on street paving and the improvement of services, later seeking unsuccessfully the presidency of the republic. The Conservatives captured the mayoralty in 1953 with Rafael Léon Larrea, but he lost his 1955 reelection bid to the *Frente Democrático*, another coalition of Liberals and Socialists. Its candidate, Carlos Andrade Marín, remained in office until 1959, although his margin was cut markedly in 1957 as the result of President Ponce's assistance to the Conservatives. Liberal Julio Moreno Espinosa succeeded him for a term in 1959, after which the Conservatives returned with Jorge Vallarino Donoso.

Following the suspension of elections during the provisional years of the mid-1960s, Jaime del Castillo won a narrow victory in 1967 over a pro-*poncista* Conservative, a Liberal, and four minor candidates. The new mayor epitomized the Quito tradition by providing solid leadership of a constructive, action-oriented, and largely nonpartisan nature. Keeping his distance from partisan conflict and turning aside queries about his own political future, del Castillo concentrated on improvement and extension of city services while working to strengthen the quality of municipal administration. A series of long-range studies were undertaken, and construction began on new buildings, street improvements, and the enlarging of major traffic arteries. Much of his interest was directed at projects enabling Quito better to adjust to growing urban needs while retaining the best of the city's traditional appearance and *ambiente*. His administration was fiscally sound and among the most effective the capital has known.[20]

[20]An interview in which Jaime del Castillo set forth his opinions on municipal development appears in "El hombre que transforma Quito," *Vistazo* (Guayaquil), Vol. 13, No. 151 (diciembre 1969), 43-46.

In the last municipal elections before Velasco's *autogolpe,* the diffuseness of *quiteño* political loyalties was again apparent. In a six-candidate race, Sixto Durán Ballén, supported by Social Christians, *poncistas,* and independents, won office with 37.9 percent of the vote. Manuel Córdova Galarza, running for the *Izquierda Democrática* offshoot of the Liberals, trailed by 5 percentage points. Significantly, official Conservative and Liberal candidates were far in arrears. Durán and Córdova, while not new to the political scene, were both relatively young and were better known for dedication and competence than for their partisan affiliations. Not only was the Quito electorate seemingly unmoved by party labels, but it was also presumably concerned about performance in office, a lesson which the republic's political leaders may soon be forced to accept seriously. Even more than in Quito, however, the potential rise of a constructive and modernizing regionalism is likeliest to originate from the coast, and the focus must inevitably center on Guayaquil.

Guayaquil Revisited. With all due apologies to *serranos* in general and *quiteños* in particular, Guayaquil clearly stands out as Ecuador's most vigorous and productive center. Rebellious, progressive, and independent-minded, it has long been a decisive factor in national affairs. Lying among the green hills along the Guayas river, it has progressed rapidly in contemporary times despite tropical inclemencies, and – with its population destined to reach one million inhabitants by 1975 – is vigorously confident of becoming one of the hemisphere's great cities. The Guayas fluvial system is potentially the best on the Pacific coast of South America, with hundreds of streams and canals penetrating from the ocean and from the Guayas. Improved port facilities are presently the best on the Pacific between Panama and Valparaiso, and the coastal production of bananas and cacao has lent economic importance to its activities. As a center for commercial and industrial production, Guayaquil is also firmly established as Ecuador's financial center.

The port city had been economically important through much of the nineteenth century. However, the generation of truly substantial income from the international market derived from cacao revenue early in the 1900s, reaching a high point during World War I.[21] The later increase from the banana was even more dramatic, as export figures reveal. In the second half of the 1920s the annual average had been 14,000 tons; in the second five years of the 1940s it had risen to 70,000 per year; in 1950 Ecuador became the world leader with 169,000 tons; and in 1967 1,260,000 tons were exported, with over 80 percent shipped from Guayaquil. As Ecuador entered the 1970s, Guayaquil banks were handling three-fourths of the country's money and 60 percent of its deposits.

At the same time, port facilities were severely taxed despite an increased capacity created by new and modern installations upriver. Sanitation and health conditions had been vastly improved, and municipal services were more extensive than ever before. Even so, a good third of the city population lived in slum hovels, while the daily consumption per person stood at only forty grams of meat and twenty centiliters of milk. Projections for population growth promised little succor in the forseeable future. The increase was especially compelling in its magnitude when seen in contrast to that of Quito. As shown by Table 14, the port city is moving toward a population virtually double that of Quito by the start of the 1980s. Thus the pressures on municipal government will be greater than ever before and, barring exceptional progress in providing services, there will be strong pressures likely to justify Guayaquil's tradition as a center for political action.

Table 14
QUITO AND GUAYAQUIL POPULATION, 1962-75

City	1962	1968	1972	1975
Quito	355,183	483,847	518,671	592,606
Guayaquil	510,785	716,600	915,693	1,077,152

Data for 1962 and 1968 come from official census figures. For 1972 and 1975, estimates are derived from the Junta Nacional de Planificación y Coordinación Económica, División de estadística y censos, *Proyección de la población urbana cantonal y de las cabeceras parroquiales, 1962-1975* (Quito: N.D.).

[21]*Guayaquileño* producers and financiers grew wealthy, and family members were educated and often lived in Europe rather than Ecuador. In 1916 cacao exports reached a high of 50 million kilograms; within a decade plant diseases had drastically reduced production, and by 1933 only 10.5 million kilograms were exported. The rise of balsa wood production took up some of the slack and then, of course, the phenomenal rise of the banana occurred.

In sheer electoral terms, moreover, Guayaquil promises to remain central for national politics, and Guayas province will also be important. As Table 15 indicates, the number of valid votes in the city constitutes roughly 70 percent of the total for Guayas province; since 1956 it has also been some 17 percent of the national vote. Similarly, in the three most recent presidential contests the Guayas provincial total has been some 23 percent of the national electorate. Given this electoral distribution, the votes of both municipality and province are clearly crucial to aspiring national leaders. Thus a capacity to win and to hold the allegiance of this bloc of voters assures great influence on national affairs. For much of the past two decades, the *Concentración de Fuerzas Populares* has enjoyed such dominance in Guayaquil and environs. As discussed in chapter 4, the CFP has been unable to move fully from a regional to national basis. As a regional organization, however, it has been strong on most of the *costa,* powerful in Guayas province, and virtually unchallenged within the municipal government except for periods of unconstitutionality.

The mayor of Guayaquil effectively rules the municipal council, despite its nominal political superiority. His powers are far more than ceremonial, for in practice the mayor may veto council recommendations when he wishes. In such matters as public works, building and construction projects, electrical and water services, and health and sanitation facilities, his authority is decisive. Moreover, he enjoys the power of appointment and removal over most municipal employees. The formal structure

Table 15
VALID VOTERS IN PRESIDENTIAL ELECTIONS FOR GUAYAQUIL, GUAYAS, AND ECUADOR, 1952-68

	VALID VOTES			*PERCENTAGES OF VALID VOTES*		
Year	Guayaquil	Guayas	Ecuador	Guayaquil, of Guayas	Guayaquil, of Ecuador	Guayas, of Ecuador
1952	40,000	59,000	357,000	69	11	17
1956	104,000	141,000	614,000	74	17	23
1960	120,000	170,000	767,000	71	16	22
1968	144,000	192,000	853,000	71	17	23

Source: Consejo Supremo Electoral *informes,* 1952-1968.
Figures are rounded off by thousands.

of major municipal offices is depicted in Chart 9, suggesting the range of activities which forceful leadership can affect. Control and utilization of the municipal budget provides additional authority and leverage for the mayor. The *cefepista* organization has exercised such powers since the beginning of the 1950s; each of its two successive *caudillos,* first Carlos Guevara Moreno and later Asaad Bucaram, has proven adept at manning major municipal positions with loyal supporters.

The origins of the CFP drive to regional strength came from the talents of its first "*jefe máximo*," or supreme chief, Carlos Guevara Moreno, as well as from the relative political vacuum left on the coast with the disintegration of the Liberals following the debacle in the Peruvian controversy and the ouster of Carlos Arroyo del Río. Guevara Moreno, a minister of government during Velasco's second administration, had been

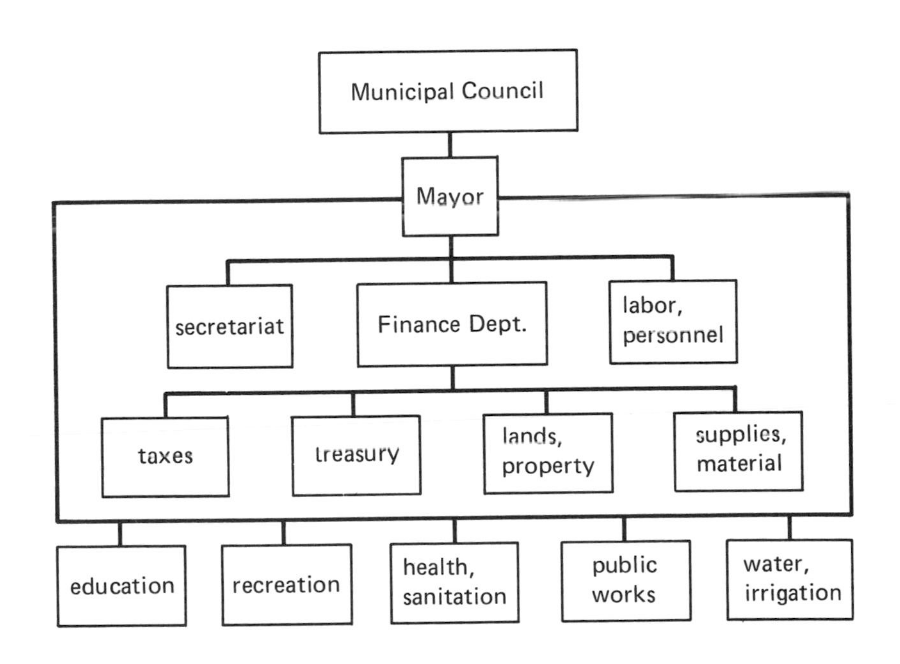

CHART 9. GUAYAQUIL MUNICIPAL ADMINISTRATIVE ORGANIZATION.

dispatched to Chile as ambassador with the overthrow of the regime. He subsequently returned to Guayaquil and joined the newly organized *Unión Popular Republicana* (UPR). In 1947 the UPR candidate for mayor, Rafael Mendoza Avilés of the University of Guayaquil faculty, ran second to a dissident Liberal. By the close of the year the UPR had been reorganized by the CFP; the party organ *Momento* had begun publication, and Guevara Moreno proceeded to build the party. Mendoza Avilés again lost the mayoralty in 1949, although the margin was small; Guevara Moreno was jailed by the national government for six months; and then in November, 1951, he polled 45 percent of the vote in defeating four opponents for the mayoralty. The CFP also won three of five contested seats on the municipal council, and from that juncture the rise of party strength was impressive.

Guevara was briefly influential within the new administration, having supported Velasco's 1952 campaign. Before long the president viewed him as a political threat; the coastal *caudillo* was exiled to Peru, and Velasco replaced Guayaquil officials with his own appointees. By June of 1954, however, a reactivated CFP won 46.8 percent in Guayas provincial elections, with Guevara Moreno leading the party's seven members on the twelve-man provincial delegation. In November of the year *cefepistas* polled 42.6 percent of the vote to the Guayaquil council. Velasco, again wary of a possible challenge, threw government influence and money into the November 1955 race for mayor. The *velasquista* candidate narrowly defeated Guevara Moreno, who nonetheless received 48.8 percent of the vote and continued to mobilize for his 1956 presidential bid.

Although failing to make the leap to national office, Guevara Moreno ran first on the coast while winning four of every ten votes in the region, amassing more than 50 percent of the vote in Guayas province. Unchallenged in his coastal authority and eager to prepare for the 1960 presidential contest, he sought to extend *cefepista* hegemony further. In November 1956 the party won 52.2 percent of the vote for Guayaquil councilmen, securing five of six contested seats and thereby controlling eight of the eleven. A year later Guevara's lieutenant, Luis Robles Plaza, captured the Guayaquil mayoralty with

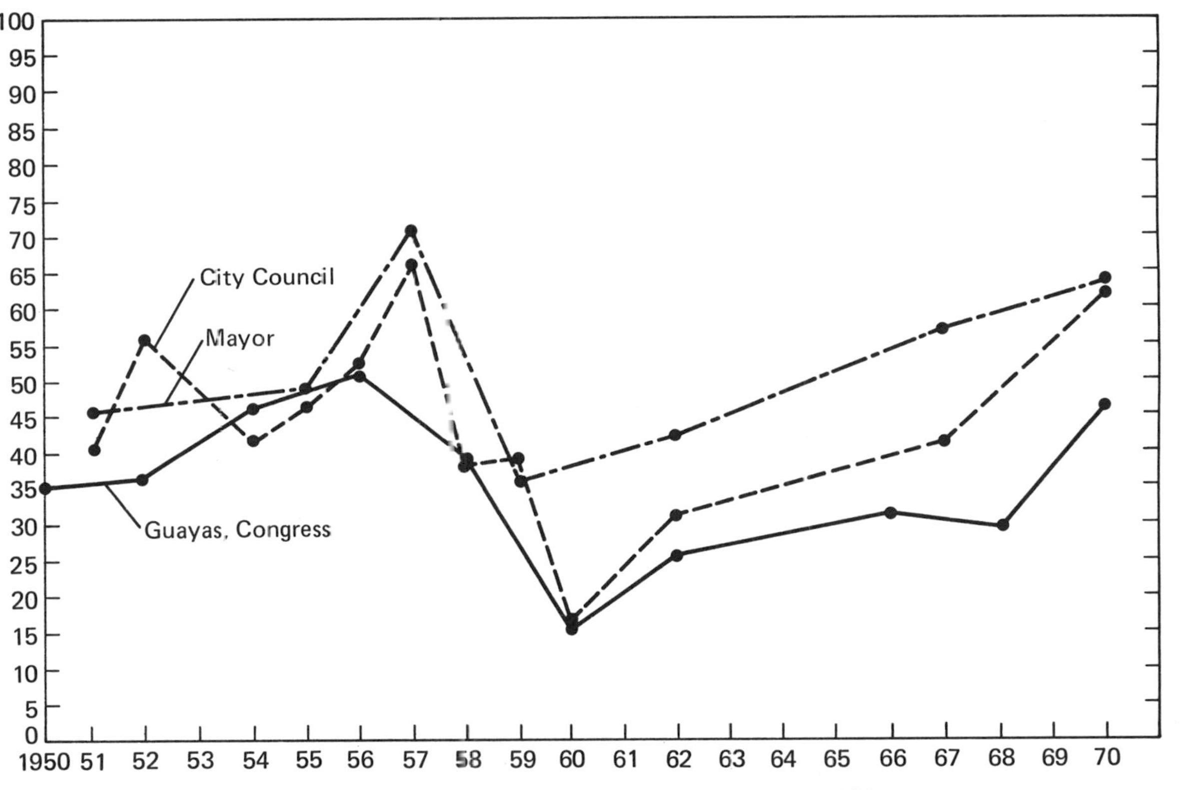

CHART 10. *CEFEPISTA* ELECTORAL SUPPORT, 1950-1970.

72.8 percent of the vote. As it turned out, this marked the high tide of *cefepismo* during the Guevara era. The Robles municipal administration, virtually unchallenged in the port city, continued an active program of public construction, but social conditions received insufficient attention.[22] Administrative miscalculations began to emerge, and conservative President Camilo Ponce lost no opportunity to whittle away at *cefepista* strength.

Guevara Moreno inexplicably turned away from Robles rather than mounting a counteroffensive, and before long rumors of administrative scandal and malfeasance were rampant. The *jefe máximo* devoted decreasing attention to party affairs, and despite his carefully cultivated image as representative of the disenfranchised coastal *pueblo,* Guevara's life style became increasingly luxurious. Electoral decline swiftly set in. In June of 1958 the CFP vote in congressional elections dropped more than ten points to 39.5 percent in Guayas, although still capturing five members of the twelve-man delegation. In November of the year the party won only one-third of the vote for municipal councilmen, although retaining eight of the eleven seats. Then in November of 1959 Guevara himself, bidding for another term as mayor in competition with five other candidates including incumbent Robles Plaza, received but 36.5 percent while running second to *velasquista* stalwart Menéndez Gilbert. A miniscule vote for Robles Plaza indicated that his smashing victory in 1957 had been the result of party strength rather than personal popularity, and from that time forward the split between Robles and Guevara was absolute.

In 1960, with the party about to divide into rival wings, it was apparent that the earlier iron will and political sagacity of Guevara Moreno was no longer viable. In congressional elections that year the CFP won a mere 15.9 percent of the Guayas vote, capturing only two of the twelve provincial seats. It received 16.5 percent in elections for municipal councilmen, losing control of the city administration to *velasquistas.* This marked an

[22]For a fulsome review of municipal activities undertaken during this period, see J. Gonzalo Orellana, *Resumen histórico del Ecuador; apuntaciones cronológicas complementarias 1947-1957,* Vol. 3 (Quito: Editorial "Fray Jodoco Ricke," 1957), pp. 147-54.

electoral nadir for the party, and its later phoenixlike resurrection from the ashes came under the leadership of a second dominant *caudillo,* Asaad Bucaram. The collapse of the movement under Guevara Moreno has never been fully explained. Numerous factors entered in, including municipal mismanagement in the late 1950s, tactical misjudgments by Guevara Moreno and, perhaps most importantly, a seeming loss of appetite for political battle on the part of the *jefe máximo.* The return to power of Dr. Velasco was also a contributory factor,

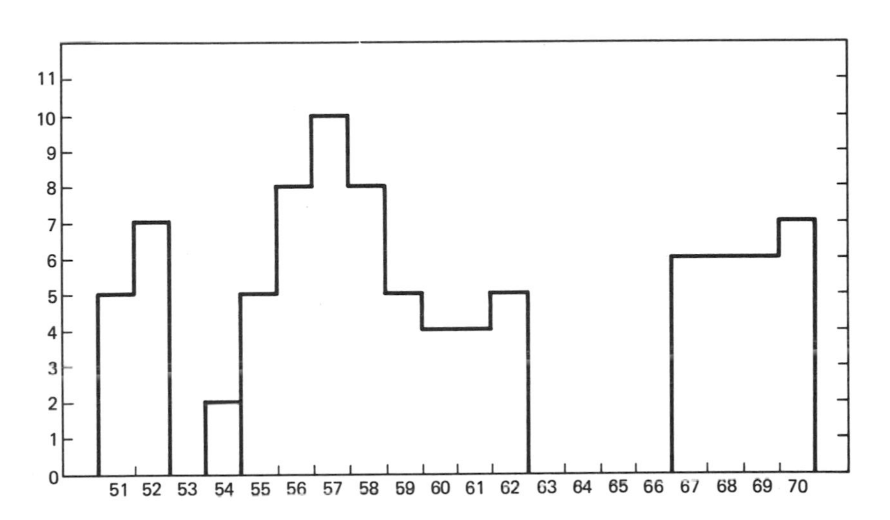

CHART 11. *CEFEPISTA* REPRESENTATION ON GUAYAQUIL COUNCIL, 1951-1970.

In 1953 and 1963-67, the Council was intervened by the national government.

as was the hardening of hostility from the Guayaquil economic elite. By the end of 1960 Guevara Moreno had resigned his party leadership and left the country. A later effort to wrest control of the CFP from his former lieutenants met with failure, and in the 1960s the fate of the party fell upon the burly shoulders of Asaad Bucaram.[23]

In Bucaram a unique figure emerged on the Ecuadorean political scene. A former peddler of Middle Eastern extraction, born in Ambato but having risen from humble origins in Guayaquil, he had been a faithful worker for the CFP; an innate intelligence and astute political instinct carried him to party leadership. Blunt, direct, simple in manner but shrewd in action, his personal touch with the masses, and a growing reputation for impeccable honesty if impetuosity of action led to his growing domination of the CFP in the wake of Guevara's eclipse. Elected to congress from Guayas in 1958 and again in 1960, Bucaram won the Guayaquil mayoralty in June of 1962 with 43.2 percent of the vote. At that juncture the CFP held five of eleven council seats, while Bucaram himself outpolled the party list by a little over 10 percent of the vote, and the value to the party of his personal magnetism was evident.

Like Guevara Moreno a decade earlier, Bucaram and council members were arbitrarily removed from office by the national government – this time in the wake of the 1963 military *golpe de estado*. When elections were next held, Bucaram led the party to victory in the race for the Constituent Assembly; the CFP ran first in Guayas, with Bucaram heading the four *cefepista* members of the thirteen-man provincial delegation. In June of 1967 he won his second term as mayor with 57.1 percent of the vote, this time running ahead of the party slate for municipal council by more than 15 percent. For this election Bucaram had entered into coalition with coastal Liberals, receiving their support for mayor while seats to the council were shared between the PLR and the CFP.

The CFP-PLR alliance was maintained in subsequent elections, strengthening *cefepista* authority over the municipal administration while catapulting Bucaram to further prominence. In June 1968 national elections, while the redoubtable Velasco won his fifth term, the CFP-PLR coalition captured five

[23]A sympathetic and thoughtful, if somewhat vague explanation of Guevara's political demise appears in Rafael Galarza Arízaga, *Esquema político del Ecuador* (Guayaquil: Editorial Alborada, 1963), pp. 131-45. A teacher and educator, Galarza Arízaga had been elected as a *cefepista* member of the Guayas delegation to congress in 1958. At the time of writing, he was not only a defender of Guevara Moreno but also wrote favorably of Bucaram.

of sixteen provincial seats in congress. Two years later the alliance fought its way to a devastating victory in both municipality and province. Forbidden under a revised electoral statute from running for immediate reelection as mayor, Bucaram stood for provincial prefect, hoping thereby to maintain his authority while demonstrating his electoral appeal at the head of the ticket. His running mate for Guayaquil mayor was the young Liberal Francisco Huerta Montalvo, who had been sympathetic to the coastal collaboration between the two parties. The victory was total. Despite concerted and explicit anti-Bucaram opposition, the *cefepista* leader swept to the post of prefect with 63.4 percent against three opponents, while Huerta received only a shade less in winning the mayoralty against four rivals. The coalition also captured four of the six contested seats to the council, thereby controlling seven of the eleven. Half of the sixteen-man delegation to congress also came from the alliance.

Although there was no way of judging quantitatively the respective contributions of the two members of the alliance, Asaad Bucaram himself unquestionably stood out as the paramount personality. Young Huerta, a medical doctor born in 1940, was inexperienced and something of an unknown quantity, while the Liberal party nationally was badly divided. Bucaram's strength on the coast was regarded as unassailable, and he was clearly *presidenciable* for 1972. As *Vistazo* noted in reviewing the results, Bucaram was heir to the coastal populism which had been mobilized by Velasco and Guevara Moreno in other periods.[24]

José María Velasco Ibarra unerringly reached the same conclusion. Bucaram, although an impassioned critic of unconstitutional intervention in the early 1960s, had carefully maintained cordial relations with the president after 1968 and was guarded in his public comments following the *autogolpe*. Nonetheless both he and Huerta were detained by government authorities in late September of 1970.[25] They were replaced by presidential appointees and, while Huerta was swiftly set free, Bucaram was

[24]"Lo que dijeron las urnas; triunfadores del Guayas," *Vistazo* (Guayaquil), Vol. 14, No. 158 (julio 1970), 34-40.

[25]For details, see *El Comercio* (Quito) and *El Universal* (Guayaquil) for September 28-30, 1970.

forcibly deported to Trinidad and soon settled in Panama. In mid-1971 he slipped back into Ecuador and was again apprehended, expelled this time to Paraguay and ending up back in Panama. His future prospects continued to be bright, but for the short run were dependent upon *velasquista* acquiescence to his return and reemergence as a public figure. In the meantime, the basically personalistic nature of the CFP was demonstrated by the party's leaderless confusion and relative inactivity following Bucaram's initial arrest and deportation. The *cefepista Comando Nacional,* headed by Aquiles Rodríguez and Jorge Carvajal, failed to rally the masses on his behalf. Much the same thing happened when Bucaram went into hiding after the February 1972 military *golpe de estado.* The existence of party structure, as with Guevara Moreno in earlier years, proved largely inoperable in the absence of its dominant *caudillo.* In this context, Ecuadorean political tradition was once more being upheld.

Only time will demonstrate whether or not either Bucaram or the CFP succeed in winning national power and propelling the republic in the direction of modernization. The decelerating forces of social and political tradition remain powerful, and the extraordinary complex of cross-cutting cleavages which so characterizes Ecuador still exists. Given the extensive economic reorientation made likely by recent subsoil discoveries, available resources should be far greater than ever before. At the same time, the challenge to reassert true nationality in the face of both external and domestic dependency relationships will be unprecedented. Moreover, the presence of a sea of effectively dispossessed Ecuadoreans endures, and it is this human element which most persistently cries for succor.

The vast preponderance of the population still survives in a variety of forms as the stereotypical "traditional man" of the underdeveloped world. Joseph Kahl, writing of all such areas, put it well:

> The traditional man . . . perceives himself as permanently stuck in a life which does not change and which cannot be controlled to any great extent. Therefore he seeks little and expects to gain little; he takes what the fates may bring; he pursues security through close personal ties, primarily with relatives but also with a few friends and with *patrones* in high

positions who will protect him so long as he stays in his place. To this exchange he brings resignation and gains safety.

It is the responsibility of Ecuador's political leadership to provide that enlightened, disinterested, and genuinely national guidance whereby the "traditional man" of the republic has cause to alter the present passivity of such fatalistic resignation.

SELECTED BIBLIOGRAPHY

The works listed below are limited to those written in English. For the Spanish-reading student, the more extensive literature by Ecuadoreans may be found by topic in footnotes throughout the volume.

Beals, Ralph L. *Community in Transition: Nayón – Ecuador.* Los Angeles: University of California Press, 1966.
A scholarly anthropological study of a Quechua-speaking village in Pichincha province; provides insight into characteristic patterns of Indian life on the highlands.

Blanksten, George I. *Ecuador: Constitutions and Caudillos.* Berkeley and Los Angeles: University of California Press, 1951.
An exceptionally perceptive treatment of Ecuadorean politics and society; although two decades old, it retains a freshness and relevance for Ecuador today.

Brooks, Rhoda and Earle. *The Barrios of Manta; A Personal Account of the Peace Corps in Ecuador.* New York: The New American Library, Inc., 1965.
A chatty account of Peace Corps activities in Manta; a good picture of daily life emerges, although there is somewhat greater emphasis placed upon the particularistic problems of Peace Corps volunteers.

Franklin, Albert B. *Ecuador: Portrait of a People.* New York: Doubleday, Doran and Company, Inc., 1944.
Essentially a travel book which depicts Ecuadorean geography well but is rather dated in other ways.

Icaza, Jorge. *Huasipungo: The Villagers, a Novel.* Translated and with an introduction by Bernard M. Dulsey. Foreword by J. Cary Davis. Carbondale, Illinois: Southern Illinois University Press, 1964.
The authorized English translation of Icaza's internationally famed novel, which first appeared in 1934; although a deliberately overdrawn portrayal of rural life, it effectively captures the frustrations and enforced passivity of the Indian in the face of traditional white domination.

Linke, Lilo. *Ecuador, Country of Contrasts.* 2nd ed. London: Royal Institute of International Affairs, 1955.
One of the brief country surveys in the old RIIA series; written by a German journalist who settled in Ecuador years ago; although much of the socioeconomic data is no longer meaningful, the work reflects Miss Linke's keenly observant eye.

Maier, Georg. *The Ecuadorean Elections of June 2, 1968.* Washington, D.C.: Institute for the Comparative Study of Political Systems, 1970.
A well-informed overview of political currents and trends leading to the 1968 electoral victory by Velasco Ibarra; also includes a listing of all Ecuadorean heads of government and presidential electoral data for recent years.

May, Stacy, and Plaza, Galo. *The United Fruit Company in Latin America.* Washington, D.C.: National Planning Association, 1958.
A review of the famed banana company which includes extensive treatment of its activities in Ecuador; an account highly favorable to United Fruit, it was widely cited by the political opponents of ex-president Plaza during the 1960 presidential campaign as evidence of his alleged uncritical sympathy for North American economic interests.

Needler, Martin C. *Anatomy of a Coup d'Etat: Ecuador 1963.* Washington, D.C.: Institute for the Comparative Study of Political Systems, 1964.
Detailed narrative of events surrounding the 1963 military ouster of Carlos Julio Arosemena Monroy from power; includes thoughtful interpretations of the roles and motives of ranking officers.

Plaza, Galo. *Problems of Democracy in Latin America.* Chapel Hill, N.C.: University of North Carolina Press, 1955.
The text of three lectures delivered at the University of North Carolina by the ex-president in 1954; the second deals directly with his own experiences during the 1948-52 national administration.

Saunders, John V. D. *The People of Ecuador; A Demographic Analysis.* Gainesville, Florida: University of Florida Press, Latin American Monograph #14, 1961.
A detailed study of demographic configurations based primarily upon the 1950 census, first to be conducted in Ecuadorean history.

Thomsen, Moritz. *Living Poor; A Peace Corps Chronicle.* Seattle, Washington: University of Washington Press, 1969.
An extraordinary account of life in Rio Verde, Esmeraldas; written by a Peace Corps volunteer with fine literary talent and remarkable understanding.

Von Hagen, Victor Wolfgang. *Ecuador and the Galápagos Islands.* Norman, Oklahoma: The University of Oklahoma Press, 1949.
A somewhat idiosyncratic and anecdotal narrative by a popularizer of Latin American history; includes a number of entertaining tidbits,

but not always historically accurate.

Watkins, Ralph J. *Expanding Ecuador's Exports; A Commodity-by-Commodity Study with Projections to 1973.* New York: Frederick A. Praeger, 1967.
Reporting a study commissioned by the military *junta* with a view to the formulation of long-range economic planning; richer on data than analysis.

Whitten, Norman E., Jr. *Class, Kinship and Power in an Ecuadorian Town; The Negroes of San Lorenzo.* Stanford, California: Stanford University Press, 1965.
Thorough anthropological study by a North American scholar, based on firsthand observation; originally a doctoral dissertation at the University of North Carolina.

Wilson, Jacques M. P. *The Development of Education in Ecuador.* Coral Gables, Florida: University of Miami Press, 1970.
A description of educational institutions; useful, although giving little stress to dynamic political behavior within the educational arena.

Wright, Freeman J. *The Upper Level Administration in Ecuador.* Quito: Editorial "Fray Jodoco Ricke," 1968.
Study directed by a North American political scientist in conjunction with a contractual arrangement involving the University of Pittsburgh concerning Ecuadorean public administration; includes findings derived from interviews, many conducted by Ecuadorean students and collaborators.

Zook, David H., Jr. *Zarumilla-Marañon: The Ecuador-Peru Dispute.* New York: Bookman Associates, 1964.
Definitive study of the 1941 conflict and its attempted resolution through the Protocol of Rio de Janeiro; by the late military historian whose work also includes a study of the Chaco War.

For readers undertaking the difficult task of remaining informed about contemporary Ecuadorean affairs, the following journals may be consulted:

Bolsa Review. A monthly publication of the Bank of London & South America, containing useful economic and financial data as well as brief informative economic reports.

Latin America. A highly useful weekly political and economic report published in London. Probably the best single source in English for such current reporting.

The Times of the Americas. A weekly newspaper published in Washington drawing substantially on wire service dispatches. Tends toward the superficial at times, but nonetheless quite useful.

World Petroleum. As the title suggests, a specialized publication. Of considerable value concerning petroleum developments in Ecuador. Many of these items are written by Juan E. Rassmus.

INDEX

928165